Paris-Amsterdam Underground

Cities and Cultures

Cities and Cultures is an interdisciplinary humanities book series addressing the interrelations between contemporary cities and the cultures they produce. The series takes a special interest in the impact of globalization on urban space and cultural production, but remains concerned with all forms of cultural expression and transformation associated with contemporary cities.

Paris-Amsterdam Underground

Essays on Cultural Resistance, Subversion, and Diversion

Edited by Christoph Lindner and Andrew Hussey

Dear David,

My thanks to you and The New School for hosting the last (and most important) month of my sabbatical in NYC.

Best wishes,

AMSTERDAM UNIVERSITY PRESS

This book is published in print and online through the online OAPEN library (www.oapen.org)

OAPEN (Open Access Publishing in European Networks) is a collaborative initiative to develop and implement a sustainable Open Access publication model for academic books in the Humanities and Social Sciences. The OAPEN Library aims to improve the visibility and usability of high quality academic research by aggregating peer reviewed Open Access publications from across Europe.

Cover illustration: Sarah Guilbaud

Cover design: Kok Korpershoek, Amsterdam
Lay-out: Heymans & Vanhove, Goes

ISBN 978 90 8964 505 0
e-ISBN 978 90 4851 820 3 (pdf)
e-ISBN 978 90 4851 821 0 (ePub)
NUR 694

Table of Contents

Acknowledgements

This book – like its subject – is the product of a series of interactions and exchanges between Paris and Amsterdam involving a group of creative and critical thinkers whose work addresses (and is sometimes implicated in) countercultural movements, moments, scenes, and spaces in both cities. The project developed from a pair of linked conferences on the topic of the underground – one held in Amsterdam in 2010 and the other in Paris in 2011 – which involved a lot of geographic and intellectual shuttling between the two cities on the part of the speakers. The benefit, we believe, can be seen throughout this book in the often surprising, sometimes strange, but always productive interconnections between the various chapters. Our thanks, therefore, to the speakers and audiences at both conferences for their energetic contributions, as well as to our respective institutions, the Amsterdam School for Cultural Analysis and the University of London Institute in Paris, for providing financial support. For serious and substantial help in getting this book ready for publication, we are greatly indebted to Miriam Meissner at ASCA, whose editorial and research assistance tied many loose ends together. Most of all, we are grateful to the authors in this book for participating with such a collaborative spirit in the extended conversation involved in the project as a whole, from its guerrilla conference roots through to its final published form.

Christoph Lindner and Andrew Hussey

Acknowledgements

[illegible]

Foreword

David Pinder

In one of the many striking images in this book, a figure scrutinizes the earth through a giant magnifying glass. A painting by Jean Dubuffet, it is one of many that he composed from the mid-1940s that depict the ground and what lies beneath. Readers of the book are often invited similarly to look downward, to consider spaces that are literally under the ground of Paris and Amsterdam. Our attention is directed to what is under the paving stones, asphalt, and concrete on which so many people daily tread. What may be found there unseen, buried, sequestered, and forgotten? How can explorations of those depths transform understandings of the urban? The vertical line down may be a relatively neglected dimension of cities, the subterranean largely an unknown realm. But the latter, in its darkness and opacity, as a place to which expelled matter and waste flows and in which secrets as well as bodies are buried, has also long been a source of fascination combined with repulsion. That is particularly the case with Paris where the underground became an obsession during the nineteenth century among many writers and artists as well as politicians and administrators as the construction of new sewers, cemeteries, trains, and other infrastructure proceeded. Traditional imagery of underworlds was reworked as spaces under the city came to harbor all manner of fears, superstitions, fantasies, dreams, and visions. Associated with danger, decay, criminality, terror, insurrection, and the demonic, it was also a site of technological accomplishment, beauty, and wonder as well as escape, shelter, and refuge (Williams; Pike).

Looking downward provides a distinct perspective on the city above, the underground even perhaps offers a key to unlock certain of its mysteries. Yet the underground cannot be comprehended through an abstract viewpoint and instead requires entering its 'shadows'. That is an observation drawn toward the end of the book from one of the most famous chroniclers of Paris souterrain, Victor Hugo. The preceding pages take us on many journeys below the surface. The underneath is at times literal, for example via train or metro. But it is also metaphorical. The underground of these pages is both a place and an idea, one that resonates in manifold ways with the histories of Paris and Amsterdam. They have become renowned for their underground movements and practices of cultural resistance, subversion, and diversion (and some of the paradoxes and recuperations involved in that 'renown' are explored insightfully in what follows). Opposing dominant power relations, these movements and activities have typically operated below dominant culture's threshold of visibility, even clandestinely.

One characteristic mode has been that of digging, grubbing, burrowing, undermining – and on occasion erupting through the surface. That is to use the terms of the 'old mole' evoked by Marx, an image he borrowed from Shakespeare's *Hamlet* to refer to revolutionary struggles in 19th-century Europe. It is also the language adopted a century later by the Situationists, who play a prominent role in this book. Positioning themselves as 'the catacombs of visible culture', they sought not to gain access to the artistic and cultural establishment but rather to undermine it (SI 'The Adventure', 79). Renunciating the 'world of the spectacle', they looked to desires, resistances, and struggles from below that threatened the current social and spatial order. 'An irreducible dissatisfaction spreads subterraneanly, undermining the edifice of the affluent society', they noted with satisfaction in 1962, adding that the 'old mole' conjured by Marx 'is still digging away' (SI 'Bad Days', 107). It was an image to which they often returned, including during the uprisings in Paris, in May 1968, when they believed 'a decisive threshold' was crossed: 'Europe can only leap for joy and cry out: "Well dug, old mole!"' (Viénet, 15).

The book focuses on the decades since the mid-twentieth century. The underground at its heart is that associated with the counterculture whose designation as 'the underground' the editors and others trace from the 1950s and 1960s. The text nevertheless resists a single track and gives free rein to the term's fluid meanings and associations. Maps are reworked, detours taken, and lines hijacked. Routes and destinations are varied. The journeys productively unsettle familiar narratives and images, most obviously those of the 'official' cultures of the two cities but also those which have coalesced around their undersides. While there is an extensive literature on aspects of the post-war counterculture, an important contribution of this book lies in its spatial as well as historical approach. Not only does it trace how cultural movements arose within particular urban contexts that also shaped them, raising questions about why and how Paris and Amsterdam have been such conducive and distinctive sites for artistic, creative, and ludic practices of resistance since the 1950s; it further addresses how, for these movements, urban space is itself a medium of expression, conflict, and struggle. Cultural creation is not sealed in specialized institutions but enters into the realms of everyday life and space, which in turn are remade. What are subverted and diverted are urban life and the definitions, uses, and production of its spaces. When in the momentous year of 1968 Henri Lefebvre declared, 'Let everyday life become a work of art!' – and when, at the same time, he articulated 'the right to the city' – they were cries and demands that resonated strongly with many artistic and cultural radicals in both cities.

The book's most vital contribution is indicated by the hyphen in its main title, which is to say its effort to think the cities and their cultural politics together. That the title suggests a train line or route is no accident for the book is deeply concerned with encounters, exchanges, and traffic. Recent work in urban studies and geography has demonstrated the importance of understanding cities not as bounded locations but in terms of their interrelations with other places and peoples, as nodes and meeting places within flows and networks. This demands looking outward, as it were, as well as downward (Massey). Through the political economic lens of global cities literature in particular, focus most often falls on cities regarded as command centers within the global economy, on their hierarchical and competitive relationships to other cities, and on the flows of money, information, and people between them in response to economic restructuring and changes in the geopolitical order. The movement and mutation of urban policies has also been examined and unpacked, including in relation to the reception of 'creative city' visions in Amsterdam (Peck; see also McCann and Ward). Addressing Paris-Amsterdam through notions of the underground, then, explicitly invites different ways of conceiving connection, movement, exchange, and place. While some chapters explore and compare movements between the cities, others address one city or the other, and the argument emerges through combination and juxtaposition.

Far from collapsing the different inflections and trajectories of underground cultures, the chapters bring out their specificities as well as interconnections. The movements they address include those that of dissident ideas and practices, for example those involved in the formation and legacies of the Situationist International, in the sexual undergrounds of Amsterdam, and in the writings of the Beats based in Paris but whose networks stretched wider. What comes through strongly is the significance of material urban spaces for these exchanges and circulations, for example the specific neighborhoods of Paris and Amsterdam whose collective exploration played a crucial role in the development of Situationist ideas and ideals. They were exchanges that literally *took place*, and a critical element of the book lies in taking that seriously.

If there is traffic of ideas, however, there is also that which ferries passengers, most particularly the metro that cuts across a number of chapters. In one chapter, for example, we follow the daily commute between city center and suburban home by a resident of Sarcelles. Attending to metro lines, stops, delays, and detours calls into question understandings of culture as travel promoted by recent cultural theorists, and enables the complexities of place, identity, and journey to be addressed. In another chapter we descend to the metro with Dubuffet to observe commuters awaiting or riding carriages. Again its ordinariness as an everyday underground space is part of its appeal, yet his metro paintings are shown to lead into a fuller exploration of the undersides of both Paris and painting, and into efforts to find a space for aesthetic contestation. A further chapter on the metro tells of the controversial construction of lines in Amsterdam during the late 1960s and 1970s, of the furious mobilizations against its 'economically-driven tunnel visions' and displacements of populations, and of the subsequent integration of some of those involved in an 'official' memorialization of the struggles. At such moments the book's concern with the multiple meanings of the underground becomes particularly provocative, directing us with new insight back to the city as a contested material and symbolic space.

A question running through many of the chapters concerns the fate of the underground as it confronts the mainstream and becomes fragmented, dissipated, commercialized, or absorbed into contrary interests. Wariness about the abilities of cultural undergrounds to avoid recuperation has, of course, been common since their inception. So, too, has the stronger suspicion that they fuel, more than challenge, fundamental aspects of the dominant capitalist order, not least in their emphasis on innovation and the new. Among the underground's sharpest critics were the Situationists, who targeted among others the Beats and the Angry Young Men for their innocuousness and also ultimately their reactionary faith in the redemptive power of literature. One response is to avoid romanticizing the lines between the oppositional underground and the recuperative powers of commerce and state, and instead to analyze their entanglements in particular situations. That is something that the nuanced account of the Amsterdam metro struggles does so well. But another task is to examine in critical detail, as a number of other chapters do, how the undergrounds of these cities have now become part of their spectacular images, and how each city trades in various ways on its renown as a center of underground culture to distinguish itself on the global stage. The very proposition of a commercial guide to the underground, considered in the book's final chapter, embodies some of the paradoxes involved in this process, as it attempts to render visible for consumption what is meant, in its designation as underground, to resist by being oppositional, marginal, and ephemeral.

Yet, if the book could slide into a longing for past undergrounds, now lost to a world of neoliberalism and hypercommodification, the authors collectively avoid this. Looking downward, they have the present conditions and possible futures of cities in mind as much as their pasts. In so doing, they encourage exploration of the underground's changing configurations as well as the varied subterranean relationships, circulations, and forces currently at work in constituting urban spaces. Included among them are perhaps those quietly burrowing away, hidden from view, awaiting their time. What forms they might take, and through what images they might best be thought, remain open questions. This rich collection of essays nevertheless reminds us of the significance of sounding these depths, and of how differently cities appear when addressed in terms of their undersides.

1. Concepts and Practices of the Underground

Christoph Lindner and Andrew Hussey

Paris-Amsterdam

The post-war histories of Paris and Amsterdam have been significantly defined by and frequently encounter each other in the notion of the 'underground' as both a material and metaphorical space. The underground traffic between the two cities has most often occurred in avant-garde movements. For example, the CoBrA movement, although centered in Amsterdam, Brussels, and Copenhagen, also exerted a strong influence on the Parisian *Nouveaux Réalistes* in the 1950s. Throughout the 1960s, the work and activities of the Situationists, Constant, and the Provos were an important part of the counterculture in both Paris and Amsterdam, often in parallel or simultaneous moments. What all of these projects had in common was a radical reinvention of city space that was both political and aesthetic.

This insight is at the center of this book, which seeks not only to interrogate the interrelating countercultural histories of Paris and Amsterdam in the mid- to late-twentieth century, but also to cast those forward to twenty-first-century realities, where the notion of the underground has also come to include the problems of violence and integration in the Parisian *banlieues* and Amsterdam suburbs, the sex and drugs trade in both cities, the re-imagining of city limits, globalized boundaries, and, in the most literal sense, the impact of the Paris and Amsterdam metros on urban mobility and the heterogeneity of city life. Shuttling back and forth between Paris and Amsterdam – as well as between post-war avant-gardism and twenty-first-century global urbanism – this book seeks to create a mirroring effect over the notion of the underground as a necessarily dissonant but also culturally-binding force in the making of the contemporary European city.

Hipsters and Counterculture

The origins of the first usage of the term 'underground' – meaning, in this context, cultural resistance to mainstream power structures – are notoriously unclear. Most cultural historians agree, however, that the word probably first took on this meaning at some point in the 1950s in the United States (see Green; De Groot; Sandbrook). Indeed the various anxieties and dissident currents which coursed in an underground fashion through post-war America were most famously given a wider public in Norman Mailer's extended essay *The White Negro: Superficial Reflections on the Hipster*, published in 1957. The aim of this essay was to give an account of young white people from the 1920s to 1940s who had fallen so deeply in love with jazz music that they had adopted black culture as their own. Mailer's essay was not the first to document this phenomenon. As far back as 1948 *Partisan Review* had published an article by Anatole Broyard called 'A Portrait of the Hipster' which hailed the Greenwich Village jazz fan as a 'kind of Surrealist' and 'an underground poet' (43).

Mailer's essay went one step further, however. Drawing upon his recent readings of Jean-Paul Sartre, Mailer defined the hipster as 'an American existentialist' (11) who rejects all forms of conformity as the enemy of real culture. More than this, Mailer's hipsters, with their own secret language (based on the jive talk of their jazz heroes) and a nihilistic philosophy of total freedom, were 'wise primitives' (11) who had declared war on the orthodoxies of the McCarthy era. From this point of view, *The White Negro* is not mere journalism, nor just the uncomfortably-titled self-indulgences of a swelling writerly ego, but also, and more importantly, a call to arms.

The sociologist Bernice Martin has described what happened next in Western society as an 'Expressive Revolution'. By this she meant the explosion of the counterculture in the 1960s, as the hip American 'underground' went 'over ground'. Across all of the arts, in politics, philosophy, psychoanalysis, the term 'underground' became a codeword to designate a way of thinking and behaving which, if it was not always totally new, was always at odds with received ideas. Martin has described this impulse as being driven by what she calls 'anti-structure' as the guiding principle of all 'underground activity', from art to aesthetics, from cinema to 'happenings' and 'anti-psychiatry' (132-3). This cuts across all oppositional movements and personalities of the era, she implies, ranging from the Beats to Timothy Leary to the Black Panthers. More precisely, she defines all of this activity as drawing together 'the pitting of freedom and fluidity against form and structure ... a long and concerted attack on boundaries, limits, certainties, conventions, taboos, roles, system, style, category, predictability, form, structure and ritual. It was the pursuit of ambiguity and the incarnation of uncertainty' (133).

The real paradox at work here, however, is the extent to which this activity made its presence felt – even visible – in mainstream culture, where it disrupted but did not dislodge established power structures. It is hard to find a better example of this than the Beatles's song 'Revolution 9', a dislocated and sinister sound collage, influenced by Stockhausen and John Cage, which was owned by millions around the world within days of its release in 1968, and then listened to mainly with indifference and boredom from a public who probably preferred commercial pop but who could also just about put up with the self-indulgent noise of the 'underground'.

This apparent problematic was one of the many reasons why so many European avant-garde groups at first kept their distance from the 'pop revolutionaries' in Britain and America, who seemed only to confirm and to consolidate the spectacle of commodity culture, against which these Europeans – many still steeped in the language of classical Marxism – had been fighting their own long war. More to the point, what this ironic dead end seemed to highlight was that the 'Expressive Revolution' of the Anglo-American counterculture was not at all the same thing as the concrete, concerted action of a real political Revolution. There was of course much talk of 'Revolution' in underground circles in the Anglo-American world, but for the most part this was focused on liberating sexuality, awakening the unconscious mind, and dreaming up myriad varieties of utopianism.

Nonetheless it was inevitable that the seismic shifts which were taking place in the 'Anglosphere' would eventually have an impact within Europe, as the sex, drugs, and rock 'n' roll culture met the dialectical rigor of European Marxists head-on. The twin capitals of this encounter were Paris and Amsterdam.

Urban War Games

In Paris, until the mid-1960s, the post-war underground most often meant resistance to the French Communist Party, the monolith that dominated working-class politics during this era. Other 'underground' movements included the French and Algerian supporters of the FLN (*Front de Libération Nationale*), which were determined to bring the Algerian war to Paris. These insurgents had their corollary on the right in the form of the OAS (*Organisation de l'armée secrete*) and their armed proxies who were fighting their own war against the French government, whom they saw as the betrayers of the *Algérie Française*. Against this background, the avant-gardists of the period – including former Surrealists, Lettrists, and Situationists – were forced through necessity to conceive of their work in hard political terms.

Similarly, in Amsterdam, the avant-gardists of the *Vrij Beelden*, the *Nederlandse Experimental Groep*, the early CoBrA group, and others had been marked by their own experience of war, occupation, and resistance. The most persistent motif in the work of these interrelated groups was building on the wreckage of the blasted cityscapes of post-war Europe: art and architecture had a political mission to replace the failures of the 'old civilization'. One of the key texts of the era for Amsterdam avant-gardists was Johan Huizinga's *Homo Ludens*, first published in Dutch in 1938. This was translated into French in the early 1950s and was devoured just as eagerly by their Parisian counterparts. Essentially, the appeal of this text was Huizinga's argument that all true civilizations emerged from play and not work. Writing in the 1930s, Huizinga seemed to have analyzed and predicted the demise of *homo politicus* and *homo economicus*. In the post-war period, to his readers in Paris and Amsterdam, Huizinga was laying out the blueprint for a new form of city, a new way of existing.

Interestingly, both Paris and Amsterdam provided a ready-made home to ludic traditions of resistance. In Paris, this tradition went back to the 1940s, to the jazz-addicted youth of Paris who hated the Germans who occupied their city with the same venom that they had traditionally directed at teachers or priests. The most fervent disciples of the American jazz masters adopted the baggy zoot suits and greasy, lank hairstyles they had seen in the Hollywood movies that made it through the German censor and called themselves 'Zazous' – apparently a Gallic corruption of the 'zah-zuh-zah' phrase used by the much-cherished bandleader Cab Calloway. As far back as 1942, a journalist called Raymond Asso had written in the collaborationist newspaper *La Globe* of the 'Zazou Menace'. Asso was referring to distinct groups of young people whose main aim in life seemed to be irritating the German authorities as much as was humanly possible.

They were mostly under twenty-one years of age (the 'Zazous' also nicknamed themselves 'J3' – a reference to the ration books which were assigned to those Parisians who had not attained the age of majority). 'Zazous' haunted the terraces of the Champs-Elysées – at the Pam-Pam or La Capoulade – or the Latin Quarter, at the Dupont-Latin, Le Petit Q or Café Cluny. They were distinguished not only by their American suits and tendency to invent slang out of the remnants of English that they took from jazz songs, but also by dandified details, such as wearing a miniscule knot in a necktie or always carrying an umbrella. Female 'Zazous' were unashamedly sexy, sporting the reddest lipstick, thin dresses adorned with big modernist squares, short skirts, and high heels. Both sexes adopted incomprehensible but modish fads as a mark of tribal belonging. These included drinking beer with grenadine or, most bizarrely of all, ordering *carottes râpées*, or grated carrot salad, with every meal.

The 'Zazous' were pranksters and teenage rebels a decade before these attitudes were properly codified in the pop culture of post-war Europe. It would be a ludicrous exaggeration to say that they represented anything like a true threat to the occupying forces, but they were a genuine nuisance and a rallying point for disaffected youths who, precisely because they were below the age of majority, were harder to police and control than other sections of the population.

Twenty years later in Amsterdam, the Provos, a group of anarchistic young people who took their name from the verb 'provoke', turned the antics of disaffected youth into a series of serious insurrections that by 1967 had become a direct challenge to the Dutch government. The Provos had their roots in the variety of anti-consumerist campaigns which became popular among students in Amsterdam from 1962 onward. One of the most playful ways to attack the rigidity of post-war Amsterdam culture during this period was to invoke magic, poetry, and play as weapons against the stultifying rationality of mainstream consumer culture. Throughout the early 1960s, mysterious graffiti appeared across the city: 'Gnot', 'K', 'Klaas comes' or 'Warning'.

The Provos at this stage probably had no more than a dozen adherents at the hard-core of the group. But their style had a massive influence – their name was adopted as '*geuzen*', a rebel name, while a new hip language emerged around it, including '*vogel*' (boy), '*chick*' (girl), '*blowen*' (to smoke a joint), '*te gek*' (crazy), and '*kip*' (policeman). Most importantly, the Provos had a firm grip on the power of signs and symbols in the culture wars of the 1960s: their occupations and demonstrations were all characterized by a willful, antic spirit which was the most effective way of wrong-footing the authorities, whether at the royal wedding in 1966, or the various riots and sit-ins at Vondelpark or Dam Square. For a generation, in the Netherlands and in the wider world, the Provos were the very emblem of underground Amsterdam made into the most spectacular forms of mutiny.

Projections, Mobility, Visibility

This, however, is not just a book about the extended, interconnected history of the underground in Paris and Amsterdam. Indeed the very notion of the underground as defined above actively militates against nostalgia. This does not mean, however, that the passage of time should eradicate memory. With this in mind, the essays that follow aim to engage with the particular nature of the underground in each city and how they speak to each other in the past and present. Reflecting the recurring concerns of the authors, the book is organized into three interlocking sections which focus, respectively, on 'projections', 'mobility', and 'visibility'.

The essays in Part 1 (projections) focus on the aesthetic, performative, and socio-philosophical strategies used by underground artists, groups, thinkers, and activists to re-imagine dominant, established images of Paris and Amsterdam in the urban imaginary. The essays in Part 2 (mobility) focus on the underground as both a material and metaphorical space of movement, diversity, encounter, refuge, and political action. The essays in Part 3 (visibility) offer new critical insights into the existing underground cultures of Paris and Amsterdam in the early-twenty-first century and reflect on these cultures' relation to the so-called 'surface', to the dominant, visible, and increasingly commodified dimensions of urban space and experience. While some essays specifically address either Paris or Amsterdam, and some work comparatively across the two cities, all retain a sharp focus on how concepts and practices of the urban underground animate countercultural spaces, scenes, moments, and movements.

The opening essays by Sophie Berrebi and Andrew Hussey begin in the 1940s and 1950s and seek to excavate from those periods a sense of the material nature of the underground. In the case of Dubuffet in the Paris metro, Berrebi identifies the central ambiguity of Dubuffet's work during this period as the slide, or swerve, between the notion of the underground as a literal space and a metaphorical experience. This ambiguity is unresolved in his painting, and therefore remains a defining tension in revisiting these works.

In a similar way, Andrew Hussey establishes the conflict and tension between the Parisian Situationist Guy Debord and the Dutch artist and architect Constant as the crucial dynamic in the early history of the Situationist International. The word 'Situationist' would of course go on to have great significance in the underground histories of both Paris and Amsterdam: this essay identifies the key debates and points of divergence and suggests that this history is still shaping debate about urban space in both cities.

In the next essay Gert Hekma looks at the history of the sexual underground in Amsterdam, tracing with a forensic eye the fast-moving and sometimes blurred evolution of the city from a provincial metropolis to the world capital of sexual freedom. This is linked to the ludic nature of Provo revolt and also the pre-history of the subcultures that preceded them – the gay youth cultures of 'Pleiners' and 'Sissies', 'Dijkers' and 'Nozems'. Here, the sexual underground is seen as the site of theory as well as activity. Reich, Sade, and Foucault are all regularly invoked by Hekma as avatars of the underground; but this is also, as he points out, a lost world in the fragmentation of twenty-first-century transnational realities.

The essays by Sudeep Dasgupta and Ginette Verstraete focus on the politics of spatiality in, respectively, Paris and Amsterdam, with an emphasis on mapping the margins as the center. In his reading of Karin Albou's 2005 film *La Petite Jérusalem*, Dasgupta analyzes the Parisian metro as the space of transition for a young woman of Tunisian-French-Jewish origins, as she journeys daily between her home in the *banlieue* and her philosophy classes in the center of the city: a journey which takes her literally and metaphorically between worlds. Dasgupta's innovation is to focus on how the film's treatment of delay, detours, and diversions disrupts the hegemonic cultural dichotomy of fixity and mobility.

Verstraete presents a compelling history of the controversial project of the Amsterdam metro line. Most significantly, she situates the varying strategies of opposition to the project beyond the power-resistance divide, demonstrating how the 'messy entanglement' between the underground and institutionalized power functions as a motif in the experience of everyday life in Amsterdam. In particular, she considers how a countercultural art movement was 'integrated' by the municipalized underground space of the metro; and how, as a consequence, resistance was moved from margin to center with conflicting results.

In his essay on 'The Beats in Paris and Beyond', Allen Hibbard establishes the Beat writers of the 1950s and 1960s as the unstable center of a shifting network of like-minded dissidents, with their headquarters in Paris, but with floating islands of influence in Amsterdam, Tangier, and beyond. Hibbard looks to Deleuze and Guattari for a theoretical explanation of how flows of communication traverse the social field into the open space of the 'rhizome', the in-between where accelerated movement propels history forward. This, asserts Hibbard, is how the underground works – a kind of anti-dialectic which carries meaning through desire rather than ideology. Hence the emergence of the transnational underground network of the Beats and their followers, for whom geography is both an accident and an inspiration.

Carolyn Birdsall and Joyce Goggin focus on the visible/audible nature of underground activity in Amsterdam – especially the city's tourist image, place-branding, and the Red Light District, the last of which is arguably the most conspicuous articulation of a normally clandestine activity. Both Birdsall and Goggin are concerned with the paradox of how Amsterdam sells itself as an underground capital, and how this process is sometimes validated, and at other times negated, by the consumerist nature of the spectacle on offer. Most significantly, both essays express an anxiety about Amsterdam's countercultural self-image as mediated through the spectacularization of the underground.

Back in Paris, Anna-Louise Milne gives an account of how illegal immigrants challenge the legal and institutional framework of the city when they make themselves visible on their own terms. She reads this activity within the register of Parisian particularity and the universalism of the French concept of the Law.

The underground she describes is not just in opposition to these forces, but is also a defining component part of them. Also in Paris, Stephen Sawyer maps the underground as a matrix of metaphors and experiences, asking questions about how much is concealed and revealed in everyday Parisian life. The underground he encounters is both a place and a mechanism. More to the point, he argues that knowledge of underground activity in the city exposes the limits of urban experience, at the same as it traces the experience of liminality.

Future City

The meaning and nature of underground activity – already a fluid and elusive concept – has inevitably evolved and mutated in the twenty-first century. Yet, as many of the essays in this volume reveal, the questions asked by so-called underground artists and activists in the 1960s and 1970s have not yet gone away. Rather, their questions about the condition and future of urban space, commodity culture, sex, money, and identity have become ever more acute in the transnational, rapidly globalizing environment of contemporary Europe. What this book reveals in the end is that the underground is not an anachronism but an integral component of how we live in cities and how we will choose to live in cities in the future. That, indeed, is one of the lasting insights of this necessarily eclectic and challenging collection of essays, which reveals Paris and Amsterdam to be, albeit in increasingly complicated and paradoxical ways, enduring epicenters of cultural resistance, subversion, and diversion.

Part 1: Projections

2. Metromania or the Undersides of Painting

Sophie Berrebi

Overhead driveways and their sprawling, spaghetti-like networks have come to exemplify in the collective visual imagination the archetypal motif of late capitalist urban dystopia. The underground railway system, by contrast, speaks of an earlier modernity, one that was born in the industrial age, and developed in the early-twentieth century, producing in that course the now classic dialectic of alienation and progress analyzed by Georg Simmel (1998).

Stepping down into the Parisian metro in the mid-1940s to paint its commuters, the French artist Jean Dubuffet (1901-1985) seemingly avoided those themes. Neither was he much concerned, in the sinister years of the Occupation, with any veiled allusion to the underground resistance movements that occasionally used the metro as a site of action. The straight-faced multicolored puppets that appeared in a large painting (*Le Metro*, 1943) and in a series of equally colorful gouaches (1943) were made in the early years of this third and successful attempt to embark on a career as a visual artist. The recurrence of the subject matter in Dubuffet's oeuvre – a series of lithographs on the metro followed in 1949 – bestows it a programmatic quality for the work that followed. Bypassing the more expected associations with modernity, the metro provided the artist with a mundane set filled with everyday characters that suited the artist's claim to avoid high culture and classical beauty and depict instead the 'common man' in his daily routines. If it were only a vehicle to convey this idea of the common man, the underground, in its incarnation of the Paris metro, would be little more than an accidental support to this idea. Yet underground as an idea recurs in Dubuffet's pictorial and verbal work after this initial period, and extends well beyond the subject matter of the metro. His interest in the ground, the soil, the undergrowth as a subject matter in the 1950s reprises this notion as a visual theme. Furthermore, 'underground', can also be used to describe the 'Art Brut' toward which he displayed a sustained interest as a collector and main theorist, after coining the word in the mid-1940s. Likewise, his celebrations of 'anticulture' – in opposition to established high culture – in particular in a lecture given in English in Chicago in 1951 to an audience of American art amateurs, institutional figures, and artists, may be understood as another oblique reference to an idea of a cultural underground.

Thus if the idea proposed by this book is to explore a certain polysemic understanding of the underground as place and idea associated with the urban my-

2.1. Jean Dubuffet. *Métro*, oil on canvas (1943).

2.2. Jean Dubuffet. *Métro,* gouache on paper (1943).

thologies and histories of Amsterdam and Paris, the term also aptly characterizes a recurring set of interests, issues, and themes that Dubuffet developed throughout his extended career. Within his oeuvre the underground, we might say, is both a place and a metaphor, and relates to both apocryphal and factual aspects of his life, work, and ideas. As such the term 'underground' sums up and resonates deeply yet diffusely with his multi-faceted practice. It can be used to define a set of thematic issues as well as technical concerns, and above all, perhaps, it suggests a way of thinking.

The aim of this essay is to examine the term underground as a key to unlock and define Dubuffet's aesthetic and, if not to iron out the many paradoxes that characterize it, at least to identify some kind of convergence in the wide constellation of his concerns as painter, writer, and collector.

Within Dubuffet's oeuvre, which spans six decades from the early and largely fruitless attempts at becoming an artist in the 1920s and 1930s to his death in 1985 after a prolific career, the depictions of the Paris underground from the 1940s constitute only the first evocation of the underground understood literally as an underground network. Soon after, moving away from the urban context, Dubuffet undertakes a series of paintings that evoke more or less abstractly the soil and what exists underneath the ground. This concern recurs in different works that suggest topographic explorations of a given area or, on the contrary, vertical cuts into the ground. In several instances, the term 'underground' appears in titles that use the French equivalent of the term: '*sous-sol*'. *L'âme des sous-sols* (*The Soul of the Underground*) from 1959 exemplifies this interest. The painting suggests – more than it actually depicts – a formless and undefined area of earth under the ground. In such a work, another idea of underground emerges, as the term might be said to refer not only to the subject matter but also to the radical technical approach to painting that is developed by the artist, who spreads and piles up thickly onto the canvas heavy, muddy substances that make the final work oscillate between the two dimensions of painting and the three dimensions of relief, or sculpture.

A sentence by art theorist and historian Hubert Damisch, one of Dubuffet's most subtle exegetes, establishes, suggestively but briefly, a connection between these two very different ideas of what the 'underground' may signify as subject matter and technique. Writing in 1962 what is, in part, a phenomenological critique of Dubuffet, Damisch remarked,

> If Dubuffet does not enjoy working with flat brushstrokes, that is because the observer of the 'dessous de la capitale' (the undersides of Paris) and the geologist that he later became, likes to work within the thickness of the ground – I mean the painting – and to disclose its undersides. (*Fenêtre* 114, author's translation)

Although Damisch does not develop this direct connection any further in his essay, it also appears in the very title of the book in which this text was reprinted, *Fenêtre jaune cadmium ou les dessous de la peinture*. The title of this book, which contains a series of monographic essays on twentieth-century artists, is

2.3. Jean Dubuffet. *L'âme des sous-sols*, silver-paper (1959).

remarkably close to the title of the book compiled by Jean Dubuffet and Jean Paulhan in 1949: *La Métromanie ou les dessous de la capitale*. The heading of my own paper brings together the titles of these two publications in order to take up Damisch's brief – but highly significant – allusion and delve further into questioning the relationship between the *undersides* of Paris and those of painting.

More specifically, my aim is to examine how the idea of underground, in all its semantic variety, can be construed as a term to define Dubuffet's practice. In turn this will shed light on how Dubuffet's work, through its continuous involvement with different kinds of underground, contributes to the definition of this term somewhat more generally in the framework of cultural production in the post-war period.

The 1940s, and in particular what I call the 'metro years' from 1943 to 1949, is a key period to look at in this context. It brackets a period of a few years during which Dubuffet raises in provocative ways the question of the human figure, of the painters' technique and materials, and of culture and its dissidences. How these different streams of interests coalesced in defining a particular form of 'underground thinking', or 'thinking of the underground' – as Andrew Hussey evokes in his chapter – that profoundly orientated and defined his practice of the following decade is what I want to investigate.

The Underneath of Paris

The metro paintings and gouaches from 1943-1945 were created in the midst of Dubuffet's series the *Marionettes de la ville et de la campagne*. The *Marionnettes* were the artist's earliest public statement and consisted of paintings, gouaches, and drawings depicting urban scenes with Parisian buildings and their inhabitants, and country landscapes complete with animals and farmers. Formally, the paintings combined flattened perspective, bright, at time unmixed colors, with coarsely outlined and schematically drawn figures. They exude a general effect that might be described as one of conscious, playful, and elaborate 'de-skilling' by which Dubuffet deliberately went against the subtle color harmonies of an Henri Matisse, and the artful and precise distortions of a Pablo Picasso, to compare him to two veteran modernists who were celebrated by important exhibitions in Paris at the end of the war, at the time Dubuffet encountered his first successes on the Paris art scene. Dubuffet followed up this theme of the metro with a series of gouaches that reprise the characteristics of the large metro painting from 1943, on a smaller scale and in ten scenes. Dubuffet hoped to assemble these scenes into a book but the project, which lingered in the publisher's offices, was ultimately rejected by Gaston Gallimard. Despite this, it caught the attention of Jean Paulhan, a seminal figure of the French literary world and for a long time, until the Occupation, the editor of Gallimard's literary journal, *La Nouvelle Revue Française*. Paulhan, a collector of contemporary art and occasional critic, had then recently discovered Dubuffet's work. His accolade brought him a certain controversial reputation, along with many acquaintances with writers and a sustained dialogue about literature and art (see Dubuffet 2004).

In this context, Jean Paulhan penned, in 1945, a series of five very short stories destined to accompany the metro gouaches. The text and paintings remained an unpublished project that was revived a few years later when Dubuffet, casting aside the gouaches, drew a series of lithographic prints alongside which he copied out by hand Paulhan's text. Anna Louise Milne has described the whimsical quality and the falsely naïve style of some of Paulhan's writing of the time, and while this certainly applies to this text in *La Métromanie ou les dessous de la capitale*, it equally reflects the character of Dubuffet's images. They depict little groups of figures outlined in Dubuffet's trademark simplified, somewhat childlike style. His characters are shown seated on benches on the train platforms, waiting, clambering into trains, and squeezed into coaches. Complete with felt hats, bow ties, and handbags, the figures closely illustrate Paulhan's text, both in subject matter and in visual impact: the pictures are embedded within the text and drawn with the same thin lines than the handwritten text. Yet while the result suggests, visually, proximity between the two authors, in reality, Dubuffet and Paulhan approached the metro from polarized perspectives.

For Dubuffet, this archetypal urban subject matter had above all a provocative dimension – first of all, in the way in which it played with the conventional notion that painting thrives on light and on representing its effect on the surfaces of things. Depicting an underground space lit with artificial light only made a clear statement about the pedestrian nature Dubuffet wished to confer to his art. If, furthermore, we read the metro series as invoking, metaphorically, an underground aesthetic, a secretive, dissident art practice removed from the mainstream, there was something paradoxical in taking as a subject matter for this purpose accidental gatherings of average, mainstream people, displaying a broad variety of human types. Grouped together and frozen still for a few minutes between two stops, they presented the artist with ready-made, constantly changing *tableaux vivants* that epitomized everyday life in all its banality and randomness. Yet these were also precisely the types he claimed were his ideal audience. Writing in January 1945 a pre-project for a conference on painting destined to a wide audience, Dubuffet explained: 'I would rather that my paintings amuse and interest the man on the street when he comes out of work, not the fanatic, the connoisseur, but the person who has no particular instruction or disposition' ('Avant-projet' 36, author's translation).

For Jean Paulhan, by contrast, the metro took on graver undertones. His short tales are allusive and metaphorical, evoking the hardship of the war, the dire economic situation of its immediate aftermath (his text is dated 20 June 1945), and the moral crisis of a society that had endured years of Occupation and emerged politically divided. Furthermore, Paulhan's allusion to the Resistance through the voice of one of his characters: '*d'ici trois mois, dit Castille, je devrais me cacher comme sous l'occupation*' ('Within three months, said Castille, I will have to hide myself, as under the Occupation'), recalls more generally the metro's historical as well as symbolic importance as a place of underground contestation of German authority. The metro indeed was the site of one of the first acts of resistance in 1941 when Pierre Georges Fabien, who later gave his name to the metro stop Colonel Fabien, shot dead a German soldier on 21 August at Barbès Rochechouart. Unlike Dubuffet, Paulhan had been an active member of the Resistance and his reference to underground secret action – even though he did not participate in the post-war cult of the Resistance – reads as another subtext in the book's otherwise more fanciful tone.

Differences, however, can be productive, and pursuing this idea of underground as resistance, the metro project can be read as anticipating a double form of underground thinking that marks an early turning point in Dubuffet's aesthetic. This change occurs through the process of translation by which Paulhan reacted to Dubuffet's gouaches of 1943 with a text to which, in return, Dubuffet responded by producing a new set of images, this time lithographs, in 1949. Translation here might imply mutual transformations of each author's ideas, and perhaps a productive misunderstanding by which the metro became something else than the sum of their diverging perspectives.

In 1949 Dubuffet was in a very different place than he had been in 1943. After resuming artistic practice tentatively in 1942 and becoming introduced into some important circles of the Parisian literary world, Dubuffet experienced controversial success with this first two solo exhibitions organized at the René Drouin Gallery on the Place Vendôme. This notoriety helped him in turn to gain a gallery representative in New York by 1947 and through this dealer, Pierre Matisse, a larger set of collectors, which was a relatively rare occurrence for an artist of his generation, but which meant, in this case, that by 1947 the Museum of Modern Art in New York owned one of his paintings. Dubuffet had also authored a volume of writings on his aesthetic views and artistic practice, which Paulhan helped to collect and publish at Gallimard under the title *Prospectus aux amateurs de tout genre*.

In the period of six years between the metro painting and the book of lithographs, *La Métromanie,* his ideas about art had clearly shifted. The man on the street to whom he wanted to reach out, as he explained in 'Avant-projet d'une conférence populaire sur la peinture' (January 1945), did not warm up much to his work, as the violence of critical reactions to his exhibitions in the mainstream press showed. Within a few years, Dubuffet's attitude changed, a modification that was reflected in both his paintings and his writings. His 'Notes pour les fins lettres' ('Notes for the Well-Lettered'), also from 1945, dealt with broad aesthetic issues but through the more reduced prism of technical issues in painting. Developing a more difficult form of painting toned down to neutrals and thickly layered onto the canvas, coupled with a growing interest in marginalized forms of art production, Dubuffet also began to develop a conception of an art removed both from mainstream culture and from the avant-garde. In an important essay from 1949, he stated: 'True art is always where it is not expected, where nobody thinks of it nor says its name' ('L'Art Brut' 90-1, author's translation). As well as endowing art with a secretive quality, in praising qualities of elusiveness and secrecy, this sentence curiously visualized a process akin to political resistance activities, and evokes the vital constant mutability and secretiveness of resistance movements as during the Second World War.

These six years between 1943 and 1949 also witnessed a shift in Dubuffet's art practice. The metro painting and gouaches of 1943 showed flattened, simplified hieratic figures evocative of medieval stained glass. These gouaches were cited in the opening plates of the lithograph book of 1949 that displays similarities of style and composition. But immediately after, illustrating the first of the four short stories or playlets by Paulhan, Dubuffet shows figures embedded in a network of lines, scratches, and smudges. Entrenched deep in the landscape (the first story takes place in the countryside), the figures appear boxed into a tight, irregular spider-like web of lines and marks. The high horizon line that leaves only a small white strip at the top of the plate tilts the scenery forward to the surface of the page, as if Dubuffet was depicting the ground simultaneously from above and in cross section. In this way, the landscape depicted becomes at the same time a background and an underground. Both the tight enclosure of the figures that presses them into the ground and the sense of dual viewpoint are repeated in several plates that follow, as one story, leading to another, displaces the action from the countryside to the city and its metro. The last illustration located in a rural environment announces literally the descent into the metro by strikingly depicting a figure seen in profile, laying horizontally face down, but less toward the ground than already half immerged into it. The following image extends this visual theme. It shows a male figure standing in front of a map of the metro, stretching out an arm as if to search for his itinerary. Although the figure is depicted in front of the map, the contours of his body subtly merge with the network of metro lines and names of stops, and partly engulf him, making

2.4. Jean Dubuffet. *Adieu vieille terre...* , on page 13 of Jean Paulhan's *La Métromanie ou les dessous de la capitale.* Lithograph on paper, transferred to stone (1949).

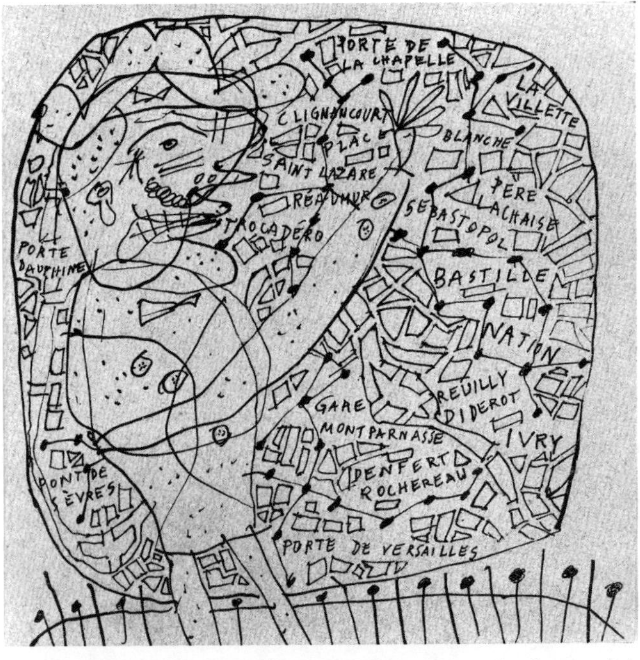

2.5. Jean Dubuffet. Plate 3 of Jean Paulhan's *La Métromanie ou les dessous de la capitale.* Lithograph on paper, transferred to stone (1949).

unclear the limit between human figure and map. In a third image that marks the transition into the metro, Dubuffet boldly juxtaposes again two views: a profile view of a figure on top of the stairs leading into the metro, and a view of the staircase and the fence around the entrance to the metro surrounding the figure in a semi-circular shape.

This bringing together of different viewpoints, made by playing with the rules of 'correct' drawing and perspective, occurs repeatedly throughout the book. Hence a few striking plates further on in the book show figures set in an abstracted space made up of irregular hatchings. Barely visible save for their faces and grinning smiles, they seem embedded very deep underground, gesticulating as if trying either to extract themselves from the murky soil or on the contrary to take a regressive pleasure in being stuck into it. The lithographs of the *Métromanie* book depict space in a far more complex way than Dubuffet's earlier representations of the metro did. In the book, the flatness has given way to a newly created depth, which originates in the juxtaposition of viewpoints that disorientate the viewer.

In a text from 1945, Dubuffet had evoked his difficulty in the 1920s and 1930s to find an entry point into painting: '*je cherchais l'entrée*', he wrote ('Plus modeste' 90). With the metro series Dubuffet finds an entrance into more experimental work, stocking up ideas experimented in linear drawing that will later be translated into painting. The metro lithographs are, furthermore, a cipher by which Dubuffet displaces his '*je cherchais l'entrée*' into an '*entrée en matière*' as

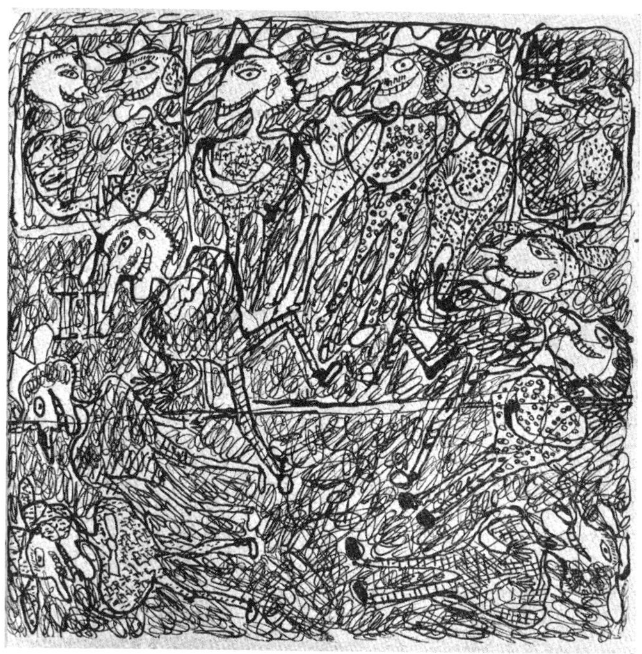

2.6. Jean Dubuffet. Plate 8 of Jean Paulhan's *La Métromanie ou les dessous de la capitale*. Lithograph on paper, transferred to stone (1949).

Hubert Damisch, playing with words in an essay from 1985, called his entrance into another form of underground, far more organic and topographic.

The Undersides of Painting

This second form of underground is concerned with the material texture of painting, which, in Dubuffet's works, is achieved through extensive experimentation with a host of fine art and ordinary materials. A series of paintings from 1945-1946, dubbed '*Hautes Pâtes*' by the artist, exemplified his interest in what I want to see as another way of thinking the 'underground'. Those paintings reprised subject matters of his earlier series, *Marionnettes de la ville et de la campagne*, but swapped flat surfaces and primary colors for complex mixes of paint, sand, straw, pebbles, and other organic materials which created thick, dark-colored paintings in which figures were gouged rather than painted. These radical *Hautes Pâtes* paintings prefigured what became, after the metro lithographs of 1949, a main concern in Dubuffet's work for the decade that followed. From 1949 to 1960, the experimental quality of Dubuffet's paintings resides in his increasingly wild explorations of the capacity of painting to absorb extraneous materials. Putties and resins complement the natural materials introduced earlier. Announced by the metro lithographs and their experimental depiction of space, the works from the 1950s combine textural inventiveness with spatial disorientation. Dubuffet explores repeatedly the ground and the underground both in design and texture and through subject matter and technical approach. The last paintings of the decade, from the so-called *Matériologies* series, represent a complete fusion of these different interconnected aspects. A few key works mark the steps of this development toward the *Matériologies*. A 1951 painting, *Le Géologue* (The Geologist) is a key work in this respect, and one that Damisch mentions in the sentence quoted at the start of this essay.

Depicting a figure peering into the ground through a magnifying lens, standing over a vast expanse of indefinable ground, *The Geologist* launched Dubuffet's interest in the depiction of the ground and what is beneath it. The many characters and types riding the metro have now all disappeared but one. This solitary figure is itself gradually absorbed, devoured by the land around it as in another painting of the same series entitled eloquently *Le Voyageur sans boussole* (*The Traveller without a Compass*). If this is not strictly true of all the works of the early 1950s – many of them depict more or less clearly little characters clambering across expanses of land – the change of focus in these works from figure to the space surrounding them defines, what Jean Luc Nancy describes as what constitutes for him, in *Paysage avec dépaysement,* the genre of landscape painting. In a letter written from New York in early 1952, Dubuffet indeed described his increasingly bare, very textured expanses of paint in which occasionally a face or a character peers out, as being produced merely '*par force d'habitude*' ('by the force of habit').

Elaborating on this coming forth of the ground, the place, in landscape painting (hence the stress on *pays*, in *paysage*) Nancy writes: 'If I wanted to push it, I

2.7. Jean Dubuffet. *Le géologue,* oil on canvas (1950).

would say that instead of painting the countryside as a place, he paints it as its underside: what presents itself there is the announcement of what is not there' (114). Although it is somewhat of a facile pun, this idea of *endroit* which is an *envers* suggestively describes the rough stretches of land that are so devoid of any characteristics that they seem to depict not only the ground but also its other side, its underside. These places might be non-places, they might be the underground, the undergrowth or the soil seen from above, and throughout the 1950s, Dubuffet's painting seems to alternate between depicting plane and underground.

The surfaces of his paintings in the early 1950s, particularly from the *Paysage du mental* series, are indeed most often not only piled up (as they were in the *Hautes Pâtes* of the 1940s) but also filled with craters and recesses created by shrinking resins. When they are not as thick as these, in the *Pâtes battues* (*Beaten Pastes*) series of 1953 and 1954 that followed, the creamy top layer is scratched to reveal an under layer painted in a different way (Damisch *Fenêtre*). A few years later, Dubuffet resorts to another strategy to evoke the interplay between underground and above the ground. This consists, in his so-called *Texturologies*, in superimposing layers of projected speckles of paint of different but similar colors that create optical illusions of depth. The series that closed the decade of the 1950s, the *Matériologies,* present a kind of climax of this depiction of the ground. Completely devoid of figures or lines, these large works by Dubuffet's standards at this time consist in aggregations of natural and artificial materials, including tin foil, resins, and straw. There is no longer any suggestion of viewpoint. In fact these are almost three-dimensional objects that evoke iron and copper ore, a chunk or slab that would have been carved out from a layer of the underground.

While these paintings go quite far in exemplifying art as underground, not only through representation, but through what this representation implies as a secretive practice, carried out in resistance against assimilation to prettiness and easy visual consumption – there is no eye candy here – there is another way to read them in terms of underground. Here we go back to Hubert Damisch and his interest in the undersides of painting. For Damisch, this notion goes back to Balzac's best-known novella *Le chef-d'oeuvre inconnu* (*The Unknown Masterpiece*) in which one of the protagonists discovers the painting his master has kept hidden for so long. Peering beneath the mess of paint layers of the failed masterpiece, the viewer calls out: '*il y a une femme la dessous*' ('there is a woman under there'), or behind this, as the plot suggests this is a double entendre. The novella introduces for Damisch a reflection on the importance of the *dessous* or underside or underneath, a term that refers to the traditional secrets of coating and layering of painting in the secrecy of studio practice, as it evokes the more modern 'cuisine' of the painter, that is, the unorthodox experimentations with materials by which artists create their idiosyncratic touch. Delacroix is mentioned in this context, along with Jackson Pollock and, more to our point, Dubuffet.

Dubuffet's exploration of the undersides of painting, his experiments with materials, his way of piling them up thickly on the surface of his canvas or board, his depictions of the ground, and his scratching and gouging of surfaces, further present Damisch with an antithesis of the definition of modernist painting as proposed in mid-twentieth-century New York, by the critic Clement Greenberg. For Greenberg modernist painting defined itself by its particular attention to the medium and its properties: paint as well as the canvas and what he called its 'inherent flatness'. Thinking differently to Greenberg, Pollock, Dubuffet and several other artists, Damisch defines the underground, or, as he calls it, the *dessous*, as an alternative to flatness, and a primary quality of modern art. It is through this attention to the '*dessous*' that the historian gains a new understanding of the way in which artists break with illusionary perspective by delving into the physical properties of painting and exposing its undersides, which are traditionally left secret or hidden. In this idea of underlayer in painting, another interpretation of the underground appears. It becomes a criteria by which modern art can be re-interpreted, against the domination of the visual sense that is predominant in the Greenbergian version of modernism. Stressing the underside therefore means both working against this domination of the visual, against an idea of pure visibility and, as Damisch argues in reference to phenomenology, it also means to conceive of painting as an activity that engages all bodily senses rather than exclusively vision (*Fenêtre* 116-17).

Underground and Avant-Garde

By way of an extended conclusion I want to return to the period of the metro to address a third dimension of the idea of underground. In the title of the book, *La Métromanie ou les dessous de la capitale*, the first word, *métromanie* – translated as 'metromania' in English – is diverted from its usual meaning of an obsession with writing verse. It is meant to signify instead the kind of dizziness that overcomes the obsessive metro rider, the passenger who, having punched his ticket in the morning, spends his entire day criss-crossing the city, riding the metro as a merry-go-round. The manic behavior described by Paulhan in his text hints to another type of obsession, closer in fact to the original meaning of metromania, the compulsion not of writing verse, but of drawing and painting. This type of compulsion, found first in individuals whose works Dubuffet began to collect in Switzerland, prompted by the famous 1922 book by Hans Prinzhorn, *Bildnerei der Geisteskranken*, began to interest him at the same time as he worked on the metro versions, and was shared with Jean Paulhan.

Art Brut (a term translated by Roger Cardinal in 1972 as 'outsider art'), became Dubuffet's version of Prinzhorn's psychopathological art, although, as Dubuffet staunchly claimed, the two were different. Art Brut for Dubuffet referred more specifically to visual productions of people he found living at the margins of society in social or psychological isolation, who had never had training in the visual arts and were in effect sheltered from mainstream culture through a diversity of circumstances such as imprisonment or confinement in a retirement home or an asylum. These were not artists in the cultural, socially acknowledged sense of the term, nor were they psychotics whose graphic productions were studied by psychiatric doctors, as in Prinzhorn's publication. Rather, what Dubuffet found so important in the Art Brut 'artists' he found and identified as such is that they were animated by a compulsion to create, something that Dubuffet believed was absent in what he called 'cultural artists', including in members of the avant-garde. Dubuffet shared this interest in Art Brut with a group of writers that included Paulhan alongside André Breton and Henri-Pierre Roché, and he federated this enthusiasm by creating in 1947 the Foyer de l'Art Brut in order to collect funds and administer the growing collection he was compiling. Paulhan was one of his early companions in this. The pair traveled across Switzerland in 1945 during an early research trip that the writer recounted in a short book, *Guide d'un petit voyage en Suisse.*

While the term 'Art Brut' does in no way apply to Dubuffet's own production as is sometimes wrongly assumed, Art Brut did constitute for him the ideal model of an art driven – as Damisch has put it – by 'inner necessity'. Dubuffet's rhetorical attempts to place himself apart from other art movements, rejecting for instance the label *informel* that came to define the more organic abstract painting of the 1950s, and his efforts to construct himself a very specific, isolated position on the contemporary French art scene testify to this idea of Art Brut as an ideal model for artistic practice

As a secretive, marginal, alternative practice of art, Art Brut constitutes, an epitome of underground thinking. If Dubuffet defined Art Brut as the opposite of mainstream art (notably in a lecture and essay entitled 'Art brut préféré aux arts culturels', from 1949), Art Brut as a notion may also help shape more generally an influential idea of the underground as a form of aesthetic resistance, following a common meaning of the term in the English language. This of course is anachronistic to some degree: the 1962 edition of the Littré dictionary does not contain the English term 'underground', although a more recent edition from Le Robert does.

In the metro pictures, Dubuffet transformed the political associations of resistance evoked by Jean Paulhan in his text into purely aesthetic ones. This transformation process, which is visible in Dubuffet's writings of the same period, was further developed in the paintings of the 1950s that evoke, in increasingly abstract terms, the underground understood literally as 'what is under the ground'. Along with the *Hautes Pâtes* from the mid-1940s, it is upon these works that Hubert Damisch's theory of the undersides of painting has rested, as a form of aesthetic dissidence in relation to the orthodoxy of flatness in modernist painting. Further, with Art Brut, Dubuffet was able to create and theorize upon a movement that placed itself far beyond the avant-garde, in a sense, as an anti-avant-garde, an ultimate, almost tautological underground, since the authors who where part of it were so estranged from mainstream culture that they were not even aware of being 'artists' or of being in a movement.

Together, these different ways of interpreting the notion of underground take steps into outlining a posture that sought to distance itself from the so called 'historical' avant-garde movements of the 1910s and 1920s of which Dubuffet was a firsthand witness, and sometimes participant in the course of his early artistic experiments in a period he later dubbed his 'prehistory'. In attempting to function *against* the 'historical' avant-garde, Dubuffet's reflection on the underground aims to locate another space of aesthetic contestation, one that he liked to call *anticultural*, as in his lecture 'Anticultural Positions'. This radical re-thinking of the avant-garde and of aesthetic dissent is what made Dubuffet a precious example for some of the artists who, in the 1950s and 1960s, also called in their own terms for an anticultural positioning. His work was hence much admired by some of the artists that formed CoBrA, for its raw visual quality and effort to 'unlearn' drawing. It also served as a model for the early Claes Oldenburg, who translated Dubuffet's idea of anti-culture in the context of the United States and its a-cultural condition (see Berrebi 'Paris Circus'). At the same time however, the source of that aesthetic, in being closely connected to that modern, industrial invention, the '*metropolitain*', remained firmly anchored in a notion of underground that the 1960s avant-garde movements, discussed in other chapters in this book, would transform in a more radical way.

3. Mapping Utopia: Debord and Constant between Amsterdam and Paris

Andrew Hussey

1.

Halfway down Spuistraat, one of the main arteries of central Amsterdam, at number 216, there is a relic of the recent radical past of the city, now fading fast from memory into history. This is the Squat Vrankrijk, one of the most iconic of the remaining squats in the city left over from the squatting boom and police confrontations of the 1980s. The busy cultural life of the Squat Vrankrijk these days is for the most part the fairly standard amalgam of hip-hop, anarchism, and skate punk. The graffiti on the exterior facades tells, however, a different, older story.

Scattered throughout the drawings and stenciled images are several slogans and indeed whole paragraphs taken from the *Internationale Situationniste*, the

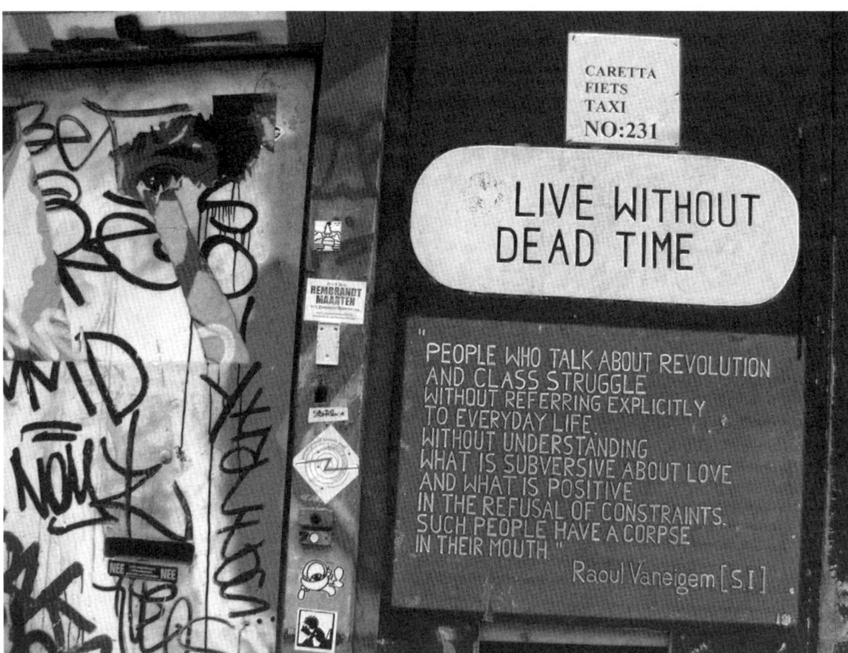

3.1. Situationist graffiti on the Spuistraat, Amsterdam. (Photo: M. Meissner)

house journal of the iconoclastic coalition of artists and intellectuals known as the Situationist International (SI), which lasted from 1957 to 1967 and which, among other things, has been claimed as the main influence on the Paris events of May 1968 and even the British Punk Rock movement (Marcus; Dumontier; Savage 15-25). Obviously, these slogans, denouncing the 'spectacle' of modern life and proclaiming the emptiness of consumerism and capitalist society, still have meaning and currency for the squatters of Vrankrijk; but there is also a sense in which they can be read as emblematic, carrying traces of an earlier moment in the history of 'underground' culture in Paris and Amsterdam, when subversive movements spoke to each other and inspired in each other differing but parallel techniques for remaking the world.

This moment is roughly the period 1955 to 1967, the years leading up to the revolt of May 68, when artists and activists travelled between Paris and Amsterdam, nourishing in both cities a growing sense of revolt and sharing revolutionary tactics and techniques. There was of course nothing unique about this traffic: during this same period young people developed their radical politics in London, Berlin, and New York, reading much the same texts, from Marx and Marcuse to Wilhelm Reich. There was, however, a very specific movement between Paris and Amsterdam of groups who called themselves 'Situationists'. Nowadays, the term 'Situationist' is usually attributed to the Paris-based group around Guy Debord, who edited *Internationale Situationniste* from 1957 to 1972 and who was without doubt its leading force and chief theoretician. It may well be argued that a great deal of activity by recent scholars of the Situationist movement has been to reinforce the already powerful and unassailable role of Guy Debord in Situationist history (see, for example, Kaufman).

The word 'Situationist', however, has also played an important role in the lexicon of subversive political and artistic activity in the Netherlands. Most notably, from 1962 to 1964 the artist Jacqueline de Jong published the journal *Situationist Times*, bringing together renegade Situationists from the Paris-based group and fellow-travelers from the UK, Germany, Scandinavia, and Belgium (Hussey, *Game of War* 172-3). The Dutch-based rebel groups, the Provos and the Kabouters, often described themselves or were described as 'Situationist', and even if they had no official link to either the Amsterdam or Paris-based groups, they also used terms such as 'spectacle' and used techniques and ideas borrowed from shared sources such as Johan Huizinga or Surrealism. But there is also a wider historical context to this discussion of the sliding definitions of 'Situationist' between Paris and Amsterdam which is related to the notion and development of 'underground' cultures in the two cities. More to the point, although it is unclear when the word 'underground' precisely entered the language in French or Dutch, it is almost certain that it was not at the same time nor defined in the same way.

The Dutch writer and historian Geert Mak traces the rise of 'underground' movements in Amsterdam to the early 1960s. This was the beginning of what he calls 'the Twenty Year Civil War', a long war of attrition fought against the government and city authorities by a variety of groups and with varied tactics (Buruma; Van Duijn). More precisely this 'underground culture' in Amsterdam was very much a homegrown phenomenon – the Provos and Kabouters, as Mak points out, were very much rooted in local contingencies and meanings. At the same time rock music and drug culture from the Anglo-American world fed into and shaped the cultural language and indeed the politics of Netherlands-based movements. As opposed to Paris, Amsterdam is where the European avant-gardes met, and sometimes dissolved into groups which in various ways blended into a 'counterculture' on the Anglo-American model, meaning that the priorities were pleasure and freedom rather than just the apparently outmoded language of class struggle.

In France, by contrast, the term 'underground' only really became popular and popularized toward the early 1970s, in the wake of the seismic cultural shifts that occurred in the wake of the revolts of May '68. During this period, the term 'underground', was commonly used as a cipher for artistic and political revolt in the journal *Actuel*, edited by the influential figure of Jean-François Bizot, and the publishing house Champ Libre under the aegis of Gérard Guégan and Gérard Lébovici (Bizot; Hamon and Rotman). Until then, through the 1950s and 1960s, through the histories of the Nouveaux Réalistes, Letterists, and Maoists, 'underground' activity was traditionally a harder political culture and was indeed more driven by the language of classical Marxism and Hegelianism and debates over the meaning of history. As such, these groups belonged more properly to the stricter notion of an 'avant-garde' that is not simply a focus of revolt but which is organized on a historical mission: traditional materialism in other words. Seen from this point of view, as twin capitals of the international 'underground', Paris and Amsterdam often seemed to be on very separate and distinct trajectories.

This is why, taking my cue from the graffiti of the Squat Vrankrijk, the historical moment I have chosen to examine is the brief but intense collaboration between Guy Debord and the Dutch artist Constant between 1957 and 1960. During this period both men were members of the *Internationale Situationniste* and thinking together to develop a working definition not of the word 'Situationist' but of what 'Situationist' theory and activity might be: in other words, this moment of collaboration was the crucible of the movement (McDonough 44; Kaufman 150-9; Marelli 123-35; Ford 50-7). The cities of Paris and Amsterdam, as I will demonstrate, were central to this process in the most literal way.

2.

Constant had first made contact with Debord in 1956 and became a key figure in the group. He was part of the editorial team on *Internationale Situationniste* 3 and 4, provided important texts to the journal during this period (1957-1960), and was given the responsibility of developing and promoting Situationist activity in the Netherlands, primarily by attracting sociologists and architects to the group. Above all, what brought Debord and Constant together in this first phase, commonly known as the 'artistic' phase, of the Situationist International was a shared belief that contemporary avant-garde movements had betrayed their original commitment to revolution (Sadler 158-9; Wigley 14-18). The Situationists aimed at reinstating revolution, not as metaphor but as lived experience, at the heart of the avant-garde program. 'Situationist' strategy, Debord argued, would, by contrast, be an endless, ever-changing series of offensive actions, which created 'situations without a future', confusing and wrong-footing the enemy (McDonough 45).

At this point in their history the Situationists conceived of the modern city as the battleground for the meaning of modernity. Accordingly, the most ambitious aspect of the collaboration between Debord and Constant was the imagined city they called 'New Babylon'. This was a series of plans, designs, maps, models, and photographs which aimed to be the concrete representation of the 'Situationist city'. The name had been coined by Debord – Constant's original title had been 'Dériville', from the Situationist activity of the '*dérive*'. Most importantly, as they exchanged ideas and theories, they were united in their belief that 'New Babylon' was at the core of Situationist theory (Wigley 31). This exchange culminated in the so-called 'Amsterdam Declaration' of 1958, a text written by Debord and Constant as a manifesto for all future Situationist activity. Constant resigned from the SI shortly after the publication of this text, an act which has led to much speculation among historians of the SI. This moment has indeed been described as the founding moment of the Paris-based Situationist movement as a revolutionary force, moving from art to politics and ultimately to the convulsions of May '68. In the meantime, the Dutch, with Constant as their leading theorist and figurehead, were dismissed by the Parisians as dilettantes, utopian dreamers, and – the worst insult of all from the lips of a 'Situationist' – as 'artists'.

This certainly is the rhetoric denouncing Constant and the Dutch group which appears in *Internationale Situationniste* after the break between Debord and Constant in 1960. My starting point in this essay is that even Guy Debord, who wrote this material, knew that this was all rhetoric and not really to be trusted as a guide to the thinking of Constant. The 'Debordist' rewriting of 'Situationist' history thus starts here, as it does in so many other instances, with Guy Debord himself (Wark 69).

The real aim of this essay, in contrast, is to trace the definition of Debord and Constant's use of the word 'Situationist' as it moves between Paris and Amsterdam during this period. Most importantly, although based on documents of the period, including recently published correspondence which sheds new light on key debates, this essay is mostly concerned rather with examining Debord and Constant as prismatic figures – more precisely, what I am most interested in here, as suggested above, is the mirroring of both cities in the thought of both men as a real, physical presence. In other words, what was contained in the cityscapes of Paris and Amsterdam, as read and interpreted by Constant and Debord in the late 1950s, and how did this make them 'Situationists'?

3.

Interestingly, the much-debated origins of the term 'Situationist' have often been attributed to Constant – this is in a slim volume published by Constant in 1953 which is called *Pour une architecture de situation*, and in which he argues that existing buildings provided identical interior spaces for wildly different internal uses: architecture should seek to create spaces for specific 'situations' and build quite different shapes for sleeping, eating, working, and daydreaming (Hussey 'Abolish Everything!').

When he wrote this text, Constant was already known in Paris to the international Letterist group, which then included Guy Debord. Crucially, he was already one of the bridges between the Parisian avant-garde groups such as the Nederlandse Experimental Groep and CoBrA. As such Constant was well versed not only in architectural theory but also in painting. Most importantly, he applied to architecture the same demands that he made of art: when Constant finally met Debord in Paris in the mid-1950s, he was in the process of turning away from painting toward urbanism and architectural theory. Most importantly for Debord, during the period of their first meetings Constant was preoccupied by the devastation of war and was working on a series of what he called 'war paintings', works which aimed at giving some sort of context to the physical destruction that he had witnessed during the war. At the same time, Constant felt keenly that painting was an insufficient medium for such a project, that it lacked what he was beginning to term a 'total experience', that it did not touch or affect ordinary existence in any real way (Wigely 67-78).

In his first letters and conversations with Debord, Constant discussed the notion that art was dead, that it belonged to the 'old civilization', and that the image itself was a form of falsification of experience (Debord, *Correspondance Vol. 1* 54, 106, 162-3). The new civilization demanded new forms of expression, 'situations' which revealed the future and its possibilities. Having acquired the term 'situations', Constant began in Paris, and then later in Amsterdam, to codify and transform this vocabulary into a conceptual language, and ultimately architectural models, which would carry the weight of their respective ideas in practical terms.

In Paris, these ideas became practice in the form of the '*dérive*' – a praxis which Debord claimed to have invented but which was also an experimental and usually collective enterprise. In all of the histories of the SI, the '*dérive*' is often characterized as an essentially Parisian activity, and it is true that the topography of Paris plays a key role in both the theoretical and practical aspects of the '*dérive*'. Typically, a '*dérive*' would begin in an obscure or half-forgotten part of the Parisian hinterland – Aubervilliers or the Chinatown in the 13th arrondissement. The first account of the '*dérive*' appeared in 1956 in the Belgian Surrealist journal *Les Lèvres Nues*, reprinted in *Internationale Situationniste* in 1958. Essentially, as this account demonstrated, the '*dérive*' was not simply an updated version of the nineteenth-century practice of '*flânerie*' but rather an explicitly political event which sought to insert the subject back into the cityscape as an active living agent. As such, and again as opposed to '*flânerie*', the '*dérive*' demanded to be recorded, not simply in text but also as an image. Throughout 1957 and 1958, Debord and the Danish artist Asger Jorn worked on maps which aimed to capture the '*dérive*' in visual form – effectively mapping the fugitive, fluid, and fleeting nature of the '*dérive*', whose central purpose, as theorized by Situationists, was to link the varying atmospheres in a given urban environment.

These experiments began in Paris, and this is where Constant, in the company of Debord, first encountered them. Debord also favored Venice as a site to explore the '*dérive*', and charged the English Situationist Ralph Rumney with the task of making '*dérives*' and maps of the Italian city (Rumney and Woods).

It was during this period that Debord and Constant turned their attention to Amsterdam. This was partly because Amsterdam was Constant's home city, and he had a deep and intimate knowledge of its intricate past and present structures. For Debord Amsterdam was also interesting because it was a modern city which contained a medieval city as a living component of its cityscape. In other words, the city – like the experimental maps that he was producing with Jorn – functioned as an authentic palimpsest, a site of multiple realities and atmospheres where the past was glimpsed in the passage of everyday life.

To be more specific, the Amsterdam which Debord and Constant encountered was also defined by the specific political realities after the Occupation. More to the point, well into the 1950s, the city was still recovering from the wreckage of the war. Although the Old Center of Amsterdam had been more or less untouched by the Allied bombing raids, which had concentrated their attention on the docks and the outlying industrial zone, the city was poor and shabby. Late in the 1950s handcarts loaded with black cardboard coffins carrying the bodies of the poor, dead from disease or hypothermia, were a daily sight on the narrow streets of the medieval center, an area which then as now traverses the red-light district between Warmoesstraat and Nieuwmarkt, as well as in the bomb-scarred landscape of the Jodenhoek, the Jewish quarter which had been almost entirely emptied of its population and which was not yet quite ready for reconstruction. This was an area populated by human detritus, whores, drunks, and drifters.

It was here that Debord would begin his wanderings around Amsterdam, sometimes in the company of Constant or Armando, another Dutch artist friend, and sometimes alone, fuelling his drifting with endless white wine or occasionally a *kopstoot* (Constant, personal interview with author, 2001). Constant and Debord were especially fascinated by the Jodenhoek, now empty and desolate, a landscape of wrecked buildings, occasionally pillaged by hard-up Amsterdammers for fuel and building materials. Even the name of the area, the 'Jodenhoek', was disappearing from history as Amsterdammers, in a whirl of guilt, shame, and forgetting, stopped referring to the area by its original name as they literally dismantled its buildings. The area was soon to be scheduled for reconstruction and a metro built to connect the Old Center with the dead modernist suburbs of Bijlmermeer, then designated by planners as the main dormitory suburb for the future citizens of Amsterdam.

Aware that the site would soon pass away into the past, Debord was particularly intrigued by the exposed interiors of the wrecked buildings in the Jodenhoek which he saw as revealing myriad, secret, and forgotten histories. The exposed innards of buildings, in their intricacy and intimacy, also functioned as a metaphor for the way in which architecture could conceal but not control individual subjective experience. For Constant and Debord, the destroyed Jewish quarter was thus the negative reflection of the aims of modern architecture which, following Le Corbusier, sought to provide a 'machine for living' and thereby 'living machines' (Constant, personal interview with author, 2001).

Constant and Debord also wandered through the area known as De Pijp, a name which came from the way in which the tall and austere nineteenth-century tenements which absorbed and concealed the most densely-packed and variegated population in the city – a population made up of mainly Surinamese and other immigrants as well as a traditionally radical working-class community – formed long and labyrinthine lines of passage. It was here that Debord planned with Constant and Armando an exhibition of Situationist work which would spread across the city, 'detourning' the commercial center around Damrak and Rokin and then through the Jodenhoek. This would be for Debord and Constant the ultimate Situationist city – a dreamscape constructed in fragments of real, lived experience, and defined, and destroyed, by the passage of time.

4.

It was against this background and informed by these experiences that, in perpetual dialogue with Debord, Constant began work on the project called 'New Babylon'. Constant worked on his models for 'New Babylon' for over a decade, aiming to build an exquisitely fabricated environment where everything would sing of humanity. 'New Babylon' was not meant to be an ironic comment on the architecture of the day but, as he claimed, it aimed at an architecture so powerful that it could have a direct impact on the body. Effectively, 'New Babylon' was a city in which town planning was abolished in favor of the 'continuous drift', the perpetual movement between spaces which reflected and recast the whole spectrum of human emotions. To this extent the models produced by Constant were the three-dimensional equivalent of the maps produced by Debord and Jorn.

In the first edition of *Internationale Situationniste*, the proto-Situationist Ivan Chtcheglov had imagined a city with a 'Happy Quarter', a 'Bizarre Quarter', a 'Historical Quarter', a 'Noble and Tragic Quarter' and so on: Chtcheglov's dream architecture was constructed out of labyrinths, covered passageways, mazes, ramparts, and stairways which led nowhere (Chtcheglov 15). In the same way, Constant made models and *maquettes* of a city in an endlessly fluid series of spaces or 'sectors', a 'floating city' defined by the imperatives of need or desire. A 'hanging sector' was suspended over the movement of traffic and commodities, allowing free circulation beyond even the most rational forms of modernist architecture; a 'yellow sector' and 'red sector' were ever-changing, 'mobile spaces' which changed according to the emotions of those who filled the space.

The guiding theories behind 'New Babylon' were laid out by Debord and Constant in a text called 'The Amsterdam Declaration'. This text was published in the second issue of *Internationale Situationniste* in 1958 and, at that time, defined the first principles of Situationist arguments on architecture and urbanism. Most notably, in 'The Amsterdam Declaration' they imagined a Utopian City based on the principles of what they called 'unitary urbanism'. This aim is achieved via the construction of situations, here defined as 'edification of a transient micro-ambiance and of the play of events for a unique moment in the lives of several persons'. 'Unitary urbanism' means above all therefore that the social and the aesthetic cannot be separated on the level of everyday life – instead of being organized, designed, and controlled by the needs and demands of commerce, industry, the circulation of traffic, and the movement of workers to workplace and home. In this way 'unitary urbanism' seeks to make the city a free space, open for play, anarchy, danger, passion. Debord and Constant emphasize especially the importance of what they call 'ambiance' – the product of '*dérive*', which is almost impossible to record in spatial or visual terms, but which is nonetheless the unifying force of 'unitary urbanism'. This notion is expressed thus in six related theses:

> 1. Unitary urbanism is defined as the complex, ongoing activity which consciously recreates man's environment according to the most advanced conceptions in every domain.
> 2. The solution to problems of housing, traffic, recreation can only be envisaged in relation to social, psychological and artistic perspectives which combine in one synthetic hypothesis at the level of daily life.
> 3. Unitary urbanism, independently of all aesthetic considerations, is the fruit of a new type of collective creativity; the development of this spirit of creation is the prior condition of unitary urbanism.
> 4. The creation of ambiances favorable to this development is the immediate task of today's creators.
> 5. All means are usable, on condition that they serve in a unitary action. The coordination of artistic and scientific means must lead to their total fusion.
> 6. The construction of a situation is the edification of a transient micro-ambiance and of the play of events for a unique moment in the lives of several persons. Within unitary urbanism, it is inseparable from the construction of a general, relatively more lasting ambience. (Debord and Constant 62-3)

Despite the apparent unity at work here, Simon Sadler, in *The Situationist City*, describes the 'The Amsterdam Declaration' as a 'brave' but 'schizophrenic document' (121). More precisely he states that Constant aims at co-ordinating 'artistic and scientific means' to make 'a perfect spatial art', while Debord sees 'unitary urbanism' as a new form of collective expression, which would eventually bring about a revolution in the way in which people live (121-2).

In other words, Constant, according to Sadler, for all his theorizing about play and experience, remained an 'artist', belonging therefore to 'old civilization'. Debord, in contrast, was a true 'Situationist', who had abandoned art for a new politics of free 'sociocultural activity' (121-2). This was in 1962. Constant was allegedly very hurt and angry about this insult.

In line with this version of events, Constant resigned from the SI in 1960. Recently published letters by Debord from the period have however revealed that this split was less acrimonious than we have been led to believe in previous histories of the SI. Indeed, as this correspondence demonstrates, there was little between Constant and Debord at the moment of Constant's resignation. Uncharacteristically Debord even pursued a friendship with Constant after the resignation and beyond politics. The real argument was over Constant's association with the Van de Loo Gallery and his recruitment of two Dutch architects to the SI who had accepted a commission to build a church (the Situationists were violently anti-clerical). This then raises the question of what the term 'unitary urbanism', as used in 'The Amsterdam Declaration', really means if it is not, as Sadler claims, a 'schizophrenic document'?

5.

In fact the term 'unitary urbanism', although coined by Debord and Constant, had its origins in the 'unitary architecture', imagined by the nineteenth-century Utopian socialist Charles Fourier. Fourier, whose career as a businessman, journalist, and thinker traversed the French Revolution, combined social philosophy, economics, and a millenarian view of the world, seeing the universe as destined to last for 80,000 years and following a curve from chaos to harmony and back again (Hussey, *Game of War* 153; Bruckner; Tacussel). In the period of harmony, Fourier wrote that the sea would become as sweet as lemonade, the North Pole as mild as the Riviera, and that the world would be geometrically balanced, with 37 million poets as good as Homer and 37 million scientists as good as Newton. 'These are approximate numbers, and no less than four husbands for each woman', Fourier conceded after being challenged about the precision of his figures (in Marshall 151-2).

Most significantly, Fourier had put his ideas into practice with the establishment of an early form of Communist society at Condé-sur-Vesgre, near Rambouillet and not far from Paris. These were ideal, mainly agricultural communities of ten families called '*phalanges*', who were to live in a set of buildings called a '*phalanstère*', a coinage which brought together '*phalange*' (a phalanx or combat format of soldiers in antiquity) and '*monastère*' (monastery). The idea behind the '*phalanstère*' was to dissolve what Fourier saw as the artificial distinction between the individual body, the family, and the self, on the one hand, and the social body, the collective authority of the group, and the system, on the other. Fourier advocated the abolition of money and free love, with men working for passion rather than money. Although both Debord and Constant disdained Fourier's naïve perfectionism, they were nonetheless interested in the careful terms in which Fourier had laid out his pre-Marxist project. Most importantly, it was self-evident to both Constant and Debord that any future architectural and urban theory of the passions must refer back to Fourier.

The significance of Fourier to 'The Amsterdam Declaration' and the 'New Babylon' project was that Fourier did not simply imagine his project as a theoretical space but as a real map of Utopia. In the same way, 'New Babylon', certainly for Constant but also for Debord, was a reality, a dreamed version of a new social space and not an ironic critical comment on existing city spaces. In particular, Constant wrote the 'metabolism' of 'New Babylon', the deep structures that maintained and shaped the ever-changing environments. These models, in other words, were not simply guides to a new form of architecture but to another form of life. This was precisely, for Debord, the meaning, the *teleology* even, of the word 'Situationist'.

6.

What Debord and Constant had in common, for the brief moment of their collaboration as 'Situationists' in this sense, was a project which aimed at a radical reinvention of city space which would be both political and aesthetic. For Debord, this would become the starting point of the theory of the 'society of the spectacle'. This is of course a specifically political reading of the city, which emerges out of the experience of the endless flow of subjective experience in city-space. To this extent, although the term 'spectacle', by 1960, has yet to enter the Situationist lexicon as defined and policed by Debord, we can already see that the experiments in 'unitary urbanism' are for Debord a necessary prelude to other theories of 'psychogeographical' activity, which eventually bring the Parisian Situationist International into its so-called 'political phase'. For Constant the adventures with 'unitary urbanism', as we have seen above, would become an aesthetic method, and part of his project to develop a Utopian architecture, or even an architecture of Utopia.

The divergent paths which Debord and Constant took after their collaboration are not in contradiction. This is one reason why, until the end of his life, despite the propaganda of Debordists, Constant always considered himself to be a 'Situationist' (Constant, personal interview with author, 2001). This was not simply by association with Situationist history; throughout his career Constant frequently emphasized that only the architect and not the artist could actually define what Situationist activity was and could be. For Constant, theory was never necessarily separate from experience; a project such as 'New Babylon' was a form of 'speculative representation' – in other words, theory made visually real – which was the way into imagining the future.

The Situationist adventure, however, has long been consigned to history. Debord and Constant are both now dead and their aim to 'Leave the Twentieth Century' has now happened. We are actually in the world which they imagined, for good or ill. Paradoxically both Paris and Amsterdam are these days widely acknowledged as world capitals of 'underground culture' in the most 'spectacular' way – indeed both cities conspicuously trade on their reputations for 'underground' art and behavior to attract tourism and participate in the globalized economy of hyper-capitalism, as Carolyn Birdsall, Joyce Goggin, and Stephen Sawyer all discuss in their chapters in this book.

Not long after the break between Debord and Constant, the Parisian Situationists would claim themselves as the only true revolutionaries of the late-twentieth century. In Amsterdam, however, Constant's ideas were not so easily dismissed and indeed became a component part of the matrix of arguments and revolts which were defined as Amsterdam's years of radicalism. Contrary to his Debordist critics, Constant was indeed no less a 'Situationist' although he no longer belonged to Debord's grouping. Arguably, Constant's influence on the counterculture in Amsterdam has been longer-lasting and more dynamic than Debord's influence on Paris, a city which according to Debord himself had been defeated and conquered by 'spectacular forces' in the 1970s.

For this reason, the most notable absentee from the neo-Situationist graffiti on Spuistraat, is Constant: the architect-dreamer who not only gave the world the word 'Situationist' but whose drawings and models ensured that the term was given a real physical shape, such as he and Debord had originally defined it in the 1950s in the streets of Amsterdam.

4. Amsterdam's Sexual Underground in the 1960s

Gert Hekma

A sleepy town turns into a sex capital

Amsterdam witnessed a radical shock in the late 1960s when it changed from a rather sleepy provincial town into a vibrant city that became one of the main centers of the occidental sexual revolution. The Netherlands had been one of the more conservative countries of Western Europe where Christian parties set norms and laws, and it suddenly developed a worldwide reputation for being among the most free and tolerant. In Amsterdam in the 1950s, a sexual underworld served local people and, as a harbor city, sailors and other foreign visitors, including American soldiers on leave from occupied Germany. Jacques Brel sang the praise of its harbor whose sailors attracted prominent gay figures like Jean Genet. Amsterdam had a red-light district that was still very white in terms of race and a small gay scene that in those years quickly developed because of alterations in policing sex. In the 1960s, the sexual underground exploded: it grew enormously and parts of it entered the mainstream, often in different forms.

This chapter begins with Dutch sexual politics and Amsterdam's sexual underground in the 1950s and moves on to the late 1960s. Amsterdam was the symbolic center of these developments and attracted many Dutch and foreign people. The sexual revolution had effects all over the country and entered into the capillaries of its culture. The focus will be on the city but will sometimes drift into the country. The period of the 'sexual revolution' can be seen as developing over the long term, and historians who focus on changes in sexual behaviors regard it as the period from the end of World War II to the beginning of the AIDS epidemic (1945-1985). I focus instead on cultural aspects and want to stress its short highpoint in the late 1960s. It is amazing how much changed in the pivotal year 1968, which can be seen as the climax of the sexual revolution. This date will repeatedly return in this chapter as moment of change on many fronts. The sexual revolution was a kind of *Gesamtkunstwerk* (unitary work of art) and resembled the 'unitary urbanism' of the Situationists (Pinder 128-30). It embraced all sexual orientations and included media, arts, literature, pop music and ways of dancing, social movements, novel types of spirituality, experiments with body, gender, and sexuality, communal and squatted housing projects, drugs, and a critique of traditional politics and religion. Dutch culture dramatically changed in a short period. An undercurrent of sexual desires suddenly came above ground but new underworlds and subcultures emerged. The chapter will end by addressing the question of how the sexual underground and revolution subsequently developed.

From the 1950s on

Since the early-twentieth century, the Netherlands was a 'pillarized' society, where four main groups (pillars) set the political and social tone: Catholics, orthodox Protestants, socialists, and liberals. From 1960 on, this system started to break down. Society democratized, individualized, and secularized. Consumption started to compete with production as a main economic activity. Many people lost their political and religious faith and wanted to be independent of pillars, even to get rid of them. The Christian pillars also changed from the inside and played a central role during the transformations of the 1960s.

In 1911, Christian parties introduced new sex laws that criminalized abortion, pornography, and pimping, and created a higher age of consent for homosexual relations than for heterosexual relations (21 versus 16 years, in Article 248bis). They wanted to differentiate themselves from those who held more liberal legal attitudes and introduced stricter legislation influenced by Christian values. This put a stamp on the Netherlands as sexually conservative country. In the 1950s, however, it was Catholic and orthodox Protestant psychiatrists and clergymen who proved to be pivotal in a change of mind that transformed society in the Netherlands. As practitioners in the newly developed fields of social work and psychiatry, they treated clients who suffered from the suffocating sexual morality of the churches: unmarried women who got pregnant, people dealing with the taboos on pre- and extramarital sex, gays and lesbians who felt rejected by religions that condemned their love. Forced marriages, illegal abortions, imposed adoptions, and other family dramas were the rule of the day (Develing). Priests engaging in pedosexual relations were unimaginable. Although liberals and socialists had more lenient attitudes toward sexuality, contrary to what one would expect, it was Catholics and Protestants who put questions of sexual morality on the social agenda (Oosterhuis). With their criticism, the professionals contributed significantly to the erosion of the pillars. Once the two religious clusters lost their rigid and dogmatic views on social morality, the constraints they had imposed on the other pillars disappeared and public opinion made a complete turn from opposing to supporting various sexual freedoms (see the surveys of Noordhoff and Kooy). This created sexual space in society.

The pillars were not the only part of society to be transformed. Like other Western countries, the Netherlands saw a radical change in its sexual culture in this period. The main transformation regarded sexual desire. While in the past, lust was only imaginable between opposite poles (male/female, active/passive, old/young, client/prostitute, butch/femme, queer/trade), the trend was in the direction of equality. Feminism and socialism that strived for gender and social equality respectively began to have influence. This meant that women should have more sexual and social autonomy. The genders became increasingly equal partners in hetero-erotic relations and women became more independent from their husbands. The feminine queers of the past who had preferred sex with masculine straight men became masculine gay men and pursued each other, while butch lesbians stopped pursuing feminine heterosexual women. A new generation of gays and lesbians wondered why an older cohort so strongly identified with the other sex while they preferred their own sex. They wanted to be normal, and as they said, they were only different in bed where sexual roles would be interchangeable (Hekma, *De roze rand*). The drive for equality was most beneficial for gay and lesbian relations that generally show more gender parity than straight ones. It was negative for those groups who desired unequal relations: pedophiles, zoophiles, sadomasochists, sex workers and their clients, and straight couples with traditional, unequal power dynamics (Hekma, 'The Drive').

When the weekly *Vrij Nederland* did a survey among 'new adults' in 1959, the young generation still expressed a conservative morality in which marriage was central. The youngsters were not asked about sex, but about going on vacation together before marriage. Yes, they responded, they could, but most respondents indicated that it should be in the company of third parties. Divorce was possible but care for children should have first priority. 'Two religions on one cushion', or sex between those of different faiths, was deemed unacceptable by 56% (Goudsblom).

Male Youth Cultures: Nozems and Provos

From the 1950s on, a male youth culture of Pleiners and Dijkers (referring to higher-class Leidseplein and lower-class Nieuwendijk), or Nozems, developed in Amsterdam. '*Nozem*', a word of unknown origin, meant that both groups were trouble makers. Nieuwendijk was close to the Red Light District, while Amsterdam's artist scene was to be found near Leidseplein, with its French existentialist penchants. This square was also the location of one of the two main gay dance halls in town, the Schakel, with Leidsestraat ('*rue de vaseline*' in gay slang) leading to the other dance hall, DOK, on Singel, in those times the main location of male street hustlers. The French style of the Pleiners was close to that of queens in Schakel and DOK while Dijkers with their macho manners resembled leather men of the newly emerging kinky scene in the Red Light District's Warmoesstraat. They were more oriented toward the United States, pop music, blue jeans, and leather than the Pleiners and Sissies, who preferred more feminine French elegance and chansons.

In the late 1950s, the first ripples of new times were visible with the Nozems. The gay scene and sexual politics of the local police also changed. While vice squads of the past harassed queer bars out of business, they now decided that it was better to keep homosexuals in their clubs than cruising on the streets for straight men, which only led to public nuisances. This policy of toleration in semi-public places, such as bars, led to a rapid development of the gay scene. Where a few transient bars existed before the World War II that were often mixed (gay, lesbian, sex workers and their clients), now the number of specialized places suddenly increased. Mixed bars disappeared and sexual differentiation between homo- and heterosexual space and identity became stricter. When social integration of gay and straight became imaginable, erotic integration faded away. Both the gay sexual use of public toilets and the visible presence of male hustlers on streets abated in the 1970s. In the 1960s the city had two co-existing gay undergrounds: on the one hand a lively but shadowy street culture of past days, and on the other a new subculture with bars that remained hidden behind closed doors. Both worlds were visited by men for whom the whole world was a 'closet' with no exit. 'Coming out' had yet to receive a meaning: it was still a straight world.

Nozem was soon replaced by Provo (provocateur) which referred to a new politicized group of young people who became active from 1965 on. Provo initiated a radical cultural and political shift and stimulated vital social changes. It has become synonymous with major transformations in Dutch society in the late 1960s such as secularization, democratization and individualization, and the rise of a youth culture. Their public activism started taking as an example the weekly 'happenings' of their predecessor Robert Jasper Grootveld whose innocuous events in 1963-1965 had made the authorities and the police very nervous. His happenings took place at the Lieverdje (The Little Darling), a statue of a street urchin on the centrally located Spui (Duivenvoorden). Anarchist Provo youth copied his street activist methods. They stood for resistance against the authorities, and were in favor of squatting, communal living arrangements, drug use, ecological solutions, 'white' (that is, free) bicycles, and public transportation instead of cars, which were both dangerous and polluting. They opposed the neo-colonial wars of NATO and support for dictatorships. Provos heartily embraced the sexual revolution. They were in favor of, as one of them said in the first issue of their journal *Provo* (1965), free love and 'complete amoral promiscuity'. The leading Provo intellectual Roel van Duijn (1985) drew upon the work not of the straight Wilhelm Reich but of the queer Marquis de Sade – whose works were translated in the late 1960s – which he liked for its libertinism rather than for its violence. In addition to creating a *witte fietsen* plan for free bicycles, they also developed a *witte wijven* plan ('white', that is, free women plan; *wijven* being a negative term for women) for female sexual emancipation, and a *witte homofielen* plan for homosexual rights (unlike *wijven*, 'homophile' was the most conventional term for homosexual; see Van Weerlee). It was a broad program that also stressed spontaneity, desire, playfulness, urban renewal, police officers as social workers, and strongly resembled the Situationist one (Pinder). In 1966, Provo became a political party and joined the Amsterdam city council with one seat. Provo received international attention through various public events, most famously in 1966 with demonstrations against the royal marriage of Princess Beatrix to a German squire. Pictures of a smoke bomb that struck the golden carriage went around the world (Kempton).

Many artists supported this counterculture of provocation. Author Simon Vinkenoog became its unorthodox spokesperson. Composer Peter Schat offered the basement of his house for meetings. Jan Cremer and Jan Wolkers – an author and a painter – wrote *I, Jan Cremer* (1964) and *Turkish Delight* (1969), pivotal literary texts of the sexual revolution (see Calis). A revolution in the art world preceded Provo: CoBrA (Appel, Corneille and Lucebert), architectural utopia

'New Babylon' of Constant Nieuwenhuis (Kennedy, Pinder), artist group Nul (Zero).

Provo was short-lived (1965-1967) but had a major impact. It inspired many groups in politics and the squatters' movement, and led to all kinds of alternative initiatives: bookshops, printing and publishing projects, bars and restaurants, galleries, pop groups, communes, and so on, often in squatted places. With the Man-Vrouw-Maatschappij (Man-Woman-Society, 1968) and the more radical Dolle Mina (Mad Mina, 1969), the second wave feminist movement started. They were mainly active in the field of gender politics while their main sex-related issue was abortion, being 'boss of your own belly' (Ketting; Vuijsje). In May 1969, students occupied the Maagdenhuis, the University of Amsterdam's bureaucratic center, and asked for more democracy – another memorable moment of the 1960s. Art students directed actions toward concert halls and theaters. Most of these demonstrations were radical and *ludiek* (playful). Urban protests concerned large-scale developments that destroyed the fine structure of inner cities. When in the early 1970s Amsterdam's government demolished parts of the old town for a new subway, violent riots broke out. In the late 1960s the city was in the mood for major changes in gender and sexual politics, the arts, city planning, and environment.

Sexual Movements

Since 1946, there were two kinds of sexual movements in the Netherlands. The Nederlandse Vereniging voor Seksuele Hervorming (NVSH, Dutch Society for Sexual Reform) had been largely concerned with family planning. In the 1960s it changed its aims to focus on sexual reform. The NVSH became a major social force in the 1960s with over 200,000 members at its high point (Nabrink). The Cultuur en Ontspannings Centrum (COC; Center for Recreation and Culture) represented the homosexual movement; it became junior partner of the NVSH during the late 1960s (Tielman).

The NVSH's political demands were formulated in 1967 in a speech given by its chair, Mary Zeldenrust-Noordanus. On a legal level she requested the abolition of laws restricting homosexuality, abortion, pornography, prostitution, and divorce, and asked for easy access to contraceptives for all women above 16 years old. She hoped this might be realized by the year 2000. In fact, most of these changes came about within a decade through either legal change or 'tolerance', meaning that the state did not prosecute those who engaged in officially forbidden acts – a typically Dutch way to deal with controversial topics. Abortion became an accepted medical practice in 1968 (Ketting). Zeldenrust-Noordanus's main point, however, was broader. She was in favor of ending gender and sexual binaries. At that time, hippies celebrated androgyny, young men had long hair and wore shiny shirts, and girls started to wear jeans – the 'masculine' trousers once forbidden to them by local regulations that also forbade male drag. There was sexual openness among the new generation, but it did not last long. NVSH may have suggested legal changes and transgressing gender and sexual dichotomies, but, while laws and regulations were abolished or modified, these binaries became in fact stricter from the 1980s on.

Parallel to these sexual movements, Amsterdam's sexual and gay scenes started to grow in the 1960s. The Red Light District developed into a tourist destination, and venues such as cinemas, sex shops, and erotic clubs opened across town. The number of gay bars doubled in this decade, with a main upsurge in 1968. To the distress of the city government, gay tourists started to flock to town as a result of its new tolerant reputation. Flower children slept on Dam Square and in the Vondelpark. From 1968 on, Amsterdam was a city of love, sex, drugs, and rock music.

Mediatization

Media contributed to the sexual revolution, television in particular. Television entered all households in the 1960s, with 75% of Dutch households having a TV in 1966. In 1964, a program featuring the poet Remco Campert was censured because he read a poem with the word *naaien* (meaning to sew, but also to screw; Calis 34). Times changed, however, and the satirical program *Zo is het toevallig ook nog eens een keer* (1963-1966) (Ferdinandusse) and *Hoepla* (1967) (Verhagen) could be more explicit. The first was made by famous Dutch personalities like author Gerard Reve, and the second by artists Willem de Ridder, Wim T. Schippers, and others. The broadcasting of both programs resulted in questions being raised in parliament, *Zo is het* for blasphemy and *Hoepla* because it featured the first appearance of a naked woman on Dutch television. In 1966, *Zo is het* is also notable as the first Dutch TV program to use the word *neuken* (fuck).

The television broadcasting company VPRO, the NVSH, and the weekly *Vrij Nederland* (Free Netherlands) were mainstream organizations or media outlets that were supportive of the sexual revolution. The largest Dutch morning paper, the right-wing *Telegraaf*, was a staunch opponent of the trend. Sex became front-page news in various ways. Jan Cremer (straight) and Gerard Reve (gay) were authors who, through their books, interviews they gave to the media, and TV appearances, injected the news with a healthy amount of sex.

The NVSH published a monthly journal, *Verstandig Ouderschap* (Prudent Parenthood), that changed its title in 1968 to *Sextant* and completely transformed its contents. The monthly developed into a mouthpiece of the sexual revolution. It offered special issues on birth control, sexually-transmitted diseases, love, pornography, and sexual dysfunctions – vacillating between tame and daring coverage in order to accommodate its broad readership. Each issue had two pages of letters to the editor and another two with questions and answers. These features were among the most popular found in the journal and provide an indication of the concerns and attitudes of its readers. Marital problems and questions about sexual preference issues were dealt with in the advice section '*Wij willen weten*' (We Want to Know), and received pragmatic medically-informed answers. The letters indicated strong differences of opinion between NVSH's more mainstream and radical members. Some opposed the attention given to pornography or homosexuality, while others complained that most of the erotic imagery was of women and not men, or that it was too tame. In the 200,000 households where the monthly was delivered, youngsters could read about information like this possibly for the first time (Röling).

In the spirit of the time, COC initiated a journal in 1965 whose name indicated its message: *Dialoog*, referring to the conversation between the gay and straight communities. Gay activists stepped out of their underground, stopped using pseudonyms, 'came out' and started to fight for social integration. A letter from Gerard Reve in the first issue became controversial because in it he imagined Jesus returning to the world as a donkey he would have sex with out of celestial love. Clergymen connected to COC protested, and a member of parliament initiated court proceedings against Reve for blasphemy. The case went from the lower court to the Supreme Court. Reve was supported by theologian expert witnesses, who claimed that the donkey fantasy was his way of expressing his beliefs. The Supreme Court accepted this view and acquitted him. The case made headlines in the media, which discussed his homosexual preferences more than the depiction of bestiality with Christ that had started the procedure (Fekkes). Through his novels and media presence, Reve became the pivotal Dutch queer who engaged in SM and polyamory, or consensual non-monogamy. He was also a conservative who embraced Catholicism at a moment that many Dutch were leaving the church. Reve's case illustrates how quickly changes came. In 1966 when the court proceedings started, he was still a weird outsider; in 1968 when he won his case, public opinion had changed in his favor. He had become a national gay icon (Maas).

Many explicit sex journals started in the late 1960s. The most famous were *Chick* and *Candy*, both dating from 1968. *Chick* (1968-2008) was the highly successful enterprise of Jan Wenderhold who started it to make money for his family. Its initial print run of 5,000 rose to 18,000 by the second half of 1968, and a major (and still existing) concern about erotica grew out of the magazine. *Chick* was more than just a porn periodical since it covered general news and offered libertarian views. The colorful Joop Wilhelmus became its editor. He started his career by publishing Provo-like journals, edited books on bestiality and sexual variation, ventured into specialized areas like child porn with the magazine *Lolita*, and started sex shops. *Candy*, still published to this day, was *Chick*'s main competitor for the new sex market. Publisher Peter J. Muller edited another major journal of the sexual revolution, *Hitweek* (1965-1969), which later became *Aloha* (1969-74). These monthlies focused on pop music, and added drugs and sex to their fields of interest.

One of the most attractive and radical products of the Amsterdam sexual underground was the English language *Suck: The First European Sexpaper* (1969-74). Among the collaborators were Germaine Greer, Bill Levy, and Willem de Ridder. *Suck* was nicely illustrated and carried the work of people like Theo van den Boogaard, a major artist of Holland's sexual revolution. Contributors sent in sexually explicit narratives that dealt light-heartedly with most sexual variations from masturbation to incest and bestiality. It seemed a competition of who could tell the strongest story. The journal published Wystan Auden's cruising poem

'The Platonic Blow', excerpts from William Burroughs's *Wild Boys* (1971), and a close-up of Greer's vagina. The final issue featured the richly illustrated 'Virgin Sperm Dancer: An Ecstatic Journey of a Boy Transformed into a Girl for One Day Only, and Her Erotic Adventures in Amsterdam Magic Centrum'. *Suck* also organized the Wet Dream film festivals.

Several papers ran ads for people seeking straight, gay, and lesbian relations. In February 1968, *Vriendencontacten* (Friend Contacts) started with a run of 1,500 copies that went up to 20,000 at the end of the year. The Dutch were hungry for sex. When *Sextant* discussed 'sex by numbers' in its January 1969 issue, it provided a long list of journals that offered such ads. Not only new papers entered this market – old ones tried to revive themselves by offering sex-related content. *Vrij Nederland* would later become the main respectable paper to carry sex ads.

Nude Shows

The sexual revolution did not only happen on the pages of papers, on TV screens, or in bedrooms. On stage, nudity and sexual representations also became available. Amsterdam developed a tradition of sex shows that began in the Eylders, a bar at Leidseplein. The happenings of the bisexual Grootveld had included exhibitionist travesties and in 1962 a public orgy had taken place in his gallery (Duivenvoorden 193, 207). The post-Provo society Kiets Konservatorium ('*kiets*' meaning 'kitsch') met at Eylders, and on one occasion – in the quintessential year 1968 – the public undressing of a woman turned into a live sex show. Members of the group made this into a 'Depressive Erotic Panorama' for the Fantasio and Paradiso nightclubs. At the same time, the youth club Appeal organized a 'Rhythmic Pornography Show'. Painter Hans Frisch set up a 'Levende Opjekten Sjoo' (Live Objects Show).

All these shows consisted mainly of *ludieke* improvisations. *Ludiek* (playful) became a code word in those years for all kinds of events. The word had been introduced in *Homo Ludens* (1938) by the famous Dutch historian Johan Huizinga, who would have been surprised by its popularity among the 1960s radicals. His work had also inspired Constant in his project 'New Babylon' (discussed at length by Andrew Hussey in his chapter in this book). The nude shows were accompanied by music and actors were often stoned. They might pretend to be engaged in sexual activities, but the main aim was social critique. Sometimes the nude objects were put up in cages to indicate sexual repression. The Appeal show included two women and one man dressed in plastic that covered their naked bodies painted in the colors of the Dutch flag while playing the national anthem. This served to ridicule Dutch nationalism. On another occasion they used the German national anthem. Hans Frisch offered his show for all kinds of places, including churches, funeral homes, parks, and night clubs. The accompanying music was intentionally bad: he declared himself to be the director of the worst orchestra in the world with its 'stutter choir'. He also offered the performers in his show for rent by the hour. It was all meant to be *ludiek* and of course to shock the petit-bourgeois, whom provocateurs called *het klootjesvolk* (testicle people).

The shows offered several sexual variations, and included not only heterosexual but also masturbatory, male and female homosexual, and sadomasochistic representations. Bestiality was only shown with toy animals that could be *ludiek*. The SM scenes that Ruud Kraamwinkel showed in his 'Depressive Erotic Panorama' were not popular with the public, so Hans Frisch left them out. Kraamwinkel's gay scenes were popular, however, in part because of his 'horse-dick'.

There may have been a new tolerance for sexuality on stage, but the shows were not always permitted. In April 1969, Kraamwinkel organized four evenings with an 'Explosive Erotic Panorama'. After the first day, the newspapers showed pictures of naked women behind bars and, at the suggestion of the vice squad, the mayor forbade them immediately. The organizers were prosecuted for public indecency and were ordered to pay a minor fine of fifty guilders each only in 1972. When the shows went into the countryside, they were forbidden in some places such as Nijenrode, the posh school of economics. Although the shows offered sex on stage, sex never took place off stage, and the presentations never became orgies, as rumors claimed.

After the mayor's interdiction, Kraamwinkel, philosopher Fons Elders, and a group of lawyers and doctors started the 'Erotisch Syndicaat' (Erotic Syndicate) that successfully brought the sex shows all over Amsterdam. The syndicate propagated tolerance and support for erotic imagery and play as a necessary antipode to the arms race and commercialization – a critical reference to militarism and capitalism, cornerstones of the existing order. They resisted sexual exploitation for anti-sexual aims. The shows included boys and girls playing school kids in shorts and with bare breasts, the boys at some point in cross-dress and wearing fetish clothing that could be bought on the spot and removed from their bodies – leaving the children nude. Elders liked qualities such as enthusiasm and amateurism in the sex shows. The city allowed these shows because the Syndicaat, as a membership organization, did not need official permission. There was too much nudity around for the city to make it stop: in 1967, the first female nude appeared on Dutch TV, actors came on stage in a 'natural state', streakers created excitement in the streets, and in 1972 the first nude beach was opened. It was amazing how suddenly the Dutch took to eroticism in 1968: with nude shows, magazines, sexual activism, or pleasures of the pavement.

The Dogmatic Turn

At the high point of the sexual revolution in 1967 to 1968, homosexual student activist groups were started in most cities. They made the same points as the NVSH, were against gender and sexual dichotomy and sexual taboos, and in favor of good sex education and abolishing antigay Article 248bis of the Criminal Code. They organized mixed dance parties for gay, straight, and in-between, and went to 'normal' discos to dance with same-sex couples – creating turmoil. And they continuously discussed sexual politics and experimented with erotic life.

In 1969, NVSH and homosexual student groups organized a 'love-weekend'.

Jos van Ussel, a historian of sexuality and the NVSH's philosopher, gave a talk and asked the organizers to replace chairs with mattresses to transgress standard, unsensual ways of lecturing. In his speech, he predicted the revolution would turn into a liberation of the penis, deteriorating into a 'narrow' sexual change and not liberating the whole human being. At night, the sixty mainly gay participants engaged in promiscuous sex. Some non-gay participants discovered their homosexual side, as the radicals desired (the reverse is not reported). But some participants also discovered something different: the group sex was forced upon them, and it was deemed an expression of the 'competition moral' – meaning the macho desire to outdo others now in bed. They in turn were criticized for still being so oppressed that they could not enjoy a night of pleasure. Mutual accusations of intolerance followed where tolerance should be preached. Sexual liberation was no easy task.

The critique of sexual liberation would become stronger and many leftist supporters saw its limitations, as Van Ussel had; it was too narrow, only partial, not a *Gesamtkunstwerk*. The great revolution for him was humanism, and for most students socialism. Sexuality could only be liberated when all of society and in particular its socio-economic foundations had changed in a socialist direction. Their sexual revolution resembled the unitary urbanism of Situationists: it should be total and not a minor change within liberal capitalism. This idea spread with the growing influence of theories of Marx, Freud, and, in particular, of the Freudo-Marxist Reich. A revolution that only included the sexual would lead to the commercialization and continued erotic misery of oppressed groups such as women in a liberal, capitalist society.

Sexual and gender repression were seen as secondary themes of socialist struggle after its primary focus on money and labor. It was unimaginable that the primary contradictions of society could be sexuality and gender, being seen as natural rather than social, or that they would have an equal status. This dogmatic leftist critique of the sexual revolution was intensified by the focus of Reich and his followers on coital sex and serial monogamy as socialist utopia. Sex radicalism weakened with leftist hairsplitting. Freudo-Marxism, and Marx more than Freud, was especially popular among a new generation of leftist students. Kees de Boer was a student leader who became the Dutch mouthpiece of Freudo-Marxism and got his own pages in *Sextant*. In those radical years, most universities devoted panels to the sexual revolution with the participation of students like De Boer, academics like Van Ussel, (anti-)psychiatrists, feminists, and gay and lesbian activists. But after all the excitement, the energy of the sexual revolution filtered out. Dogmatic Reich won out over free spirit Sade, socialism over libertinism. This quibbling, typical for many leftist and alternative groups, surely reduced their political success but not their symbolic influence.

Rise and Fall of the Sexual Revolution

From the moment of the Provos onward, Amsterdam had an important political and sexual underground. Young hippie tourists flocked to the city and slept in its parks. In addition to sex, narcotics (and, in particular, the tolerant soft drugs policy) became an important attraction. An emerging gay scene and the redeveloped Red Light District were other pull factors. Out of the squatting scene, an alternative world of communes, cultural institutions (the world famous live-music venues of Paradiso and Melkweg date from these years), galleries, cinemas, publishers, bookshops, bars, and restaurants developed. These underworld spaces facilitated new sexual possibilities like sex parties or nude shows. The city exploded erotically, but after the wild years of the late 1960s, most people went back to normal. An underground survived after the heyday of the sexual revolution, and its messages linger on to this day. In some cases it came above ground – as the music temples did – and drastically changed. The squatter movement shrunk noticeably because many squatted buildings were bought by the city or by tenants. In 2010, squatting was finally outlawed.

Nude shows, papers, and discussions of the sexual revolution abated in the 1970s, or continued without much innovation. The changing membership of the NVSH gives a clear indication of this decline of interest: after climbing from 10,000 per year in 1946 to 200,000 per year in 1965, it tumbled down to 170,000 in 1970 and 75,000 in 1975. Most heterosexuals simply left because most of the aims had been achieved, like access to abortion, contraceptives, divorce, and erotic material. The Rutgers Foundation, which was founded in 1969, quickly had 60 centers offering help to people with sexual problems, while the Schorer Foundation was addressing gay and lesbian life issues since 1968. The idea of a general and integrated sexual revolution (the *Gesamtkunstwerk*) was contradicted by what happened within the NVSH that lost its straight members but survived thanks to new subgroups with an interest in specialized erotic variations: SM, exhibitionism, pedophilia, and transexuality. Homosexuality remained the territory of the COC. Rather than integration, differentiation along lines of sexual and gender preference was the future. For many people the excitement of those years was formative, but most soon fell back into the routines of earlier generations.

As previously mentioned, a major influential critique came from the new left. Roel van Duijn had quoted Sade as his inspiration in Provo in 1965, but in 1970 the marquis's work was seen as pornography rather than as political philosophy. The new stars were Freudo-Marxists like Wilhelm Reich and Herbert Marcuse. Their followers saw the sexual revolution as partial, and being more about money than pleasure. The sex industry now sought profits while disregarding the real desires of people. Sexuality was used for exploitation. There could be no revolution except one that included all fields and layers of society, Reich and Marcuse argued: the sexual revolution needed to be part of a total socio-economic change but it was not. Following Marx, Freud, Reich and Marcuse, the left lost its *ludieke* and anarchist character and became dogmatic and socialist. The left had always been rather conservative in its sexual morality with a focus on the straight, nuclear family. Reich's radical and Freud-inspired goal had been greater heterosexual freedom for young people. He wanted divorce to be allowed for couples who had made wrong choices in love. But otherwise sex should be (serially) monogamous and heterosexual. Reich rebuked sex work, promiscuity, homosexuality, and other erotic variations. Many in the new left followed in his footsteps. From a quite different perspective, Michel Foucault gave a deathblow to libertine activities and promises by underlining the disciplinary and controlling outcomes of all talk about sex. Where defenders of the sexual revolution had seen progress and utopias of liberation, and Freudo-Marxist exploitation, he focused on greater controls by disciplines such as medicine and the social sciences, although his critique was voiced in the name of sexual pleasure against domination.

The sexual underground has a complex history. The Red Light District and the gay scene of the 1950s came above ground due to the sexual revolution after 1968. They remained distinct from the Provo movement that created its own underground, including issues of gender and sexuality. The avant-garde of CoBrA, Constant, Situationists, or group Nul was part of another, parallel but older generation. Gay and lesbian students groups were more inspired by Provo than by the gay scene or COC and created their own alternative spaces. Like the old underground, the new one got socially integrated. Subcultural institutions entered the mainstream, Provos continued their political activities in regular political parties, squatters had their high point in 1980 with the riots around the coronation of Queen Beatrix and witnessed decline afterwards. The gay movement gained political influence in the early 1980s, in particular in relation to the AIDS epidemic. Undergrounds of the 1950s and 1960s became mainstream or, just as often, disbanded. And while old ones disappeared or moved up, new ones emerged: queer groups like Lesbian Nation and Red Faggots in the 1970s, alternative galleries like Aorta in the 1980s, the discos Roxy and Mazzo, and kinky parties in the 1990s. They were less spectacular and influential than their predecessors of the 1960s who had to make a larger jump, but they continued Amsterdam's underground.

The sexual revolution has a controversial and ambiguous history. Nowadays, many people deplore the so-called individualism or excessive freedoms of those years and argue that they have had a negative influence on present-day Holland, but at the same time sexual freedom and women's rights, which were won in those years, are regarded as characteristic of Dutch culture today. On both sides of the equation, the elements are highly dubious: both how individualized and also how gay- and women-friendly the Dutch are. The underground saw a quick and radical development in the 1960s, and while many dreams remain unfulfilled, others lingered on and were sometimes enshrined in laws, social conventions, urban practices, and self-images. Utopian desires followed the road of continual change as the Situationists imagined.

Afterword

The year 1968 saw a revolutionary situation that exploded in Amsterdam: an unexpected, brief wild fire that burned bright and ignited many people. In an underground of alleys, parks, bedrooms, bars, galleries, and magazines a revolution started. It was so successful and subversive because it embraced so much: a critique of state, religion, and personal life. Old politics and traditional religion were blown aside while a more liberated intimate gendered and sexual life became prominent. Unlike the Arab Spring of 2010-2011, where revolts were mainly against a 'secular' state while getting support from religious forces, and politics did not in general get personal, the 1960s revolution in the West was a *Gesamtkunstwerk* with the various critiques reinforcing, not opposing each other. The fire soon petered out but its results are still there: more openness for female and gay sexuality, legalization of sex work and pornography, politics reshuffled, and religion losing influence. While red-light districts once were the quintessence of vice in a city controlled by religious taboos and political regulations, sex is now more generally available all over the city, in the media, and online. This sexual explosion was soon smothered by dominant forms of feminist and socialist critique that fitted well with the ideas of recuperating political and religious groups that feared society getting lost in a decadent flood of sex and drugs. Quite another world got lost, however: utopian queer dreams about how sexual and gender dichotomies would break open.

Although the sexual revolution may have prevailed in many ways, and although several groups have profited from its results, the fight against commercial and familial sexploitation was lost. The *Gesamtkunstwerk* that the sexual revolution had hoped to realize was broken down into its constituent parts. The old sexual margins that were concentrated in red-light districts got grudgingly tolerated while new sexual undergrounds began as rhizomes elsewhere in the cityscape and on the Internet – or in other cities, like Berlin. Foucault may have analyzed the disciplining consequences of sexual liberation, but he also saw the erotic possibilities of resistance, friendship, dandyism, and the leather scene. Ideals of underground and revolution may have slowed down, but they continue to sprout new ways of thinking and doing in various locations.

Note

This chapter is based on Hekma, 'Kermis in Amsterdam'. The research was done in the International Institute for Social History where the archives of the NVSH and *Suck* are kept and based on interviews with people involved in the sexual underground. My thanks to Sasha Albert who helped with my thoughts and my language.

Part 2: Mobility

5. Detours, Delays, Derailments: *La Petite Jérusalem* and Slow Training in Culture

Sudeep Dasgupta

Culture as travel

In his essay 'Travelling Cultures', James Clifford emphasized the mobility of cultures in opposition to the anthropological tendency to localize and fix its location. Critiquing the tendency in ethnography to 'privilege relations of dwelling over relations of travel' (99), Clifford rightly problematizes oversimplified localizations of culture, yet his casting of culture as travel risks moving too fast in the opposite direction. The essay opens with a quote from C.L.R. James: 'it's not ... where you are or what you have, but where you come from, where you are going and the rate at which you are getting there' (qtd. in Clifford 96) that matters. Maybe, but the construction of oppositions ('not') betrays a desire for movement whose urgency and speed will often be deflected and delayed precisely by the location ('where you are') and what determines and undermines the speed at which one gets somewhere. Travel, mobility, the fleeting, and the liminal: these have by now become the modes through which culture is understood. That is, a consensual formation has developed that figures culture through the metaphor of travel and mobility as a broadly left and progressive response to the violently exclusionary and right-wing solidifications of cultural discourse as fixity, traditions, roots, and belonging. Routes rather than roots, that is. The airport lounge, the hotel and motel, the ship: these have become some of the sites through which the dimension of speed and the experience of transiency further an 'anthropology of supermodernity' and the valorization of 'non-places' (Augé).

The aim of this essay is not to refuse the important interventions these arguments conducted. I do not aim to revalorize the local, the fixed, and the traditional and pose these concepts as a truer account of contemporary cultural formations. Rather, the purpose of my argument is to slow down the speed by which we arrived at conclusions of culture as travel, in an attempt to pause and reflect on the journey itself, and the locations implied in the notion of a journey. Traditions, as authors from Walter Benjamin and Stuart Hall to Edward Said and Eric Hobsbawm have reminded us, are anything but stable. Precisely for this reason, the opposition between movement and connotations of modernity, destinations and the future, cannot be opposed to dwelling and tradition, fixity, and uniformity.

My reading of the film *La Petite Jérusalem* (Karin Albou, 2005) aims at inducing a pause in the speed by which we understand culture as travel, and attend to the temporality of culture as lived and embodied within a complex nexus which articulates the past, present, and future across multiple spatial trajectories, above and below ground. This does not mean that travel does not figure in the argument. It does, in the form of the metro (Réseau Express Régional or RER) which connects Paris to its suburban environs, and that the protagonist, Laura, travels on between Sarcelles, 'Little Jerusalem', and Paris. But the film, rather than staging culture as encounter between two points on the metro, also stays, pauses, and dwells on other spaces, experiences, and encounters, which are linked to the underground though not exclusively captured by it. Speed, transiency, fleetingness are crossed with detours and delays which prolong the arrival at a destination and slow down the rate at which intellectual desire seeks to cast 'culture as travel'.

This crossing, or junction between speed and slowness, travel and fixity, is indebted to a more dialectical understanding of the problematic of culture. Instability, fleetingness, transiency (what Clifford calls a 'postmodern' and 'postcolonial' phenomenon) might become problematic precisely because in their own way, these discourses of culture produce a paradox signalled by Fredric Jameson. In *Valences of the Dialectic*, Jameson argues:

> One may very well welcome the current slogans of anti-foundationalism and anti-essentialism [discourses on cultural identity have been predominant here] without ignoring the obvious, namely that these pre-eminently theoretical slogans and programs have already themselves become thematized and reified – in other words, have themselves begun to turn into foundationalisms and philosophical systems in their own right. (10)

My argument seeks to explicitly acknowledge this paradox of foundational anti-foundationalism and focus on what gets lost in the rush to thematize speed and travel.

The argument seeks to reframe the figuration of culture between the binaries of fixity and movement, stasis and travel, tradition and modernity, by pausing, dwelling, and reflecting on what happens at both ends of the journey, and in the journey itself. This inclusion of delays, detours, and possible derailments does not reinstall locality, fixity, and tradition, but factors into the discourse of culture as travel the already living complexity of culture as belonging *along the points* through which the metro figures culture as travel. Contradictions encountered on the way from one point to another slow down, deflect, and rearrange the trajectories which mark culture as travel. Acknowledging and holding these contradictions together, and maintaining their tense signifying and experiential dimensions furthers a dialectical understanding of traveling cultures without rushing toward a narrative denouement whose destination is knowable in advance.

Delays, detours, and destinations have spatial and temporal dimensions. The coordination, or rather the problematic alignment of space and time, is inseparable from what Peter Osborne calls 'the politics of time'. A political understanding of temporality, and its attendant manifestations in experiences of travel as markers of modernity, underwrite this essay's emphasis on delays, detours, and the articulation of temporality to spatiality. Teleological time in particular has acquired a negative valence, as the narrative articulation of progression through space and time toward a goal. But, as Mary Ann Doane has argued, the contingency of time is also a necessary condition for the political reordering of modernity. In other words, the contingency of time is precisely what lends it to manipulation in the context of modernity. Travel can be spatially mapped as the temporal movement of bodies whose contingency is crucial to the experience of modernity. Doane argues that temporal contingency, which in my argument is exemplified in detours and delays, is crucial for the political management of time and space. Delays and detours, as experiences of contingency, undermine the teleological movement through space toward a destination.

If contingency undermines arrival at a destination, then the discourse of culture *as* travel needs to acknowledge the thickened, embodied, culturally complex experiences of contingency – detours and delays – within modernity. The underground emblematizes both cultural complexity and contingency. In many western metropoles, the underground is not just a channel or space for the transportation of bodies. It is also the spatial ordering of class, race, and other social hierarchies, as Mike Davis argues in his 'excavation' of the city of Los Angeles in *City of Quartz*. The predominantly white city center of Amsterdam, too, manifests surface racial and class homogeneity while underground, in that it serves as a hub for transporting classed and ethnically distinct commuters back and forth to urban concentrations in the suburbs. Paris possesses a similar spatial dynamic: the *banlieues*, while not predominantly 'colored' or composed of immigrant communities, are themselves segregated. Accidental encounters, delays, and detours as contingent temporal experiences take place within the space of the underground. The surface-depth, center-periphery spatial axes of the cities also harbor potentialities for temporal contingency signalled by Davis's counterintuitive phrase 'excavating the future'.

The narrativization of these contingent temporalities poses a problem. While rightly arguing that contingency is a *necessary* dimension of time crucial for politically-motivated organization, Doane constructs a dichotomy between contingency and narration: 'Contingency introduces the element of life and the concrete ... Description is a capitulation to the vast and uncontrollable, and ultimately meaningless realm of the contingent' (12). She goes on to argue: 'Narration, on the other hand, has an intimate relation with the past (it "recounts") and is therefore able to testify to necessity and inevitability' (12). In the encounters and experiences which take place on both ends of the metro line, and on it, however, the delays and detours which interrupt a teleological narrative are contingent precisely because they articulate the past to the present.

The 'element of life and the concrete' visualized in *La Petite Jérusalem* is far from being meaningless and acquires a specific resonance in the narrativization of travel as culture, by constructing a specific nexus of past-present-future. While the suburb, the metro, and the movement of peoples are indeed markers of modernity, contingent encounters, temporal delays, and spatial detours connect and give meaning to the disparate histories and geographies of the protagonists. This resonance produces meanings which, while related to the past, do not testify to either the necessity or inevitability that teleological narration presupposes. The time of modernity in the space of travel is both contingent and meaningful. The uncontrollable realm of the contingent and the narration of past histories intersect, and the time of this intersection is the time of delays and detours.

Detours as Delays

While the metro repeatedly emerges as the site of Laura's travel, notions of encounter, travel, and mobility are not the meanings attached to the metro. The film opens with a location, Sarcelles, which is produced through an overhead establishing shot, very similar to the panoptic, traditional ethnographer's gaze which disturbs Clifford in his critique of ethnography. The location is further specified through a particular ritual, linked to a form of Judaism. In a sense, then, the opening of the film suggests exactly the opposite of travel and transiency. At this end of the metro, the film seems to fix a location, and ascribe cultural tradition to a space producing a homogeneity shared by a community marked by religious belief. This establishing shot could be seen as also establishing a discourse on culture in two ways. Firstly, this is a unified homogenous culture on one end of the metro, at the other end of which is another culture which, when encountered, will set the cultural situatedness of the protagonist Laura into motion. This would be the figuration of culture as travel, and this opening shot, the first location on the railway line of travelling culture. Alternatively, this figuration of culture could be seen precisely as the opposite of culture as travel, as the production of an image of a closed-off, 'other' community in the tradition of the anthropology of Boas or Malinowski.

The speed with which Clifford's critique of location – and his valorization of travel – moves is striking. While he acknowledges that there are numerous internal differences *within a location* he feels obliged to rush through and emphasize travel as the mode through which culture needs to be understood. The film, on the other hand, pauses and fleshes out the lived complexity of the location, at one end of the metro, prior to the experience of travel. A location is of course not an abstract space, but a lived material space marked by conflictual relationality. In this case, it is the relations between the members of Laura's family that the film starts outlining, rather than some speed-induced dizzying destabilization of her culture triggered by the metro. Laura's family consists of her elder sister and husband, and her mother who moved to France from Tunisia. The family's location is spread out across the unstable signifiers of 'France', 'Tunisia', and 'Jewish'. While the relations between the two daughters is close, the marriage between the husband and his wife (Laura's sister) is fraught with problems. Throughout the film he plays the patriarchal role of a man governing a household of women and maintaining their cultural 'heritage', though it also emerges that he is involved in a sexual liaison with another woman. This 'impure' element, as it were, in a seemingly pure and homogenous cultural unit, makes 'Little Jerusalem' not exactly live up to its designation as the location for a certain kind of orthodox Judaism. The husband's adultery opens a gap between marriage as social institution and religion as basis of cultural fixity. His wife, instead of broaching his adultery with him, seeks the counsel of an elderly woman who seems to be the leader of a community of Jewish women in Sarcelles. There she is told that if her husband is adulterous it is her responsibility to repair the damage by making herself sexually attractive to him, and responsive to his sexual needs.

Gender and sexual politics, and their interruption of a figuration of community as a unified and homogenous whole, interrupt any temptation to figure the starting point of the metro (Sarcelles) as a static point in a trajectory of culture as travel. Travel (within the diegesis) does not seem to initiate a complex and diversified understanding of culture. Difference, change, conflict, and shifting power relations accrue within one space *prior* to any considerations of travel, speed, or transiency. It is as if before the train has started to take culture on a voyage into speed, complexity, and hybridity, it is already problematized at the point of embarkation, in Sarcelles. Clifford suggests that instead of location in terms of dwelling and home, travel and speed need to be emphasized. He suggests the hotel as a chronotope of culture precisely because it emphasizes temporality, encounters, conflict, and transiency. Approvingly quoting Meaghan Morris here, he cites this argument of hers: 'Motels, unlike hotels, demolish sense regimes of place, locale and history. They memorialize only movement, speed, and perpetual circulation' (qtd. in Clifford 106). By pausing to dwell on the place of the home, on family, gender and sexual relations, and religious belonging, the film does not fall within the binarism Morris relies on between maintaining or demolishing, preserving or destroying. Rather, the figuration of Laura's family, at the origin point of the RER's trajectory between Sarcelles and Paris, complicates and internally diversifies the 'sense regimes of home, locale and history'. Further, it does not memorialize speed and perpetual circulation but thickens up and exposes the sedimented and unequal relations of power which structure cultural identity *before* the question of travel comes up.

Further, the unequal power relations that accrue within the home are themselves traces of prior movements: Jewishness here is explicitly linked to diasporic movements (Tunisia). The starting point then is also the destination point, depending on what time scale frames the spatial trajectory of the family. Or rather, the home is both the point of embarkation and the point of arrival. The origin is also the trace. The complex temporality of the term 'origin' is pithily described by Walter Benjamin:

> Origin [*Ursprung*], although an entirely historical category has, nevertheless, nothing to do with genesis [*Entstehung*]. The term origin is not intended to describe the process by which the existent came into being, but rather to describe that which emerges from the process of becoming and disappearance. (*Origin* 45)

Sarcelles is not the beginning point of a journey, and of the film, but figured at the start as also the bearer of a process begun long before, in the experience of diaspora and that of 'disappearing' from a certain place, Tunisia. Genesis and genealogy are not defining of movement however. The play between appearing and disappearing, being in the present and becoming in the future refract the spatio-temporal dimensions of culture as travel.

While the underground trajectory of a train journey suggests a beginning and an end point, the cultural experience of travel figures a railway line as also so many points of transit in the multiple trajectories of movement. The complex temporality of the origin also implies a visual and spatial dimension. A moment is not just a temporal point, but revealed from the perspective from which it is perceived within space. The perceptual orientation from which a point on a journey is grasped reveals a specific aspect of the term 'origin'. The origin is the starting point of a process of becoming, but when perceived as an aspect of the experiential dimensions of the body, casts the latter also as the bearer (*Träger*) of multiple histories. This double-meaning is neatly captured in Edward Said's autobiography *Out of Place*. A temporal orientation ('place') is also a subjective, psychic, and spatial disorientation (being 'out of place'). The lived complexity of an internally-fractured cultural identity and the spatio-temporal complexity of the physical space of the home are linked. Such an understanding complicates the meaning of the end-starting point of the metro: it is both the starting and end point, *and* also the combination of both with a transitory stop in a journey which moves in *many directions*, as we shall see.

Destination as Detour

The film does go on to figure travel through the space of the metro that Laura takes to the university in Paris. By now bringing in another space, and the metro as a link between the place of home and the place of the world outside, the University in Paris, the film suggests a staging precisely of culture as travel. One could be tempted to start seeing the function of the metro, and the place of the University, as elements in a further destabilizing of the locale of home. This becomes even more apparent when we see Laura attending a lecture on Immanuel Kant. The two opposite elements, or spaces, with the metro as the medium of encounter and transfer *seem* to emerge – Laura in the space of family, tradition, and religion in Sarcelles, 'Little Jerusalem', and Laura in the classroom in Paris encountering not tradition, but critical reason in the writings of Kant and therefore the fruits of rationality rather than religion.

However, such an opposition between the two end points of Laura's travel is undermined by the film. The origin, as we have seen, is also the bearer of prior travels and the marker of a transition point. No unified, homogenous culture (whether Jewish, suburban, religious) can be located at the origin. The meaning of the encounter with Kant in the Parisian classroom at the other end of the railway line is thus not one side of a binary between tradition and modernity. Kant's casting of the Enlightenment as a critical deployment of Reason, exemplified in the interrogation of tradition, has already begun around the sexual politics of conjugal fidelity within a specific Jewish orthodox tradition on the other end of the train line.

The film undoes a simple opposition between the two end points of Laura's journey. The destination is not an opposition, but involves a relay between the two locations. Such a figuration of their interrelationship, while complicating the meaning of destination, also partakes of a further intensification of the meaning of travel – in particular, travel as detour. The notion of detour implies movement but also deflection. The point of origin (Sarcelles), as we have seen, is itself a transition point between past (Tunisia) and future (an elsewhere not yet determined). Before we can begin a consideration of the destination in the future, Sarcelles, and the space *between* it and Paris, detours, that is, deflects, a theoretical desire to cast culture as travel while precisely deploying the metro as a motif. For in Sarcelles, and in the train between Paris and Sarcelles, Laura encounters Djamel. Djamel, an Algerian, lives and works, in Sarcelles and as the film progresses we realize that he is a colleague of Laura's, both part of the cleaning staff of a school. Cultural encounter and mobility do not emerge (yet) in the space of Paris. Rather, it is the encounter with Djamel in Sarcelles that intensifies the figuration of cultural complexity, just as the sexual politics of her sister's marriage does. Paris as destination then, is actually a detour in the narrative emplotment of the film, in the sense that if one is tempted to see Paris and Sarcelles as the two spaces the metro links, the film turns back to Sarcelles – but not a Sarcelles as locale of the fixity of Jewish tradition, a 'Little Jerusalem', but as the location where relations between Djamel and Laura get established and their consequences start getting explored, slowly.

'Detour' here describes the intellectual waylaying of the discursive temptation to characterize culture as travel and mobility, and not just a detour in the focus of the film. The detour produces a pause, a staying in place, yet this staying in place has a temporality that summons up the recent and distant past and articulates it to the complexity of the present. One of the strengths of the film lies precisely in the centralizing of the metro or underground which becomes the mode to paradoxically figure the importance of locale rather than travel, slowness and detours rather than speed and destinations. The sequences of Laura traveling on the metro are distributed throughout the film, often accompanied by dialogic silence yet accompanied by the rumble of the wheels echoing in the tunnels of the RER. At one point, the train stops in the middle of a tunnel, the lights go out and as they flicker back on, a close-up reveals her fingers clasped around the hand of another on the same handrail. The image, and the time of its taking, visualize the focus of my argument. In the stillness of the train, paused between destinations, two hands meet, one white (Laura) and the other darker. The time of delay is the point of meeting. The image in the underground visualizes on a broader spatial level the encounter above ground between Laura and Djamel, moving the space of the encounter into the time of waiting, before arriving at a destination.

An encounter above ground produces the complex temporality and an articulation of the underground with the suburb. While Djamel and Laura are working together cleaning the halls of the school one evening she is called to an emergency. She and Djamel rush to a football field where her brother-in-law, and some other people, identifiably Jewish by the yarmulkes they wear as they are being attacked. The scene is clearly an anti-Semitic attack. As Djamel rushes to help, he suddenly pauses and walks away quickly as the police arrive, in the middle of the violent attack. The meaning of that swerving away from the scene is not immediately explained. It suggests to the viewer (and Laura) possible conclusions. Does Djamel turn away because his liaison with Laura is a secret and her family would encounter them together here and notice something? Or, does Djamel turn away because the people on the football field are Jewish? No immediate explanation of his sudden withdrawal from the scene is forthcoming. Later, in a conversation between Laura and Djamel the reason is revealed. Djamel is an 'illegal' (*sans papier*). The arrival of the police to protect the (Jewish) players being attacked signifies at the same time the threat of discovery for Djamel, and possible deportation. The incident brings Laura and Djamel together to another space, while separating them at the same time, a separation which has less to do with 'culture', whether Jewish or 'Muslim', than with legal status and social security. By showing and not immediately telling, the incident exemplifies the process of producing scenes and retracting meaning, a forward and backward movement in visualization and signification, anticipation and explanation. The film seems to stage certain paradigmatic scenes of cultural exchange, encounter and mobility, and then detours our desire to rush to a conclusion by bringing up unexpected reasons for what we see. It provokes frozen mobility, and functions as the visual analogue of the temporality of philosophical engagement with culture as travel by figuring 'the irregular rhythm of the constant pause, the sudden change of direction' (Benjamin, *Origin* 197). The insertion of Djamel's legal status rather than his ethnic or religious identity diverts us from ascribing the encounter to that of cultural specificity and conflict and inserts the question of the state into the scene, fixing him into a state of suspended mobility.

Sarcelles as the site of delay which detours the arrival in Paris as destination is a place, a locale, but one which makes visible in the play between showing and (not) telling other spatial and temporal trajectories marked by diasporic settlement on the one hand and transient contingency on the other. Place does not imply fixity but the spatial location of intersections of different temporal trajectories of past, present, and possible futures.

Some Terminal Points

The origin or point of departure of a journey is the space where the time of the past gathers. The origin emerges as a point of transition rather than a beginning. The journey toward Paris gets delayed by returning the viewer to the transition/origin point to gather together more temporalities borne by the bodies of Djamel and Laura. The film as literal transporter through time for the viewer gathers speed and moves toward its ending, yet what it figures is not one, but multiple terminal points, moving in different directions and producing different meanings of the term 'travel'. Djamel and Laura's secret affair unravels. Dependent on the silence of his extended family that is sheltering him from discovery by the police, Djamel must accede to their demands to end his liaison with Laura, though typically, his explanation of the break-up is couched in cultural terms. Her female agency in resisting her own family's displeasure is countered by his lack of agency in the face of familial and state power.

The consequences of the events (conjugal infidelity, anti-Semitism, the uncovered affair across cultures) induce the patriarch in the family, Laura's brother-in-law, to decide to move them to Israel. When he announces his decision (there is no discussion) at the dinner table, his mother-in-law, Laura's mother, stands up and walks away in silence. The meaning of her exit from the room is not explained. The family scene, its staging and fissuring, visualizes the politics of mobility. The differentiated gender, class, and religious experiences of travel, the motivations for choosing destinations and the meaning of movement coalesce around this patriarchal decision. The historical predicament of diasporic settlement produces specific conundrums when embedded in hostile environments. The term 'hostile' is itself politically loaded, particularly for the family in 'Little Jerusalem'. Does the family as a single unit experience hostility? How does traditional patriarchal power authorize itself as the motor for movement? If the dinner table scene stages family, continuity, genealogy and tradition, the mother's exit from the scene suggests a distancing from her son-in-law's decision. The silent comment becomes voluble when Laura expresses her desire not to move with the family to Israel. Her refusal breaks the link between genealogy, race (based on blood) and place, or rather return to a place. Patriarchal authority and genealogical continuity demand travel, yet here it is not 'culture as travel', but travel as stasis, continuity and fixity that is being invoked by the 'father figure'. While the underground, through the RER, has been the only mode of travel figured in the film, toward the end it is the airplane that emerges as the absent presence. Both modes of travel, under the ground and up in the air, take on specific meanings. These meanings introduce an ambivalence in the meaning of travel (and settlement).

Travel, forced or voluntary, produces exile, yet the responses to exile (*galut*) in the Jewish case are anything but unproblematic. While the underground represents movement to Paris, the capital of a country whose staunch republicanism emphasizes national universalism rather than ethnic particularity, the flight to Israel *combines* the two, equalizing racial/genealogical continuity with national belonging. In their critique of Zionism, Daniel and Jonathan Boyarin articulate exile, that is, settlement outside Israel, as the specific Jewish experience of diaspora. For them, Zionism is 'the subversion of Jewish culture and not its culmination' (712), the return to Israel cast as the 'capturing of Judaism by the state' (713). Paradoxically then, in the time frame of the present, diaspora means settlement, and culture as fixity of location defines Jewish culture, though from a longer historical perspective travel marks the 'origins' of the Jewish diaspora. Jonathan Boyarin goes on to argue:

> We Jews should recognize the strength that comes from a diversity of communal arrangements and concentrations both among Jews and with *our* several others. We should recognize that the copresence of those others is not a threat, but rather the condition of our lives. (129, emphasis added)

The discourse of cultural fluidity and mobility is predicated on the positing of divisions such as tradition and modernity, fixity and travel, essentialism and non-essentialism. The conclusion or destination of such a discourse is the grasping of culture's non-fixity and the privileging of travel. Keeping in mind Boyarin's argument, the conclusion, or destination of the film's argument, reverses and complicates this discourse. The underground links multiple others that inhabit the same space, both at either side of the train line and through the space in between. Laura's refusal to move is an avowal of a desire to move, yet the movement she aspires to is predicated on the possibilities opened up by the 'copresence' of others. Strikingly, Boyarin writes '*our* several others'. The 'other' implies alterity but by conjoining alterity with 'our' he undermines a division between self and other while acknowledging the difference. Further, where hostility is the frame through which the male head of the family understands 'copresence', for Laura this copresence is not a threat but the condition of her life. Sarcelles, and her decision to stay (and move to Paris, as we shall see) is a consequence of her casting hostility into the non-threatening possibility of cohabitation with *her* others. Culture is both travel and fixity, genealogy and history, the complexity of location (Sarcelles) and the simplicity of dislocation (return to Israel). 'Jewishness', the Boyarins argue, 'disrupts the very category of identity because it is not national, not genealogical, not religious, but all of these in dialectical tension with each other' (721).

The dialectics of mobility explicitly rejects a teleology of narrative completion (return to Israel and end of exile). It thinks the 'not only' and the 'and' together. It transforms the one into two, rather than the two becoming one, as Guy Debord put it, in his deployment of dialectics as the methodological instrument of permanent political critique (35). To think travel and fixity together is to think cultural identity through *both* rather than through the transformation of one into the other at a higher, later stage. This thinking of the two, dialectically, is a process of permanent transformation, of the unexpected swerve from the path, of a detour that leads elsewhere which is always a *some*where. The delays and detours are a consequence of holding together and maintaining tensions ('our others') rather than fleeing from contradictions. The underground links contradictions rather than transcending them and 'these contradictions must be held together' (Boyarin and Boyarin 721) – this is what a dialectics of delay and detour means.

The closing episode of the film links destination with dissemination, the endpoint of the narrative combining destination as arrival with multiple departures. The spectator has followed the narrative to its end, but where we arrive, at the end, is a bifurcated journey about to begin. This birfurcation articulates time and space, history and geography, counter-intuitively. Laura's decision to stay in France is supported by her mother, who gives Laura her wedding ring to help finance her move to Paris. The ring is linked to a past, in Tunisia, and a marriage of which Laura is an offspring. The past enables a future journey rather than a return back, and the bearer of that past, Laura's mother, facilitates it. Routes rather than roots, where genealogy generates spatial movement rather than blood ties. The family splits, moving in opposite directions, yet one side of the family facilitates the other's move in an opposite direction. For the family, travel is not the mode for the unfixing of culture's essentialist ideology but becomes the mode through which notions of the origin, the promised land, closed identity, and purity emerge. France, when seen as the location of Laura's life, takes on precisely the opposite meaning, travel from Sarcelles to Paris furthering a future of encounters with multiple others. The location of France where the film is set becomes precisely the location for cultural mobility, while travel to Israel becomes the way in which the family establishes cultural fixity. The metro and the airplane cross places, one enabling an airborne return to the source and the other a subterranean journey into the future.

Only at the very end of the film does the metro come to signify the space through which a break from fixity into a future of mobility and encounter gets figured. If one compares this to a discourse of traveling cultures, the beginning of this discourse, setting off on travel, emerges in the film right at the end instead. The length of the film is thus a preparation for a voyage rather than the staging of culture as travel. Spending time fleshing out the complexity of cultural encounters and internal differences on one end of the metro line, the film suggests the need precisely for pausing, reflecting, and acknowledging that speed, travel, and mobility are inseparable from detours, delays and the ambiguities of destinations.

6. Underground Visions: Strategies of Resistance along the Amsterdam Metro Lines

Ginette Verstraete

Introduction

The association between Amsterdam and the underground is rather ambiguous to say the least. On the one hand, the Netherlands, and Amsterdam in particular, are proud to present themselves as hospitable vis-à-vis alternative 'underground' cultures – a legacy from the 1960s and 1970s when feminist, gay, hippy, student, and squat movements were dominating the social and cultural scenes. The global tourist reputation of Amsterdam as the capital of sex, drugs, and rock 'n' roll has largely been built on the legacy of a 1960s underground culture that was leftist and avant-garde.

At the same time, however, the other notion of the underground in the sense of the 'subway' or 'metro' has been much more controversial for several decades. Since the 1960s the words 'underground metro' (*ondergrondse metro*) stand for social, economic, and spatial disasters, for the power of a hierarchical authority completely blind to the needs and daily experiences of its local citizens. The underground in this sense, then, stands for the opposite of what the word usually means: instead of (leftist) openness to other views and lifestyles, the underground-as-metro stands for market-driven tunnel visions. Instead of a commercially exploitable notion of freedom and tolerance, the underground-as-metro has accrued mostly negative connotations of mismanagement, incompetence, and intolerance, even to the extent that the word 'metro' has long been put under taboo in Amsterdam, both among inhabitants and policymakers (Breebaart). Instead of 'metro' one prefers to speak of 'fast tram' (*sneltram*). The difference is that 'fast trams' mostly run above the ground, while 'metros' go underground. And in Amsterdam for metros to go underground means to go below acceptable levels, in various ways. With the metro, at or below water level, the popular qualities of Amsterdam – as underground culture – get complicated, if not reversed.

Interestingly, despite these contrastive associations of the Amsterdam underground – one liberation-minded, the other repressive – there are also crucial connections. For as I will illustrate, the most significant opposition against the metro in the 1960s and 1970s was largely carried out by members of the underground scene: by artists, squatters, and ex-Provos. They were provoked by a repressive governmental and police apparatus and so their at first playful acts of resistance became grim and sharp, while the reactions of the authorities were disproportionately violent. In this clash between power and dissent a messy contamination of forces took place with lasting effects even to this day. Instead of a fixed opposition between hegemony and counter-hegemony, capitalism and agitprop, emerged a complex flow and entanglement of power that raised questions about the legitimacy and co-optation of the avant-garde. By focusing upon this hybrid nature of countercultural Amsterdam in the particular context of the first metro line I hope to provide a more nuanced account of a certain 'underground scene' that problematizes easy generalizations. It is through a careful analysis of particular, time- and place-bound, cultural practices that I will accomplish such a situated reading of the Amsterdam underground in the firm belief that taking culture into the sociality and materiality of urban space is a good way to resist the naïve notion that counterculture is either autonomous and oppositional or that it is inherently compromised by the powers of commerce and institutionalization. The truth lies somewhere confusedly in the middle.

This is an essay in three parts. I will first present the historical context in which the city council of Amsterdam decided to build the first metro line to the east of the city in the late 1960s (see *30 Jaar Metro*; Meiners; Jolles). I will then discuss the long, at times grim, protests against this project from 1970 onward and the intolerance with which forces of the government and the law responded (see Mamadouh; Hoeben). In this section it will become clear that the particular forms of activism and contestation that emerged against the metro ran parallel to the structures, technologies, and procedures of those in power such that the difference between authority and resistance started to dissipate. Finally, I will end by analyzing the memorials and the film that some of the protesters made during the completion of the line in 1980 as tributes to the violence that preceded it. My analysis will focus on how a countercultural movement was 'integrated' by the multi-million underground space of the metro and hence how resistance moved from margin to center, so to speak. What happens when resistance movements literally go underground and use their symbolic capital – the power of their words, images, and cultural interventions – to commemorate their struggle in the architecture of a metro station? Can they retain a critical distance vis-à-vis the walls that support their works and that, in turn, their works support?

History, Part 1: The Origins of the Amsterdam Metro

The decision to build a metro line to the east of Amsterdam dates from 1968 and was inspired by different concerns. Since the 1950s, Amsterdam was growing immensely, mostly in economic terms. Offices and services of all kinds had spread throughout the city and the urgent question rose as to how these economic activities were to be combined with the social reconstruction of the city after World War II, more particularly the need for more social housing and better living conditions. Moreover, traffic by car was increasing exponentially and, since Amsterdam had so many narrow historical streets and so much water, there were problems of congestion and parking space. What to do with the cars?

In the 1950s and early 1960s the answer to these joint problems was simple, but to contemporary ears also somewhat shocking: move the people out of the various post-war derelict areas (such as the Jordaan and Nieuwmarkt) and into new housing projects outside the center. Demolish their houses so that space is opened up for four-lane streets along which can flourish not only office buildings, hotels, and stores, but also decent transportation by car. Construct metro lines underneath those lanes to guarantee long-distance connections with the new living premises in northern Amsterdam, and in Bijlmer and Amstelveen in the south. For it was in those areas at the outskirts of the city center, including the 'garden cities' in the west and the agricultural zones of Purmerend, Zaanstad, and Lelystad further north, that the evicted people from the inner city ideally lived. Once displaced from the center to the outskirts, those people from Amsterdam at least deserved a good underground connection back to where they came from.

The author of what has come to be known as the Amsterdam Expansion Plan (*Algemeen Uitbreidingsplan*), which actually dated from the 1930s, was the Dutch architect and urban planner Cornelis van Eesteren (1897-1988), who became a member of *De Stijl* Movement in 1923, was master builder of Amsterdam between 1929 and 1959, and chairman of the *Congrès Internationaux d'Architecture Moderne* (CIAM) between 1930 and 1947 (see Somer). As the promoter of international modernism in architecture, CIAM defended rationalization and standardization in living based on rigid functional zones with green belts in between, high-rise apartment blocks for housing, provision for traffic, and space for recreation. Heavily inspired by the Bauhaus and Le Corbusier, Van Eesteren wanted to rebuild Amsterdam in accordance with his concept of the Functional City: a city designed on the basis of the social 'problems' to be solved, and divided by the functions of living, working, recreation, and transportation (Jolles).

It would take us too far to analyze these modernist ideas about city planning in detail. Suffice it to say that although much of Van Eesteren's Expansion Plan was realized spatially, the mass evictions from Amsterdam were eventually not carried out. By 1968 the city government had encountered so much public resistance that those plans for removal were only selectively implemented. And while the living machines in the Bijlmer district *were* built as extensions of an overpopulated city center, it was not the people from Amsterdam but those newly arrived from Surinam and other Dutch colonies who went to live there, with all the attendant social problems that the Bijlmer has come to symbolize. And while some of those big lanes in the heart of the city were constructed and many houses demolished – in the Weesperstraat, Wibautstraat, Jodenbreestraat, and parts of the Vijzelstraat – the old neighborhoods of the Jordaan and the Nieuwmarkt were not demolished as originally intended. Finally, and most importantly for our purposes, in the 1970s the metro line to the east of Amsterdam (today's Lines 53 and 54) was actually built to connect the Bijlmer district with the city center, but the other lines which were conceived at the same time were not constructed until much later. Line 50 (connecting south-east with north-west), the ringline (*de ringweg*), and the north-south line were drawn on paper in 1960 and accepted in a city council meeting in 1968, but it took more than twenty years before these plans were executed. By the late 1970s the 'metro' had been made taboo to the extent that the word itself was banned from public discourse. The north-south line is only being built today and, reading about all the things that have gone wrong with it so far (Bakker; Breebaart; *Metropijn*; *Rapport*), we now know why it took so long. The financial, political, and spatial disaster that it has become recalls what happened in Nieuwmarkt forty years ago. It is part of this ongoing story that I want to reconstruct in this essay.

History, Part 2: The Nieuwmarkt

The Nieuwmarkt, 'New Market', is the market place at a 5 minutes' walk to the south-east of Amsterdam Central Station. It is a large square housing the famous *Waag* building (the Dutch word '*Waag*' means 'scale'), many restaurants, cafés, and coffee shops. There is a daily general market, but on Saturdays mainly herbs and spices are sold. Nieuwmarkt is part of Chinatown and lies in between the Red Light District and the Jewish quarters. The area has a mixture of private homes and various social housing projects by the Dutch architect Aldo van Eyck.

The *Waag* building to the north of the Nieuwmarkt is now a bar and restaurant but used to be the Saint Anthony's Gate in the defense walls around the city in the fifteenth and sixteenth centuries (see Rambonnet; Van Blokland). Around that gate many foreigners – mostly tradesmen from the sea, but also Jewish exiles from Spain – who were not allowed into the city had their illegal dwellings in temporary, self-made housing. Their boats were anchored along the Waal River just outside the walls. When the city tore down the medieval fortress walls in 1614, the gate and the surrounding area became part of the city but they kept the links to trade, migration, alternative belonging, and forced displacement. In the seventeenth century the gate was turned into a weighing house (hence the reference to *Waag*) and a guildhall where bricklayers, painters, carpenters, textile workers, and others would meet and conduct their business. Because of this trade-related function of the Waag – close to the harbor – the canals around it were filled and a big market place (called the New Market) arose, housing stalls for selling cheese, fish, herbs, silk, and clothes. Side streets with places for dwelling and trading were built around the square and gradually a larger neighborhood, called Lastage, emerged. In the Golden Age, Holland was flourishing not least because of its colonial wealth, and thanks to Amsterdam's reputation of relative religious tolerance, people from all over the world arrived. This is the time when hundreds of Armenians – trading in carpets and silk – and thousands of Ashkenazi Jews – employed in silk, diamond, tobacco, medicine and in sugar refinery, all professions outside the guilds from which these migrants were banned – settled in and around Nieuwmarkt. The place constituted the literal and figurative margins of Amsterdam. When, after the seventeenth century, a crisis in trade set in, many of those migrant merchants left again.

Despite the fluctuating fate of the Nieuwmarkt ever since, it is safe to conclude that it has always been a very lively commercial place, with lots of little shops, a vibrant market, and, thanks to the nearby harbor at the IJsselmeer, many close connections to the fishing and shipping industry. Around 1900, several thousand

Chinese migrants settled here as well, most of whom were illegally hired as seafarers or stokers by the shipping companies. When not at sea they maintained little businesses in food, mostly peanuts. Many of those Chinese, however, were forced to leave during the crisis of the 1930s, while those who stayed were involved in the restaurant business which greatly expanded after World War II, along with gambling halls, opium dens, groceries, and boarding houses. Because of the persistent connection to seafarers, traders, and migrants, Nieuwmarkt has had an ethnically-diverse population which was not very affluent to say the least. In the nineteenth and early-twentieth centuries the area even had a reputation for poverty and criminality, and several attempts were made to 'sanitize' the area, all with little success.

Nieuwmarkt is now considered part of Chinatown, but it was once seen as the 'Jewish quarter'. At the time of the German invasion in 1940, about 80,000 Jews lived in Amsterdam, only 25% of whom survived the holocaust. While the Jewish proletariat lived in the quarters to the east of Nieuwmarkt, the Jewish middle classes had gradually moved out to other areas in the center, in southern Amsterdam and in Buitenveldert further to the south. Not surprisingly, the concentrated area around the Nieuwmarkt and Waterloo Square was explicitly targeted by anti-Jewish measures during the German occupation and since the people were poverty-stricken, they lacked the money to buy possible hiding places. The neighborhood was turned into a ghetto (*Judenviertel*) during the war, was hit by two bombs and various *razzias* in 1940, and in 1941 it was turned into the place where the first Jews were gathered and deported. Gradually Nieuwmarkt and its surroundings became a deserted, derelict area, so that when in the winter of 1944-1945 (known as the 'winter of hunger') the people from Amsterdam were practically starving and freezing to death, they ripped off the wooden panels from the houses that the Jewish and Chinese population had left behind. When the Germans finally left, not much remained of the area and many people had gone. Those who had survived were utterly poor.

Little wonder, then, that in the post-World War II period two main groups of people clashed over the future of Nieuwmarkt. On the one side stood the local people who wanted a reconstruction of their neighborhood and long-needed decent housing. They were supported by cultural heritage circles, but also by social housing movements, and by squatters, artists, and students who had gradually moved into the empty premises in the late 1960s and had given the neighborhood a new cultural and political boost but no financial investment. On the other side stood a mayor (Ivo Samkalden) and an alderman for public works (Han Lammers), both from the Labor Party, eager to implement Van Eesteren's plans: they first wanted to move the last inhabitants to social housing projects and then clean up the place at last by turning it into a city highway flanked by office buildings, stores and hotels, underneath which would run a metro line to take the citizens back and forth between the center – the place where they used to live – and the Bijlmer district, their new home. The social-democratic mayor had the support of the chamber of commerce (*Kamer van Koophandel*), the storekeepers' association and, interestingly, the Communist Party as well.

Protests and Activism in Nieuwmarkt

Much has already been written in the Netherlands on the New Market riots (*Nieuwmarktrellen*) of 1975 (Naeyé; Hoeben; Bosma, Boersma and Nijenhuis; Boersma *Onverklaarbaar*). It is a well-documented phase in the history of Amsterdam, in the first instance because of the city council's non-democratic decision-making process and the extremely violent actions that accompanied it, which drew the attention of the national press. Secondly, the riots are well-known because the protesters were politically, socially, and culturally articulate and had a wonderful distribution and information network. Thus they made themselves visible in public space while producing lots of writings, sounds, and images, most of which have been donated to libraries: together with a widespread presence in the city they built up a public memory in various archives. Finally, their actions managed to enter the spotlight because they were part of larger well-known countercultural and social movements that had developed in Amsterdam for over a decade. In fact, the group coordinating the resistance from Nieuwmarkt was an immediate heir to the highly mediatized Dutch Provo movement (1965-1967), in which the ex-Situationist Constant was an important figure (see the chapter by Andrew Hussey in this book). Since the early 1960s Provos and other protesting movements had been staging political and cultural campaigns for more and better housing conditions and more employment; and against the Vietnam war, an authoritarian Dutch government, members of the royal family who wed dubious right-wing husbands (from Germany and Spain), and a particularly repressive Amsterdam police force eager to break up any demonstrations by the left. Thanks to Provo's bizarre and anarchist actions in the streets of Amsterdam and their peculiar sense of publicity (see Pas), the activist group from Nieuwmarkt could fall back on, and thus sustain, an emerging tradition of self-conscious collective rebellion through media and urban performances. This has culminated in today's commercial image of Amsterdam as the Mecca of counterculture, which is quite paradoxical given the anti-capitalist sentiments that lay at the heart of the riots. It brings us back to the main point of this essay stated at the beginning, namely that we need to read the reputation of countercultural Amsterdam as not simply against but also as *deeply entangled with* the powers of government, commerce, and indeed of capitalist urban and social transformation.

The battle over Nieuwmarkt can be described as a complex cat-and-mouse game between the city council and the protesters – but also within the ranks of the council, the political parties and the protest movement themselves – which took several years but gradually evolved into nothing less than civil war. What happened? In 1964 the local citizens were outraged because the city had bought and demolished the first houses even before official decisions on the future of the area were made. Moreover, in 1968 the city council of Amsterdam neglected the growing criticism and accepted the plans for a full metro system. This is when the first protests were organized and the early squatters arrived. Despite increasing mass demonstrations, fierce criticism by the architects Van Eyck and Herman Hertzberger, and a significant dissent within the political parties themselves, the construction works started at the southern part, between Wibaut and Bijlmer and

Gaasperplas. In 1973 the engineers meant to tackle the northern part – between Wibaut and Central Station – but here the project met with growing resistance since the metro line was to cut straight through a densely-populated area around Waterloo Square and Nieuwmarkt. Because of the method of construction more than a hundred homes had to be demolished, and hence residents displaced first. While the city council had already been forced to alter some of its original city plans due to immense social pressure by 1973 – there would be no highway but social housing – it held on to its evacuation plans for the sake of the metro line.

In reaction to this authoritarian decision, various protest movements, headed by the squat movement *Woonburo de Kraker* (The Squatter Housing Agency), with ex-Provo members such as the printer Robert Stolk and artist-archivist Tjebbe van Tijen, stepped up their activities in Nieuwmarkt and occupied all the buildings due for demolition. Interestingly, however, the *Woonburo* was run like a semi-governmental agency itself, with a repertoire of rules, regulations, technologies, and somewhat chaotic decision-making procedures. Besides public meetings and debates, they produced manuals on how to invade houses, keep them intact, and serve the neighborhood. They gradually also formed committees to decide which occupant was to get which house and for how long, and under what conditions local citizens could count on their support. As Van Tijen puts it, as the pressures on and responsibilities of the activists increased, the need for structure and authority became manifest, even if this ran counter to their anti-authoritarian goals (in Bosma, Boersma and Nijenhuis 32).

Although the squatters' interventions were meant to give support to what was considered a good cause, not everybody was happy with their presence. As is clear from the archives I consulted,[1] while many local inhabitants collaborated, others firmly distanced themselves from these 'extremist' activities because they were eager to leave their houses in good condition in return for the government's money and better living premises. And there were more reasons for disagreement between the local citizens and the activists. The former feared that the latter's illegal actions precipitated rather than prevented the mayor's countermeasures in the area. People also begrudged those youngsters (often from abroad) who were simply in search of cheap housing, alcohol, and drugs and greatly disturbed the fragile social fabric. And then, of course, there were generational conflicts over modes of living together, public behavior, and expressing disagreement. Most importantly, several groups clashed over the future and tactics of the neighborhood: while older socialist and communist inhabitants supported the council's large-scale interventions in the city and aimed for political dialogue rather than actions, the youthful protesters fiercely and, according to some, dogmatically, responded with pamphlets, street actions, demonstrations, and other public transgressions. In sum, not everybody wholeheartedly embraced these kinds of countercultural interventions in the name of Nieuwmarkt and to several local citizens the protests appeared as aggravations of rather than solutions to the problems. Interestingly, though, these dissenting narratives largely remain unheard in the official historiographies of the neighborhood.

But besides squatting and barricading the neighborhood, the protesters in Nieuwmarkt also engaged in regular political activities, greatly aided by the city council's internal division over the financial mismanagement of the metro system and the concomitant growing debt. The political section of the underground movement nicely played the rules of the game and proposed alternative means of transportation, calculated less harmful and less expensive metro lines, interpellated the Ministry of Transportation in parliament, and organized leakages of secret documents in their activist newspapers. When that did not yield any results, they resorted to street protests, sit-ins, sleep-ins, and teach-ins; barricaded Han Lammers's home; and sabotaged the equipment of the demolition firms.

Much of their activism was also socially and culturally organized in the established tradition of Provo. Like their predecessors, the activists were good entrepreneurs who built up all kinds of networks and infrastructures. For instance, they had a central financial fund to support the squatters and their families, an unofficial day-care service, and even a school. They also possessed a smart publicity machinery: a printing press for newsletters, magazines and pamphlets, and a silk-screen printing press and copying machines for a broader and faster circulation of more expressive and often humorous posters, illustrations, and cartoons, which were either distributed by hand or pasted on public walls. They organized information and publicity evenings and exhibitions; painted messages, graffiti, and poems on buildings, or performed protest songs in the streets. They also broadcast updates on the events through their own radio station called Mokum ('*mokum*' is Yiddish for 'place' and refers to Amsterdam). Add to this the fact that Dutch newspapers and television crews reported on the increasingly violent tensions between militants and military force while several activists were interviewed on radio and television, and we may well conclude that this was a highly mediated protest movement aiming at instant free expression but also public visibility in media and urban space.

Since, as mentioned above, much of their instantaneously produced material was from the start strategically preserved and archived in libraries, it also greatly contributed to the installation of a public memory for future generations. Although engaged in place-based political activities around Nieuwmarkt, their collaboration and distribution networks guaranteed wider circulation, thereby lifting the activities to a broader publicized, indeed marketable, level. Little wonder, then, that some of these posters and pamphlets recur in many publications on the recent history of Amsterdam, and on the Nieuwmarkt riots in general. These locally produced political documents have begun to function as nothing less than standardized icons of the countercultural movements of the 1970s, which is ironic considering that they are supposed to stand for the opposite of standardization: freedom of expression, creativity, political activism, immediate action.

A similar tension between immediacy and mediation, avant-garde practice and institutionalization, local activism and larger reproduced culture, can be seen in the work of one of the photographers among them, Pieter Boersma. He not only photographed the activities, events, and the actual demolitions of houses (Boersma *Onverklaarbaar*),[2] but also visited libraries to take pictures of old archives on the Nieuwmarkt, which he then turned into collages to be used during teach-ins and exhibitions. By thus inscribing his instant photographs in a longer history of documentation on the neighborhood, Boersma executed a joint practice of (trans)media activism and official commemoration.

In the end the protesters delayed the demolition processes for about two years but they could not stop them. As police interventions grew more persistent, so did the resistance movement. In December 1974 several police officers were wounded in the first serious attempt to evict people from the occupied houses. When two months later extreme right-wing rioters carrying an actual bomb were arrested in the vicinity of the Bijlmer, the mayor blamed the protesters from Nieuwmarkt, even though they had nothing to do with it. In this hateful climate all dialogue stopped, and the clash between the parties escalated and culminated in what has come to be known as a day of civil war or 'Blue Monday'. Blue stands for the color of the police costumes and for the gas they used (Naeyé). On Monday, 24 March 1975 (and again on 8 April), hundreds of police officers – supported by 500 military policemen, and protected by dogs, horses, armored cars, water cannons, tear gas, sticks, and truncheons – invaded the Nieuwmarkt to literally beat the protesters out of the premises and let the bulldozers and wrecking balls do their work. Several people were wounded and arrested. For more than two years after this attack over two hundred people tried to bring the police force to trial for unlawful use of physical violence against them, but nothing resulted from those claims (Naeyé). Luckily much of this clash of forces was recorded by the camera and hence available for future research.

No wonder, then, that the 'underground metro' in Amsterdam has had this reputation of violence, repression, mismanagement, spatial disaster, economic tunnel vision, and fierce social, political, and cultural opposition; and that it took until the 1990s before the other three lines entered the public debate again. To many citizens, the metro continued a tradition of forced displacement of people – migrant traders, Armenians, Chinese, Jews, the socially disadvantaged, the homeless – that had marked Nieuwmarkt since the Middle Ages. It was left to a group of artists to enter the literal underground space and retain the memory of that painful legacy for future underground travelers.

Memorials in the Metro: Greetings from the Nieuwmarkt

In that same year of escalating violence, 1975, a semi-official public work group *Kunstzaken Metro* (Artworks Metro) was appointed by the city council to integrate visual art in the spatial environment of the metro stations. The group asked the inhabitants of all the districts covered by the metro line – including Nieuwmarkt – to propose artworks to that purpose. The Nieuwmarkt residents at first indignantly refused to co-operate, but in 1978 the question was posed again and after a tumultuous public meeting it was decided that a team of artists chosen by the people would participate in close collaboration with those that had lived and had protested there. If *they* did not produce that artwork, some anonymous artists would do it for them (Steenbeek). The following artists-activists were involved: the painter Jan Sierhuis (close to the CoBrA movement); the filmmaker Louis van Gasteren; Nieuwmarkt resident and media producer Roel van den Ende; long-time activist and part-time poet from Nieuwmarkt Tine Hofman; and visual artist Bert Griepink, also a central figure in the squatting movement. They acted as mediators between the local citizens and the patrons who commissioned the art and they worked together with other activists, but also – much more controversially – with the architect(s) and engineers. From the start it was agreed that the end result would be the integration of old 'material' rather than the creation of art. No decoration but documentation. And instead of closure they would instigate further debate.

Together this team produced a collection of monumental works and a documentary film, called *Groeten uit de Nieuwmarkt* (*Greetings from the New Market*). While the works in the metro were dedicated to the violent history of the neighborhood, the film captured 'the making of' and concentrated on the artists and their process of production. The monumental works in particular have been fiercely criticized for failing to bring to life the legacy of the protests, aiming at travelers rather than residents, and for supporting the infrastructures of power instead of continuing the fight (Steenbeek 46-52).

The final part of this essay, therefore, will investigate how these works deal with the tensions between activism and institutionalization, resistance and collaboration, past protest and material preservation, documentation and decoration.[3]

At the entrance to the north of the station hangs Jan Sierhuis's replication of a demolition ball, as a reminder of the destruction of the neighborhood. To the extent that the ball threatens to destroy the wall of the tunnel – there is already a dent in it – it also symbolizes the resistance movement. The ball presents demolition of houses and resistance against the metro in one blow, so to speak. Bert Griepink has filled the holes in the wall with blown-up photographs taken from the (well-known) archives on the eviction process. We see houses being demolished and squatters nearly crushed by bulldozers. Since the photographs represent what happened above ground prior to the construction of the metro tunnel, they expand the space of the tunnel to encompass what lies in the past and outside. Hence, the three layers of wall around the pictures indicate a multilayered spatial archive. The wall and the photos open up to a time and space that mark the destructive beginning of the metro line and thus situate the station in a larger – temporal and spatial – surrounding that is also completely lost to the present. In that sense the holes open up and close off at the same time, while the photographs literally and figuratively 'cover' what is no longer there. They represent and mask, document and decorate, make present and absent, include and exclude. The walls are made to act as an entrance to something (else) and as a terminal or dead end, much like the metro station opens up a space for travelers – it enters onto the huge space of the tunnel – while closing off the space of the residents above ground.

Something similar happens at the southern entrance of the station, where we find Louis van Gasteren's 'Roots of the City'. Here, about twenty wooden piles protrude from the ceiling and are supported by a steel buttress, which acts as a simulation of the technical support that the engineers promised to build underneath the foundations of the houses – a promise, however, that was never kept. Instead the foundations of the houses – the poles in the water on which they were built – were eliminated and the houses and their residents had to make way for

6.1. Jan Sierhuis. Wrecking Ball. (Photo: G. Verstraete)

6.2. Bert Griepink. Photograph of Squatter. (Photo: G. Verstraete)

6.3. Louis Van Gasteren. Roots of the City. (Photo: G. Verstraete)

the metro lines. Van Gasteren endows the ceiling of the metro station with a fictive foundational and supportive structure that would have saved the area above ground if only the construction had ever been real. Insofar as the steel simulation presents a construction that could and should have materialized, its fictive status raises ethical questions about the methods of building used, or, as Van Gasteren puts it in the film discussed below, his steel and wooden art project inscribes a belated 'respect' for the neighborhood, and its historical roots, that the authorities and engineers never expressed. Underneath Van Gasteren's roots project lie the broken walls of the seventeeth-century homes that were not saved. Again, in the holes, blown-up reproductions are placed: this time they concern reproductions of the posters, poems, and graffiti that the artists (including Griepink) and protesters had left behind on walls due for demolition. With the physical erasure of the buildings, the graffiti and posters were destroyed as well. The words and images by the underground movements disappeared along with the neighborhood they covered, even protected, in vain, and now they only survive in or as these photographs in the metro station. Mediated by these monumental photographs, the past writing on the wall gets reinscribed – preserved – into the walls of the underground station. Ironically, the metro functions as an archival place for conserving the things it has destroyed.

Interestingly, contemporary graffiti has been written over the reproduced posters and has thus made illegible the (past) writing on the wall. Like most graffiti tags, the text is inaccessible to the public and thus displacement has set in

6.4. Graffiti on Bert Griepink's collage. (Photo: G. Verstraete)

again, as if someone has tried to put the relation between the past and the present, between history and memory, between figurative underground culture and literal underground station through a stress test of sorts. It is as if some graffiti artist wanted to ask: does a memorial dedicated to Nieuwmarkt and hosted by the metro line help us to remember or to erase the past? How can we hijack these privatized walls of the tunnel and challenge their claims to represent the truth about what happened? How to give back to the protest movements of the past, the often illegible, rhythms of the original events? I will return to this at the end.

In between the two exits are four panels (triptychs) by Roel van den Ende, titled *Groeten uit de Nieuwmarkt*. These hang on both sides of the wall, over a length of about a hundred meters. Strolling the length of the platform one walks over Tine Hofman's motto engraved in the floor: *Wonen is Geen Gunst Maar een Recht* ('Having a home is not a favor but a right'). As Hofman explains in the film: the words on the platform evoke a history of this neighborhood being walked over. Two of the triptychs, one in the north and one in the south, contain collages of blown-up photographs or enlarged copies of paintings on the history of the Nieuwmarkt, particularly its combined history of commerce, political rallying, and forced displacement.

While the panels with the enlarged pictures focus on the past, two other triptychs focus on the present. These hang on the walls in the middle of the station and are made of black frames containing scraps of mirror and many empty spaces in between. Moving from the entrance (along the works just discussed) to the

6.5. Roel van den Ende: Groeten uit de Nieuwmarkt. (Photo: G. Verstraete)

heart of the station we move from fullness to emptiness, figuration to abstraction so to speak. What is more, while the works at both entrances represent the outside world from the past, the mirrors in the middle reflect what happens inside and in the present: the metro trains and the travelers as they wait or pass by in the here and now. Yet because of the broken surface the reflections are uneven, fragmentary; the scraps of mirror seem to produce motion continuously, even when you stand motionless in front of them. They constitute a constellation of spatial optical movement that is typical of life in the subway, characterized as this is by mobility, speed, cursory surface glances, fragility of contact.

The fragmented mirrors, however, are disrupted by huge blank intervals – spaces where there is nothing but the grayish white wall of the station, patches of framed emptiness and immobility. If all the other works just discussed can be said to 'symbolize' (humanize?) the steel, the wood, the stones, the bricks, the pipes, and the panels by making them witnesses to a social past – and if all the other works at least make the walls of the station speak and communicate with us travelers – here in the middle, in front of these absences the wall remains blank and refuses to mean or reflect anything. At best the large spaces of grey concrete simply close off. They remind us that a lot remains unsaid, excluded, and inaccessible. It may be true, as Roel van den Ende says in the film, that there was not enough money to fill the whole frame with mirrors. But to me at least, these gaps raise the difficult question as to whether metro works as grand and famous and publicly accepted as *Groeten uit de Nieuwmarkt* do not in the end repeat the mistakes of the past. Do commemorative, monumental acts such as these, which

6.6. Roel van de Ende: Triptych with mirrors. (Photo: G. Verstraete)

are completely integrated in the architecture and history of the metro station, not end up homogenizing and emptying for future generations what is, or should be complex, multiple, time- and place-bound? Instead of witnessing to a conflict-ridden action in a particular, tumultuous period in the history of the place, *Groeten uit de Nieuwmarkt* has consolidated the official monumental tribute to the past, hosted by the metro line. Here we get to see a past completely dominated by one straightforward narrative, namely that of the metro and the resistance against it. As Jan Sierhuis asks in a self-critical move at the end of the documentary film: 'Did we fail in making something that could be so easily appropriated by the institution against which we fought?'. Insofar as the artists worked within the material structures of the station, their documentary practice was from the start inert, destined to become integrated but also lifeless and passé. It is left to the film to present us with a time-based view on what the works in the metro have had to leave out: transience, movement, contestation, and inevitable disappointment.

The Film

Groeten uit de Nieuwmarkt (1980) is a documentary by the Dutch director Guus van Waveren about the construction of the works discussed above.[4] Van Waveren interviews the five protagonists between 1978 and 1980 as they execute their project in the physical space of the metro station. Many of the interviews take place in the darkness, and noise, of the underground, as surrounding construction workers plaster walls, lower steel buttresses, cut mirrors, paint wooden panels, and so forth. At times the documentary seems more about the building of the metro station than about the production of the memorial in it, and it is precisely this thin line between critique and institutional incorporation that lies at the heart of what we see. The latter part of this essay will address how Van Waveren's film functions as the site where uncertainties about the commemoration are played out. While this loss of clarity is contested by some protagonists in the film as they loudly reclaim the utopian impulse of their project, there are moments when the meaning of what we see is much more ambiguous.

The film mainly consists of interviews of isolated talking heads: Sierhuis, Hofman, Van Gasteren, Griepink, and Van den Ende appear in front of the camera less as an artistic collective than as a group of individuals with stories of their own. The protagonists are mostly framed in the context of the metro station in 1979, during the time they execute their works while the tunnel is being completed. In those scenes they somewhat heroically testify to the meaning and reasons of what they are doing (in the present). Of course those utopian explanations inevitably lead them to recall the events of the past, namely the resistance against the metro line and the violent displacements that ensued. As their narratives in the present return to a time period prior to the making of the film, the latter cuts back to older footage to show the viewer what is being talked about: mostly TV images in black and white dating from 1975 or images from books; but we also get to see drawings, posters, photographs, graffiti on buildings, that is, the activist pictures once used during the protests of the past and now partly preserved in the metro station (and in libraries, films, and history books). Along with a return to 1975, the film switches from moving images in the present to archival (static) media from the past, and from color to black and white, as if it wants to counter its own movement – and the drive of the artists at work – with a time and space for retention. It inevitably raises the question: what is the relation between the activist documents back then and the film right now? We will come back to that later.

Besides this play with time, and between old and new media, the film poses questions about place. While most of the documentary is shot in the tunnel, at times the men are interviewed in what seems like a room. We also get to see Tine Hofman, the only woman in the picture, in the street where her house once stood while she shows Van Waveren (and us the viewers) pictures and books about what is no longer there. This change of location from below to above ground also turns out to have temporal dimensions since at the end of the film it becomes clear that the shots in the room and some on the street are actually recorded after the projects have been completed, right before the official opening of the metro station in 1980. They are to be considered moments of reflection rather than action or activism. This means that shots from 1980 (the time 'afterwards', the time of reflection in the room and the street) alternate with those from 1979 (the time 'during which', the time of the work in the metro station) and the time of the footage from 1975 (the time 'before', the time of the riots in the streets). In the spatial movements between upper and lower ground, the film cuts back between past, present, and future as well as between street activism, artistic and material production, and critical reflection. Or to put it differently, going up and down spatially the film passes through layers of time in various directions while alternating between immediate action and the memory thereof. The result is the evocation of a non-linear living in the wake of where immediacy and mediation are hard to separate.

Thus, central to the dynamics of the film is a constant play with time and space, and with the meaning of what we get to see. The film abandons the progression of past, present, and future and cuts back between them while also moving back and forth between places below and above ground. We could say that the linearity typical of a metro line, but also of a dogmatic political view (for or against the metro), is disrupted by a cyclical movement back and forth, between here and there and then and now, thereby installing a level of complexity, but also the possibility of reconnecting irreconcilable moments, places, and perspectives.

It is all the more significant, then, that in the final shot, back in the setting of the room, in the time afterwards, Van Gasteren predicts what will happen to their works in the future, let us call it the time of my writing. The works in the metro station, he says, will be appreciated by the audience, appropriated by the authorities, analyzed by students and critics, and all revolutionary or critical connotations will be lost. This is when Sierhuis self-critically asks whether they have succeeded in producing *art* (commissioned by those in power) but failed in the maintenance of resistance (in the name of the people from Nieuwmarkt). In the time afterwards – above ground – things are not that clear anymore and disillusionment sets in. The contrast with the heroism of the time of production – in the underground – could not be starker.

It is important to note that the temporal and spatial motion discussed above happens in conjunction with a recurrent switch between the medium of the film and the older media mentioned before. As mentioned earlier, the documentary heavily relies on the integration of black and white footage, and of texts, posters, drawings, and photographs dating from the time of the protests and now partly preserved in the station, as if Van Waveren wants to suspend the motion of moving images in the present and evoke the persistence of other media left over from the past. In several ways, this technique reminds us of the collages and cut-ups used in the streets of countercultural Amsterdam, when texts, illustrations, scraps of newspapers, and photographs were glued together for political commentary and public memory. In the best of those moments of crossmedial encounter in the film, the viewer cannot tell whether she is watching a shot in Van Gaveren's film or someone else's durable picture from the past. As when in scenes 5'02"–5'30" we see a shot of the wrecking ball in the metro suddenly transform into a sketch that was made of this project prior to execution. Or we see a filmic shot of the tunnel fading into a photographic still of a man waiting on the platform. In those crossmedial moments the film momentarily freezes and captures the traces of the past – and of the slightly outdated media – quite differently from the way the works in the metro station do. Here archival moments or documents are allowed to linger on not by consolidating them (for instance into a wall or museum) but, precisely, by momentarily destabilizing the medium of Van Gasteren's moving image. It is in moments of filmic uncertainty (in the present) that the words and images from the past reappear most surprisingly and intensely. Through the fleetingness or fragility of the moving image, not through its institutionalization, the past is momentarily retained in the present. Like the activist interventions in the streets of Amsterdam, the act of commemoration here is ephemeral, instant, and bound to disappear or become illegible like the graffiti tag discussed above.

Something similar could be said about the performance of the protagonists in front of the camera. While all five of them tell their own version about what has happened in the 1970s and their role in the production of the memorial, it is not in what they say but in their momentary appearance that we are able to get a glimpse of how the past lingers on in the present. Although Sierhuis and Van Gasteren did not actually participate in the riots and were not affected by the metro line personally, they verbally dominate the mise-en-scène. At a distance from the past, they play the roles of articulate spokespersons who heroically – in the case of Van Gasteren also theatrically and pedantically – evoke what happened. They eloquently imitate what was once said, gestured, and done while emphasizing the importance of their current work, or, alternatively, blatantly questioning it at the end. This is not the case with Griepink, Van den Ende, and Hofman, all three of whom were active during the protests and lost their homes. Speaking with the slightly pained, sometimes cynical, restraint of someone who has suffered, they appear much less involved in the film. Neither do they openly criticize their work in the metro station. They seem more hesitant and critical about their role in the film and about what can be said about the past *tout court*. Most striking, in this respect, is the appearance of the clearly less articulate Tine Hofman, always a bit shy, holding on to her handbag as she reads out one of her poems of protest with a strong local accent and an uncomfortable smile, as if the power given to her by the camera cannot but remind her of how this falls short of the kind of power that made her homeless and her poetry superfluous. It is in the hesitancy of her performance in the spotlights that we get an intimacy of how the past lingers on in the present.

Conclusion

This essay has examined a particular phase of countercultural Amsterdam in the context of the first metro line in the city and the fierce social and cultural protests against it. Studying this particular underground movement of the late 1960s and early 1970s in a spatial and temporal context of urban transformation and political conflict has enabled us to 'situate' its strategies of opposition and relate them to the larger structures of capitalist power and authority being fought against. The way the protest movement operated and organized itself in Nieuwmarkt, the manner in which it occupied media and urban space, the various connections it established way beyond its immediate field of action, its modes of distributing and institutionalizing its own legacy through archives – all of this invites us to reconsider the notion of underground activism beyond the power-resistance divide. This also means questioning the uniformity that is implied in the prevailing modernist narratives of city planning in Amsterdam and the protests against it.

The truth is much more complex and heterogeneous. Far from marginal figures in the history of Amsterdam, the activists from Nieuwmarkt have played an active role in the fate of the city and in the way the riots and displacements have been remembered. As I have argued, their visual tactics via posters, pamphlets, and the official monuments in the metro station have contributed to a certain mode of standardization. What dominates the discourse on the late 1960s and early 1970s is a vision of an area torn apart by the heroic clash between a huge capitalist infrastructure and a stubborn grassroots movement that could not stop the metro but at least prevented the arrival of highways and more metro lines. It is left to the film by Van Waveren to bring in some nuance in the picture by showing us the messy entanglement between underground and above ground, avant-garde and power, subversion and institutionalization.

Notes

1 I consulted Tine Hofman's archives (1940-1993) at the International Institute of Social History in Amsterdam, where most of the archives on Nieuwmarkt are gathered. Tine Hofman (1924-1993) was one of the leading figures in Amsterdam's activist movements of the 1950s, 1960s, and 1970s. While living in Nieuwmarkt she was a member of Wijkcentrum d'Oude Stadt, a civil society movement that is still active today and that works to improve the living and working conditions of people in Amsterdam. The Wijkcentrum collaborated closely with Aktiegroep Nieuwmarkt in the fight against the eastern metro line. Hofman was one of the citizens who lost their homes; she was forced to move with her husband and children in 1975. Hofman's archive contains public letters, pamphlets, minutes, photos, posters, and many other documents concerning all the protests she was involved in during her lifetime.

2 Many of Boersma's pictures can be seen at his online archive: http://www.pieterboersmaphotography.com/album2/index.html

3 The following has benefited from *Van Metro tot Beeldbuis*.

4 All my thanks to Bert Hogenkamp at the Instituut voor Beeld en Geluid for first drawing my attention to the film and then providing me with a copy of it.

7. Underground Circulation: The Beats in Paris and Beyond

Allen Hibbard

Upon my return to the United States from Amsterdam in November 2010, after the first of two symposia on the 'Paris-Amsterdam Underground', I found myself once again, as so many times before, winding through customs and passport control lines. In one line, trained dogs, obviously in the employ of the state, though without badges or uniforms, sniffed around arriving passengers' feet and luggage. One of the dogs circled the passenger in front of me – a young man in his early thirties, it seemed, dressed in T-shirt and jeans. The pace of the dog's sniffing increased, and the young man's nervousness became palpable. Perhaps, it occurred to me, this young man had spent time in one of those Amsterdam coffee shops, and the smell of marijuana had seeped into his clothing. Customs agents spent a little more time than usual with this passenger, asking him to open bags, dumping out contents, and searching for false bottoms, or secret hiding places. Fortunately, the dog showed no interest in me. Evidently it detected no evidence of transgression.

This scene suggests certain characteristics and dynamics associated with the underground and how it operates. It is at checkpoints and border crossings that heightened vigilance is exercised, and elaborate, sophisticated mechanisms are imposed to police and restrict the movement of certain substances, people, or activities. What is permitted (allowed to circulate fairly openly above ground) in one place (Amsterdam) is forced or driven underground elsewhere (in this case, the United States). Amsterdam, of course, is known for its permissive policies toward prostitution and the use of marijuana. One can do things in Amsterdam that one could not do in the United States without fear of being caught and punished. Cultural and historical context, thus, to a great extent, determines what kinds of activities and thoughts are forced to occupy underground spaces. At borders, norms and laws of particular societies are visibly announced, signposted, enforced. At borders and checkpoints attempts are made to curb perceived threats and dangers. Luggage is x-rayed. Documents are examined and stamped. Identities are checked against terrorist watch lists. Bodies are scanned, sometimes patted down, and (in some instances, at some borders) cavities are searched. The power of the state is forcefully and visibly asserted; the consequences of getting caught for violations of law are serious – fines, trials, jail time. Yet, despite these measures and possible consequences, there are those who – for financial gain, political purposes, or other reasons – assess risks and determine to attempt crossings, seeking ways to hide contraband substances, disguise identity, disrupt detection mechanisms, or ferret out porous, unpatrolled points of entry.

The underground is often a place to stay put, simply in order to survive: a place to hide out or seek sanctuary until conditions change, allowing for safe movement, or until safe passage can be assured. Historically, numerous examples can be found in which people (revolutionaries, fugitives, asylum-seekers) have sought cover and hidden out in some safe place outside their home countries, waiting for a time to return home, when circumstances were propitious. We might think of the Russian revolutionaries exiled in Geneva in Joseph Conrad's 1911 novel *Under Western Eyes*, or Vladimir Lenin's real exile in Switzerland from 1914-1917 (first in Bern, then in Zurich) where he finished *Imperialism: The Highest Stage of Capitalism* before his famous train ride back to St. Petersburg where he anticipated the role he would play after the Bolshevik Revolution. (This period of exile has taken literary form, in Tom Stoppard's play *Travesties* and Alexander Solzhenitsyn's *Lenin in Zurich*.) And, later in the century, in 1978, the Ayatollah Khomeini (who had first lived in exile in Turkey, then Iraq), briefly took refuge in Neauphle-le-Château, on the outskirts of Paris, where he made influential speeches before his return to Iran, to jubilant crowds, after the fall of the Shah. Mobility (or at least the expectation and projection of mobility) is, thus, inherently associated with the notion of the underground. The ultimate purpose of the underground is to move something – people, ideas, or things (e.g., books, weapons, documents, films) – from one place to another, as safely as possible, without being detected, under the threat of surveillance, apprehension, and punishment.

When one occupies an underground space there is usually something at stake, should one be detected, forced to surface, so to speak. Angela Davis, for instance, the American Communist 1960s revolutionary, went underground for several months (from around 14 August 1970 to her arrest on 13 October 1970) when she was charged with aggravated kidnapping and first-degree murder and placed on the FBI's Ten Most Wanted Fugitives list, after a gun registered to her was used to kill a judge. (She was later tried and found not guilty.) Those involved in political resistance in countries with tight authoritarian regimes could be slapped in jail if caught, if their activities were exposed. In the face of such a restricted way of living – in fear of being apprehended and curtailing movement, speech, and production – some understandably have chosen or been forced into exile, living in a diasporic space outside a repressive homeland.

To cite just one example, among countless others, we might consider how three contemporary Iranian women have chosen to work outside their homeland, more openly, creating or promoting work in ways they could not do in Iran: Marjane Satrapi, author of the graphic novel *Persepolis*; Sharmush Parsipur, author of *Women without Men*; and Shirin Neshat, who made a film loosely derived from Parsipour's novel. Neither these women nor their works would be officially let back in Iran, yet somehow (though banned) their work circulates there, perhaps even creating more interest and demand because of its taboo status. Despite border control mechanisms, some things seem always to manage to slip through.

The underground, as undetected space remaining outside surveillance systems, we must note, carries at the same time the potential for damage and destruction as well as the potential for progressive social and political change. Going underground can be a strategy for carrying out terrorist attacks, or – as in the operation of the Underground Railroad and the French Underground during World War II – for liberating slaves and providing refuge or means of escape for Jews.

In my own thinking through the underground here in this chapter, I continue with an examination of one specific instance of what might be conceived as underground activity – the American Beats in Paris in the late 1950s and early 1960 – and move to a consideration of how the productions and ideas of the Beats subsequently circulated, before turning to some theoretical reflections and considerations, and concluding with a consideration of the present possibilities for underground movement, above and below the ground as well as in cyberspace.

The Beats in Paris

From 1958 to 1963, a group of Beat writers that included William S. Burroughs, Allen Ginsberg, Gregory Corso, and Brion Gysin (at various times) set up temporary residence at 9 Rue Gît-le-Cœur, dubbed the Beat Hotel, where in the summer of 2009, at a marvelous celebration of the 50th anniversary of the publication of *Naked Lunch* in Paris, a rowdy crowd of Burroughsians gathered to unveil a plaque in honor of the Beats on the wall outside what is now a very fashionable hotel at the address. For a thin slice of history, the Beat Hotel served as a kind of underground outpost for these American expatriates who no doubt found the atmosphere freer and more conducive to creative activity than the United States was at the time, bound by Puritan morals, haunted by Communist witch hunts, and writhing in the clutches of the Cold War.

Though they were not forcibly exiled, the group of Beat writers who congregated in Paris in the late 1950s and early 1960s might, like some of the examples mentioned above, be considered a kind of transnational displaced underground, seeking a temporary place of haven where they could sojourn in anticipation of changed conditions that would allow return or further movement. Above all, these people chose Paris because they thought it would be a good place to live and work, and because it allowed possibilities for collaborative exchange. It might seem to be a stretch to call this 'underground' activity, because of its relative openness and visibility. Yet while perhaps not a part of the French underground scene, we might consider this Beat enclave as a kind of displaced underground vis-à-vis the United States.

Of course, historically Paris has been a favored site for American expatriates, serving various purposes for various figures at various times. We might recall Henry James's quintessential expatriate novel, *The Ambassadors*, set primarily in Paris, in which our middle-aged protagonist Lambert Strether comes to rescue and send home the young Chad Newsome, only to succumb himself, belatedly, to the city's (and perhaps Chad's) charms. And of course Gertrude Stein's salon at 27 Rue de Fleurus is legendary, as is the significant shaping role she played in the modernist movement as well as her long-time commitment to her companion

Alice B. Toklas, famous for her brownie recipe as well as for 'her' autobiography. Stein and subsequent women writers who sought refuge in Paris (such as Djuna Barnes, Jean Rhys, and Nancy Cunard) are the subject of Shari Benstock's fine study *Women of the Left Bank*. Similarly, Michel Fabre constructs the history of African American writers who made Paris their temporary home, among them Richard Wright, Chester Himes, William Gardner Smith, and James Baldwin. Somewhat ironically, Americans have often found a freer atmosphere in Paris than in the 'land of the free and home of the brave'. Many have seen Paris as a place where they could escape racism, puritanical morality, and rigid gender roles.

As we consider the experience of the Beats in Paris, we must look at what it was that had to remain underground, what the surface resisted and suppressed. It largely came down to radical political views, illegal drugs, and sexual preference. 'Many of them were gay', as Barry Miles notes in *The Beat Hotel*, 'and they could lead a freer life in France, and most of them using illegal drugs' (4). This underground locale provided a kind of cover, or sanctuary, in which these writers felt free to experiment and produce works they likely would not otherwise have produced. I propose here that writing (especially a kind of avant-garde writing that challenges established forms and norms) is an especially potent mode of underground activity, both in its means of production and its sometimes unpredictable, rhizomatic means of dissemination.

The Beat Hotel was the site of production of a number of significant works of American literature that at the time might have been considered avant-garde but now are recognized as part of the tradition. In Paris Ginsberg wrote 'At Apollinaire's Grave' and a significant portion of *Kaddish*, a long homage to his mother Naomi, written after her death at a mental institution. And Corso wrote 'Bomb' – an explosive poem, innovative in content and form, 'shaped on the page like a mushroom cloud of an atomic bomb' (Miles 5). It was in Paris that Burroughs finished *Naked Lunch*, worked on a number of collaborative projects, and (under the influence of Brion Gysin) developed the cut-up technique, producing *The Soft Machine* and part of *The Ticket That Exploded*.

My focus here will be primarily on Burroughs because I believe his work is most pertinent to an inquiry of underground, while I admit that an examination of Ginsberg, Corso, and Gysin could be productive as well. Burroughs, along with poststructuralist French theorists who were developing and refining their ideas at the same historical moment, thought about how dominant systems could be resisted. One key tactic Burroughs experimented with and developed at the Beat Hotel is what has become known as the cut-up technique, whereby portions of texts or tapes were cut, rearranged, and interspersed with portions of other texts and tapes to create wholly new patterns and meanings: break conventional, established flows of narrative; create new possibilities and meanings; 'Storm the Reality Studio'; reshuffle material formed by traditional modes of production. Contemporary mythologies, world views produced electronically and disseminated widely, were formed and functioned much in the way Greek myths, or tribal myths, once worked in smaller societies. The cut-up had the potential to disrupt, mix and – thus – critique established narratives and world views. In 'The

Cut-up Method of Brion Gysin' (the Canadian artist-writer who introduced Burroughs to the technique), Burroughs describes the process:

> The method is simple. Here is one way to do it. Take a page. Like this page. Now cut down the middle and across the middle. You have four sections: 1 2 3 4 ... one two three four. Now rearrange the sections placing section four with section one and section two with section three. And you have a new page. Sometimes it says much the same thing. Sometimes something quite different – cutting up political speeches is an interesting exercise – in any case you will find that it says something and something quite definite ... Cut-ups are for everyone. Anybody can make cut-ups ... Cut the words and see how they fall. Shakespeare Rimbaud live in their words. Cut the word lines and you will hear their voices ... All writing is in fact cut-ups ... The cut-ups could add new dimension to films. Cut gambling scene in with a thousand gambling scenes all times and places. Cut back. Cut streets of the world. Cut and rearrange the word and image in films. (Burroughs and Gysin, *Third Mind* 30-2).

Brion Gysin, explaining the cut-up technique, writes: 'What are words and what are they doing? The cut-up method treats words as the painter treats his paint, raw material with rules and reasons of its own ... Painters and writers of the kind I respect want to be heroes, challenging fate in their lives and in their art ... So if you want to challenge and change fate ... cut up words, make them a new world' (qtd. in Miles 195-6).

A number of critics have commented on the revolutionary potential of the cut-up method. Noelle Blatt, for instance, notes how the method disrupts conventional relationships between signs and meanings:

> *Il est important, au moment où l'on cherche à évaluer le role et la valeur du cut-up, de ne pas oublier l'objectif qui motive son emploi, à savoir libérer le sens en rendant au signe sa pleine fonction signifiante et en permettant à nouveau un libre exercice des rapports paradigmatiques et syntagmatiques entre les termes de la langue.* (14)

And, as Timothy Murphy points out, the method has political implications: 'Cut-ups were a form of practical demystification and subversion that could uncover the ideology at work in the political lines of the media – for example, revealing the structural collusion between the police and the drug market in the US and UK' (39).

The extent to which these Beat writers were aware of and interacted with the contemporary French scene around them has been a topic of debate. Being underground does tend to produce a kind of tunnel vision, because one is cut off and often obsessively concerned for one's safety. Sometimes, as we have seen, movement is restricted out of fear of detection, or worse. One gets the sense from Barry Miles's book that the Beats did not venture far from the Beat Hotel, other than to museums, bookstores, or in search of various (mainly forbidden) pleasures. 'As non-French speakers', Miles writes, 'they had no involvement with

French culture and the issues of the day, nor were they restricted by rules with which the French lived, simply because they were ignorant of them' (19). He goes on to quote Jean-Jacques Lebel: 'They were on an island, isolated in this magic little paradise full of rats and bad smells' (19). Later Miles does acknowledge that the Beats, even though relatively isolated from French politics, could not help being aware of the war in Algeria and the heated debates surrounding the Algerian question.

Recent essays by Andrew Hussey and Timothy Murphy focus directly on the importance of Paris on Burroughs's work and thought. Both Hussey and Murphy dispel the conventionally held view that the Beats were hermetically sealed within their hotel and had no interaction with contemporary French culture. In '"Paris Is about the Last Place ...": William Burroughs In and Out of Paris and Tangier, 1958-1960', first delivered in the form of a paper at a 2008 conference in Tangier, Hussey makes a strong case that in Paris the writer consolidated strands of thinking begun earlier. The Paris Burroughs arrived in was in the throes of conflict over the Algeria question, with ferment among various avant-garde political organizations. Hussey shows how Burroughs would have been aware of (and perhaps influenced by) movements such as the Situationists (Guy Debord) and the Lettrists (Isidore Isou), groups with whom he would have found a good deal of affinity, both in terms of philosophy and method. Indeed, what Burroughs found in Paris 'was a matrix of avant-garde movements, all of them deeply marked by the tensions of their age and with an absolute belief in revolution as real experience rather than metaphor or theory' (78-9).

Timothy Murphy, in his essay 'Exposing the Reality Film: William S. Burroughs Among the Situationists', similarly points to 'Burroughs's and Debord's parallel sensitivities to the postwar economy of the image', as well as to the pivotal connective role between the two played by Alexander Trocchi. Flows of communication would have gone from the Situationists to Burroughs, Murphy notes, with cautions that claims for direct influence remain speculative. Nonetheless, Murphy usefully draws comparisons between the key Situationist notion of spectacle and Burroughs's notion of the reality studio. Murphy cites Debord's description of the spectacle as 'not a collection of images; rather, it is a social relationship between people that is mediated by images' (qtd. in Murphy 34) It is, furthermore, 'the self-portrait of power in the age of power's totalitarian rule over conditions of existence' (qtd. in Murphy 34). At once, then, we realize a shared concern for the operation of power, particularly through the careful construction and distribution of images, with corporate mass media playing a key, intermediary role in the process. 'The reality studio,' Murphy writes,

> like the Word or the spectacle, is a totality that is not so much a set of words that we speak or images that we watch as it is a general condition in which we are immersed, even and especially when we are apparently not focused on words or images. (34-5)

Murphy compares the Situationist technique of *détournement* (breaking up previously constructed films – Brecht-like – inserting disruptive material that calls attention to fictive constructions of reality, bursting its bubble, so to speak) to Burroughs's cut-up method. Both are experimental techniques with aesthetic and political effects and consequences. Both Burroughs's cut-up technique and the Situationist practice of *détournement* envisioned a transformation of everyday lived experience, springing from a consciousness of shaping forces and optimizing capacity for individual self-determination.

Barry Miles's *The Beat Hotel*, published several years after the death of Ginsberg and Burroughs, in 2000, has a rather nostalgic tone. The vitality and poignancy of the underground at the time it is operative becomes diffuse and less poignant, loses its edge, once it is relegated to the status of history. A revolutionary mood was in the air, with the spring of 1968 just around corner. 'By the spring of 1960,' Miles writes,

> the beginning of the most explosive decade of cultural experimentation since the turn of the century, the Beats of the Beat Hotel had already paved the way with routines, Cut-ups, flicker, and scrying; they had had visions and hallucinations, experimented with hashish, marijuana, Diosan, codeine, morphine, and heroin, and had engaged in orgies and other sexual practices that were probably illegal and were certainly frowned upon in their own countries. (224)

Their innovations, practices, and philosophies, as we will see, continued to worm their way beneath the seemingly stable surfaces of societies.

Beat Circulation

Ideas and works originally contained within the space of the Beat Hotel later spread in unpredictable, unforeseen ways, inspiring others and effecting cultural change. The immediate, intended audience, as is usually the case with diasporic, expatriate, and exilic communities, was back home. The liberatory lifestyle and literary production of the Beats circulated widely in the United States in the 1960s, providing fuel for countercultural movements. Subway ads for *Evergreen Review* in the early 1960s featured Allen Ginsberg, with Uncle Sam hat and caption reading 'Join the Underground' (Morgan 310). Impulses and sensibilities that had, in the 1950s, been repressed, became dominant in the 1960s, a decade that brought student protests against the war in Vietnam, drugs, rock 'n' roll, sexual experimentation, civil rights, the rise of feminism, and Stonewall.

More unexpected was the influence Burroughs had on the Dutch writer Gerard Reve, influence that eventually circled back to Amsterdam. Reve encountered Burroughs at the International Writers' Conference in Edinburgh in August of 1962, where the American writer spoke on panels on 'The Future of the Novel' and 'Censorship.' Reve and Burroughs appear on the list of conference participants, along with James Baldwin, Marguerite Duras, Lawrence Durrell, William Golding, Aldous Huxley, Norman Mailer, Mary McCarthy, Henry Miller, Alberto Moravia, Nathalie Sarraute, Muriel Spark, and Stephen Spender

('Reality Studio'). While at the time Burroughs was not well-known outside small circles, Reve had already established himself with his acclaimed 1947 novel *De avonden* (The Evenings), 'considered now to be a classic of modern Dutch literature' (Wood).

Apparently Burroughs – both his physical presence and his remarks – made an impression at this conference, enhancing and broadening his reputation. Speaking of the future of the novel, he suggested that writers needed to keep pushing the limits, exploring new territory, like contemporary ventures in space. He spoke specifically about his own experimentation with the cut-up technique. His remarks on censorship, made just prior to the *Naked Lunch* censorship trial, were prescient and relevant to our consideration of the underground: 'In any form censorship presupposes the right of the government to decide what people will think, what thought material of word and image will be presented to their minds – I am precisely suggesting that the right to exercise such control is called in question' ('Reality Studio'). Burroughs went on specifically to talk about sex and censorship:

> The anxiety of which censorship is the overt expression has so far prevented any scientific investigation of sexual phenomena – Few investigators have asked the question: What is sex? – and taken the necessary steps to find the answers – So far as I know the only scientific work on this subject was done by Doctor Wilhelm Reick [Reich] – As a result he was expelled from a number of countries before he took refuge in America where he died in a federal prison – His experiments indicate that sex is in all likelihood an electromagnetic phenomena, that physicists and mathematicians could discover precise formulae of sexual energy and contact leading to a physics of sexual behavior – It would then be possible, on the basis of precise knowledge, to determine what sexual practices were healthy and what practices were not healthy with reference to function of the human organism. ('Reality Studio')

We can imagine that Reve listened sympathetically, with open, eager ears, to Burroughs's words, for they reflected his own views on literature and sexual freedom. After the conference, Burroughs returned to Tangier, where he finished *Nova Express*. Reve soon went to Tangier, evidently hoping to see Burroughs. Though he missed Burroughs, Reve notes that he did meet Alan Ansen, Burroughs's acquaintance who was associated with many of the Beats, in Tangier (Maas 84).

Soon after these encounters and travels, the young Dutch writer published some of his most bold and provocative works, including *Op Weg naar het Einde* (Approaching the End, 1963 and *Nader tot U* (Nearer to Thee, 1966)). Often deploying epistolary form, these works frankly and openly portrayed homosexual behavior, and displayed iconoclastic views toward religion that were shocking to many at the time. A major controversy involving Reve erupted in 1967, after the writer's conversion to Catholicism, when 'he was officially charged with blasphemy for writing an article in the journal *Dialoog* that characterized Christ as a donkey with whom he wanted to have sexual intercourse' (Wood). The scandalous description appeared in his 'Letter to My Bank' (1966), bearing the address of a bank in Morocco and noting that his portrayal of this act of bestiality was prompted by his sympathetic observation of the animal's cruel treatment in rural Spain and Portugal. Needless to say, the scandal brought Reve fame and notoriety he otherwise would not have received.

Critical observers have noted the wider cultural implications of Reve's bold, subversive writing. As Mattias Duyves has written, 'in my perspective [this incident was] a crucial cultural opening moment – a turning point – in a redevelopment of relations between status quo and underground.' Perhaps propelled by the example of Burroughs, just following the period he spent in the Beat Hotel in Paris, Reve made public and visible that which before had remained unstated, repressed; thus, his work no doubt played a role in the loosening of traditional Dutch values in the 1960s.

In the meantime, Burroughs and his work, neither of which had been much known by the French during the time the writer lived in Paris, gradually was folded back into French culture as well. *Naked Lunch* appeared in French as *Festin nu*, translated by Eric Kahane and published by Gallimard in 1964, five years after its first English publication in Paris and two years after its first publication in the United States. Soon thereafter, other works by Burroughs began to appear in French, often within a short time after their publication in English. Translation can thus be seen as another means by which ideas are moved from one cultural/linguistic scene to another, often creating fresh and invigorating meanings in the new scene. The gradual emergence of the 'French Burroughs' was followed by critical studies in the 1970s, such as those by Philippe Mikriammos and Serge Grunberg, that introduced Burroughs and his work to French readers, placing him within the context of French avant-garde writers such as the Marquis de Sade, Lautréamont, and Artaud, as well as the thinking of Marx, Lacan, and Bataille.

Theorizing the Underground

Any consideration of the underground, it seems to me, must first confront and wrestle with the question of human agency, a particularly vexing issue in contemporary theory, made all the more compelling in modern and postmodern discourse where notions of what constitutes a self become especially salient and contentious. And, associated with agency, a key motivation often propelling underground activity is the desire – indeed, the imperative – to effect meaningful political or social change. One way of thinking about the underground is to conceive of it physically – not only metaphorically – as an enterprise that will, through its loosening of the ground beneath the surface, through the creation of tunnels and caverns, inevitably, at some point, result in an alteration of the contours of the surface, perhaps even resulting in the toppling of certain established structures, opening the possibility for building new and different kinds of structures.

What then are the limits and possibilities of human action? Have the limits and capacity for exercising agency changed over time? These are questions we must examine over and over again, from moment to moment, from generation to generation. As one reviews, reads, and reflects upon modern and contemporary thinking about relations between individuals and surrounding social and political situations, one frequently encounters theories that seem to allow for very little room for human latitude. Louis Althusser and Michel Foucault come to mind. The fundamental question for Althusser in *Ideology and Ideological State Apparatuses* is why capitalism has remained such a resilient system. How are ideologies reproduced? His analysis reveals a tight, interconnected system of social and political controls that integrates (in varying degrees, depending on the society) forcible means of control (repressive state apparatuses), and softer means of control (ideological state apparatuses). The former would include police, military, and sometimes legal systems. The latter: religion, education, family, media, cultural institutions, etc. Into these systems the subject is born or cast, literally called into being, and that being is defined and restrained by these powerful forces of ideology – so powerful that it seems difficult if not impossible to step outside of them. This perhaps is the postmodern bind, one that Adorno anticipated: can we ever find a position outside the systems we are apart of, from which to critique or act? Or, are we forever inextricably bound by those systems/ideologies? Is genuine resistance possible?

The same questions arise as we read Foucault, who likewise (though with different inflections) analyzes the power of systems and the potential of human agency. As Foucault describes and accounts for the various modern institutions (jails, mental facilities, schools) that channel and normalize (often with punitive threats) human activity – employing phrases such as 'carceral archipelago' and 'regimes of truth' – we may easily be left with the impression that there is 'No Exit', no way out. Of course Foucault, aware of this bind, does try to pry open spaces and possibilities for movement and change, for example in his delineation of the 'specific intellectual.' While he seems to back off of the possibility or desirability of change on a grand scale – such as a Marxist revolution that supposedly would overturn if not obliterate class distinction – he holds out possibilities for acting within our specific local theaters.

For help in thinking through the underground, I turn to Deleuze and Guattari, who provide powerful metaphors and vocabulary for moving through the binds I have just described. We are all no doubt familiar with key terms and concepts proposed by Deleuze and Guattari: lines of flight, rhizomatic vs. root thinking, smooth/striated space, producing machines, desiring machines, body without organs, etc. Orphans, atheists, and nomads all show us the way to separate ourselves from calcified normative structures: traditional patriarchal families, dogmatic religion, and modern, bourgeois notions of property and territoriality. Their project – paralleling and extending the work of other poststructuralists such as Derrida, Kristeva, Lyotard – examines and critiques powerful paradigms of thought proposed by Marx and Freud. Their goal is nothing short of chipping away at, if not completely dismantling, fascist tendencies, collective and individual, by analyzing 'the flows of desire, the fears and the anxieties, the loves and the despairs that traverse the social field as intensive notes from the underground' (Seem xviii).

'What flow to break? Where to interrupt it? How and by what means?' (38)

ask the pair of theorists in *Anti-Oedipus*. And the translators in the introduction to *A Thousand Plateaus* write:

> [A] plateau is reached when circumstances combine to bring an activity to a pitch of intensity that is not automatically dissipated in a climax. The heightening of energies is sustained long enough to leave a kind of afterimage of its dynamism that can be reactivated or injected into other activities, creating a fabric of intensive states between which any number of connecting routes could exist. (xiv)

Deleuze and Guattari are the great philosophers of the middle: in the final paragraph of their intro to A *Thousand Plateaus* they write:

> A rhizome has no beginning or end; it is always in the middle, between things, interbeing, *intermezzo*. The tree is filiation, but the rhizome is alliance, uniquely alliance. The tree imposes the verb 'to be,' but the fabric of the rhizome is the conjunction, 'and ... and ... and ...' ... Kleist, Lenz, and Büchner have another way of travelling and moving: proceeding from the middle, through the middle, coming and going rather than starting and finishing ... The middle is by no means an average; on the contrary, it is where things pick up speed. *Between* things does not designate a localizable relation going from one thing to the other and back again, but a perpendicular direction, a transversal movement that sweeps one *and* the other away, a stream without beginning or end that undermines its banks and picks up speed in the middle. (25)

This approach, I propose, is a useful way of thinking of how the underground works, always beginning where we are, in the middle, and moving out in various directions, propelled by desire and physical force, probing the softest, most porous membranes, and pushing our way through. The underground, as we have noted, is a place 'between', neither here nor there, neither starting point nor destination.

Earlier in this introduction to *A Thousand Plateaus*, once again contrasting root/rhizome thinking, Deleuze and Guattari apply their metaphors to urban landscapes, referencing one of the cities that is a focus for this volume:

> We are tired of trees. We should stop believing in trees, roots, and radicles. They've made us suffer too much ... Nothing is beautiful or loving or political aside from underground stems and aerial roots, adventitious growths and rhizomes. Amsterdam, a city entirely without roots, a rhizome-city with its stem-canals, where utility connects with the greatest folly in relation to a commercial war machine. (15)

It occurs to me here that one of the various directions our thinking could take would be a line of flight that examines and traces the ways urban space is constructed, and – accordingly – the ways those constructs either foreclose or provide access to underground activity and movement.

Just a few pages into the introduction of *A Thousand Plateaus*, amid a presentation of the notion of rhizomatic as opposed to root-thinking, Deleuze and Guattari invoke Burroughs: 'Take William Burroughs's cut-up method: the folding of one text onto another, which constitutes multiple and even adventitious roots (like a cutting), implies a supplementary dimension to that of the texts under consideration' (6). That Burroughs and Ginsberg were among the voices Deleuze and Guattari listened to attentively as they thought their way through the legacies of Freud and Marx, seeking to understand and provide ways of resisting fascism of the mind and fascism of the body politic, is perfectly fitting, for these two American writers (among others), as we have seen, were involved in a compatible, parallel project.

Possibilities for the Underground Today

I now take my final turn to a consideration of possibilities for the underground today, during an historical period that has commonly been thought of (using Deleuze and Guattari's terms) as increasingly striated, with a vast interconnected network of checkpoints, surveillance systems, and laws checking civil liberties, often in the name of preventing terrorism and insuring security. Indeed William S. Burroughs lamented this historical condition, the shrinking of freedoms he saw occurring over the past two centuries and in his own times, in the 'Fore!' of *Cities of the Red Night*, the first of his last trilogy, published in 1981:

> There is simply no room left for 'freedom from the tyranny of government' since city dwellers depend on it for food, power, water, transportation, protection, and welfare. Your right to live where you want, with the companions of your choosing, under laws to which you agree, died in the eighteenth century with Captain Mission. Only a miracle or a disaster could restore it. (xv)

Despite this gloomy prognosis that might seem to ring true, there are still examples of what we might consider fairly traditional modes of underground resistance to rigid borders and law. Residents of Gaza bore tunnels beneath the border between Gaza and Egypt to transport a wide array of goods, including disassembled vehicles, appliances, food, and (no doubt) weapons, circumventing the tight stage imposed on the tiny sliver of territory. Drug traffickers construct tunnels from Tijuana to the United States side of the border, south of San Diego.

Still the possibilities for effective movement through the physical underground, seem to be increasingly circumscribed and unreliable, particularly given the development of sophisticated counter-measures on the part of powerful governments and organizations. As one kind of space becomes more striated, the site of underground movement shifts toward smoother, more porous space. Certainly cyberspace, in our times, opens new channels for conveying suspect, elicit information. I would like to survey various possibilities for underground activity, looking briefly at a number of specific instances. The list is by no means comprehensive; rather, I mean for it to be suggestive.

1. Flash mobs/Smart mobs

In his 2002 book *Smart Mobs: The Next Social Revolution*, Howard Rheingold describes the potential for using new forms of mobile communication devices and computing systems to effect social change. He notes that these technological innovations provide opportunities for good and ill alike. The Smartmobs.org website points to the anti-World Trade protests in Seattle in 1999 as one instance of this phenomenon, and to the toppling of Filipino president Joseph Estrada in 2001, 'through public demonstrations organized through salvos of text messages', as another. The website goes on to describe how smart mobs work, and suggests their revolutionary potential:

> The people who make up smart mobs cooperate in ways never before possible because they carry devices that possess both communication and computing capabilities. Their mobile devices connect them with other information devices in the environment as well as with other people's telephones. Dirt-cheap microprocessors embedded in everything from box tops to shoes are beginning to permeate furniture, buildings, neighbourhoods, products with invisible intercommunicating smartifacts. When they connect the tangible objects and places of our daily lives with the Internet, handheld communication media mutate into wearable remote control devices for the physical world. ('SmartMobs')

Flashmobs are similar. Social networks are used to mobilize crowds to show up at particular times at particular places to stage some kind of demonstration. One recent example took place in November of 2010:

> A crowd of about 200 gay men and women in Barcelona staged a massive make-out session in front of the Pope Sunday as he was driven through town in the bullet-proof Popemobile on his way to celebrate mass at one of the city's basilicas.
>
> The monster spit-swap was organized by a Facebook group called Queer Kissing Flashmob, which sought to protest Pope Benedict XVI's visit to Spain and the Catholic Church's policies about homosexuals. (Caulfield)

More famous and significant examples of the use of social networking to effect political change have been seen recently in the Middle East. Following the Iranian elections in June of 2009 efforts were made to organize protests to challenge results that proclaimed Mahmoud Ahmadinejad the winner over Mir-Hossein Mousavi and other opponents. Videos of the shooting of the young Iranian woman identified as Neda Agha-Soltan were spread virally on Facebook and YouTube. Twitter was used to organize protests and post lists of people allegedly killed by the Islamic regime. Social networking has been used as well in recent popular uprisings in Tunisia, Egypt, Syria, and elsewhere. Of course, these activities have not, until now, always resulted in the kinds of changes hoped for.

2. Feral Trade

A short piece in a recent issue of *Adbusters* describes a new means of challenging paradigms of global commerce, feral trade, begun by artist Kate Rich in 2003:

> Rich utilizes social networking (the old-fashioned, sentient kind) to find and contract with producers in nations outside the rubric of established global trade. Through this system of acquaintances, she procures items like coffee from El Salvador and sweets from Iran and then moves those good into the UK via another social network: a loose collective of artists, curators, musicians and relatives, people whose lives dictate a fair amount of international travel. The items essentially hitch a ride with travelers, entering the country via luggage and circumventing traditional channels of freight. Once in the UK, the goods are traded within social spheres: moved between people and organizations that bear a relationship to one another beyond the trade ... Rich maintains a database through which the movement of all goods is tracked. On first inspection, it appears mechanical – nothing more than a logbook detailing the movement of a product between points. But a closer look reveals that the data is actually a story ... The database is both record and narrative, following a product as it passes through human hands. The result is more than a map of trade routes: it's a schema of relationships, one that contextualizes a commodity in social terms. (Nardi)

3. WikiLeaks

In July of 2010, WikiLeaks rose to national and international prominence – lauded by some, vilified by others – when the cyber-organization 'defied the Obama Administration by publishing seventy-six thousand intelligence and military field reports from the Afghan war.' And 'in October, it posted nearly four hundred thousand secret documents generated on the front lines of the Iraq conflict' (Coll 27). When Julian Assange launched his digital enterprise in 2006, he described his purposes in a sort of manifesto: 'We must understand the key generative structure of bad government. We must develop a way of thinking about this structure that is strong enough to carry us through the mire of competing political moralities and into a position of clarity' (Coll 27).

WikiLeaks provides information on the conduct of current, on-going wars that has not previously been widely accessible: 'important new facts about civilian casualties, the torture of detainees by our allies, Iran's exported violence, the disruptions caused by private contractors, and the debilitating patterns of clandestine warfare in two benighted regions' (Coll 27). Not surprisingly, Daniel Ellsberg, who was responsible for making public the 'Pentagon Papers' in the 1970s, has endorsed these actions. WikiLeaks tactics, however, have been controversial. In the realm of cyberspace, WikiLeaks operated nomadically, with no fixed address, rather like small guerilla insurgency groups, though there are reports, mentioned in a column in *The New Yorker*, that WikiLeaks 'has recently been in discussions with lawmakers in Iceland about trying to concoct the world's most extensive press-freedom regime there. The idea apparently is to transform Iceland, in the aftermath of its recent, disastrous experiments with offshore banking, into the Cayman Islands of First Amendment-inspired subversion' (Coll 28).

What these various tactics share is a commitment to move goods or ideas from one place to another, avoiding usual channels, or bringing to the surface things that before were hidden from view. At the same time groups and individuals explore new means of circumventing control mechanisms, authorities step in to exert control of these new realms, rather like the way Burroughs's Nova Police try to route out the Nova Mob. National security organizations sift through communications and snag anything suspect or potentially 'dangerous.' The Chinese government blocks Google. The Egyptian and Syrian governments shut down the Internet. The Iranian government stops Internet access for 45 minutes during the most volatile period of protests, reopening with lower bandwidth. It also interrupts mobile phone services and blocks access to the BBC and *The Guardian* websites. There were also reports of intelligence service infiltration of and use of Twitter. WikiLeaks is publicly denounced by the Pentagon and Assange becomes a fugitive.

The central paradox of invisibility/visibility, thus, lies at the heart of the operation of the underground. From the perspective of those in power, for whom underground activities pose a potential threat, there is the question of whether it is best to monitor and permit underground operations rather than apprehend suspects and bring them to the attention of the wider public, for risks can be associated with making the invisible visible. Blatant censorship, for instance, can call attention to material that otherwise might have gone unnoticed. Government suppression of Ginsberg's *Howl*, or the fatwa levied against Salman Rushie's *Satanic Verses* certainly catapulted these works (and thus the ideas they contained) to the forefront of public consciousness. Some – not without reason – have suggested that the United States was better off leaving Osama bin Laden an underground fugitive. Apprehending and killing him, while producing catharsis and cause for jubilation among many in the United States, could possibly result in elevating his profile and propelling his cause in the long run.

This paradox of visibility/invisibility takes on somewhat different meanings when viewed from the point of view of those within the underground. Ultimately, the aim is to stay alive, or at least keep certain ideas alive, in order to effect conditions that will no longer necessitate the need to remain underground. And to reduce risks of being detected, underground units usually are kept small. Yet, there is the acknowledgement, at the same time, that if the number of individuals involved in the underground were to increase dramatically, that if the flow were to become great enough, it might put sufficient pressure on control mechanisms to break them.

The unfolding of events in 2011, in what has become known as the Arab Spring, reminds us that these issues are more than theoretical, academic. Many who have been oppressed and forced to remain underground for many years in places such as Tunisia, Egypt, Bahrain, Yemen and Syria, have courageously dared to come to the surface, into the streets and public squares, vulnerable to bullets and brutal recriminations. While these events may inspire us and remind us of the viability of resistance, at the same time we see how tenacious, intransigent and brutal oppressive regimes can be, how difficult it is to dislodge authoritarian systems. Those who have had power and benefited from it are reluctant to give it up. And they can often muster military support for their position.

In the face of all the obstacles and challenges, we pursue various lines of flight. We still might envision communication and transportation systems in which neighbor can connect to neighbor, and any one party in one place connect to any other party in another place without being forced to follow pre-existing channels, thus breaking boundaries and hierarchies and, simply by making connections, establish new relations, rhizomatically.

Note

I thank Andrew Hussey and Christoph Lindner, organizers of the symposia and editors of this volume, for inviting me to participate. And I thank fellow participants for challenging and pushing my thinking. My former student and colleague Aaron Shapiro I thank for talking with me and providing me material on smart mobs, feral trade, and WikiLeaks. At the Amsterdam symposium Mattias Duyves brought my attention to Gerard Reve; in later conversations and correspondence, he and Gert Hekma pointed me to specific sources used here. And, my fine friend and colleague Oliver Harris, Burroughs scholar par excellence, supplied me with leads for exploring the 'French' Burroughs.

Part 3: Visibility

8. (In)audible Frequencies: Sounding out the Contemporary Branded City

Carolyn Birdsall

The notion of the urban *underground* – in contrast to earlier associations with political and countercultural movements – has gained currency in an era of intensified city-marketing and cultural entrepreneurship. With this development, subcultural artforms and arts festivals are often deployed to hype and generate cultural capital for the city. This commodification of the underground is accelerated by contemporary trendspotting and cool hunting, whether in informal networks and social media, or by the marketing and advertising industries.

In the contemporary 'conquest of cool' (Frank), one of the artistic forms that has received undue attention and reproduction is that of graffiti or street art. The graffiti artist – a cultural figure that already emerged in the 1980s – is primarily associated with both playful creativity and rebellious acts of urban vandalism. While graffiti culture has long been linked to music and art scenes, its entrance into mainstream culture has also led to uses of graffiti aesthetics or stencil techniques for viral marketing campaigns. Following earlier precedents – such as Keith Haring and Jean-Michel Basquiat – graffiti and street art have generated interest within the international art market. The numerous high-profile auctions and exhibitions in art institutions since 2000, however, have simultaneously emphasized the ephemeral yet intransigent nature of this artform, given that most works cannot be easily archived or exchanged.

Against this backdrop of street art as a lucrative cultural commodity, one of its most well-known, although anonymous practitioners – Banksy – has offered a powerful critique in his recent film *Exit Through the Gift Shop* (2010). This Oscar-nominated film is largely constructed from footage by would-be filmmaker Thierry Guetta, who is fascinated by underground street art scenes in Los Angeles, New York, Paris, and London. As the story goes, Thierry is so inspired that he decides to become a commercial street artist and stage his own 'underground' art show in Los Angeles. In the lead-up to the event, Thierry is shown creating a Warhol-style factory of kitsch pastiche, and then busying himself with the task of generating hype through print media, attracting visitors, and making sales. The scenes from the exhibition opening include interviews with punters and art world figures, all of whom wax lyrical about how special the event was, and how they were one of the lucky few (or thousands) who could be part of the 'buzz'.

Guetta's commercial success under the pseudonym of 'Mr Brainwash' is ultimately ridiculed in the film, which was subsequently defined as a mockumentary in reviews. Banksy pokes fun at the contemporary art world and its hunt to unearth and exploit underground art scenes. The willingness to validate recycled art and popular cultural symbols, which are rendered empty if not meaningless, is revealed as undiscerning and opportunistic. Viewers are thus reminded not to uncritically accept such a depoliticized rendering of street art, whereby social critique is downplayed in the pursuit of print, poster, and postcard sales.

Banksy's film offers a useful departure point for this essay, which reflects on how art (and arts festivals) are increasingly used for the marketing and branding of places as vibrant, 'creative cities'. My focus is mainly on the Dutch capital Amsterdam, where the normative discourse of the 'creative city', as promoted by Richard Florida, has been self-described as a guiding principle for the city government, both in the planning and branding of the city (Franke and Verhagen).

My overall interest is in attempts to re-enchant the contemporary city, and question how music and, more broadly, sound are increasingly implicated in this process. This raises the immediate questions of why the city would need re-enchantment, and how that might be achieved. By way of response, I will first examine the rise of city-marketing and place-branding, and investigate the ambivalent attitudes toward Amsterdam's niche in the global tourist industry. It would seem that plans to cater for the new Amsterdam tourist would necessitate an inner city that is marketed as 'vibrant' with cultural festivals, exhibitions, and historic buildings, although still (ethnically) segregated and cleared of squats, drugs, and prostitution. In the second section, I investigate recent attempts to facilitate special, re-enchanted experiences of the inner city – for tourists and locals alike – as illustrated by the case of the Nuit Blanche festival concept. The strong presence of the international advertising industry within the city from the 1990s, I argue, has put a stamp on the new breed of cultural entrepreneurs marketing, and perhaps even cancelling out, the underground. I will then zoom in to the specific phenomenon of city promotion on the basis of music, and show how the city is not only consumed through postcards or photography, but also through (personalized) audio tours. Lastly, I examine two artistic projects that go against the grain of these commercial appeals to sensory experience, and instead, offer small interventions in generating mobile listening activity in urban space.

The City as Brand: City-Marketing and the Creative City

The emergence of mass tourism from the mid-nineteenth century has been bound up with *place-selling*, which Stephen Ward defines as a 'broad entrepreneurial ethos or ideology' for imbuing a particular place with meanings and associations, and then promoting and selling it as offering distinctive tourist experiences (3). The selling of a place to potential tourists is different to the standard marketing of consumer goods, since it is the tourist that moves, rather than the product. In the recent bid to attract visitors, as Susan Fainstein and Dennis Judd pointed out in *The Tourist City*, cities:

> have adopted image advertising, a development that can hardly escape any traveler who opens an airline magazine and reads its formulaic articles on the alleged culinary and cultural delights of Dallas, Frankfurt, or Auckland. Each city tries to project itself as a uniquely wonderful place to visit, where an unceasing flow of events constantly unfolds. (4)

In other words, cities are sold on the basis of their unique selling points within a global tourist economy. Since branding and logos should give consumers a clear and identifiable association, it is often quite selective, if not uni-dimensional elements that are highlighted in city-marketing.

In much of the scholarship on global tourism, discourses of uniqueness are partly attributed to the emergence of niche markets, as a result of the large-scale shift from mass *production* to mass *consumption*. In the shift to post-Fordism, cities became less reliant on finance and industry as sources of revenue and could generate alternative sources of wealth by way of cultural and service industries. This shift has been characterized by an emphasis on individualism and free choice, and intensified global flows of people and capital, both of which have fuelled tourism, urban restructuring, and heightened competition between places. Such developments have led to a more active role of urban politicians and policy-makers to orchestrate place-selling through more integrated marketing strategies.

Amsterdam's unique selling point – to put it in the terms of city-branding – partly derives from its role as an anti-establishment city in the 1960s to 1980s (with counterculture and squatters movements). However, there are a number of other factors influencing its marketability as a place of fun and consumption – for tourists and locals alike. As geographers Pieter Terhorst and Jacques van de Ven point out, the historical formation of irregular streets and building formations has leant itself to small-scale activities, such as restaurants, bars, galleries, and boutiques (90-1). In the 1980s, the priority of city government and urban planners was on social housing provisions. Nonetheless, the priority given to housing also allowed for gentrification in the historic inner city, following the conversion of lofts and offices into housing. The subsequent increase of prosperous residents, too, gave a boost to leisure and consumption services, which made the city more attractive to tourists and domestic visitors (96-7). Moreover, the availability of a large student population (to work in service industries) and the appeal generated by relaxed drugs policies were other contributing factors to the establishment of Amsterdam's tourist and leisure industries.

Already by late 1980s, American and British scholars noted the rise of entrepreneurial ethos among urban planners and policy-makers, and the increased interest in funding culture (Harvey; Zukin, *Loft Living*). In Amsterdam, early efforts at city-marketing can be discerned, but they did not have a large impact on planning, nor was there a coherent strategy for attracting tourists in the 1980s. However, the reduction of state grants in this period led to a shift from the welfare state toward pro-growth strategies. The Dutch geographer Jan Nijman, writing following his return to Amsterdam in 1996 after a decade in the United States, observed the commodification of the city's image as a tolerant place in the era of globalization and mass tourism:

Tolerance, perhaps Amsterdam's most prized commodity, is increasingly packaged and labeled to meet the demands of mass tourism and instant gratification. In the process it has become something of a perversion, in the sense that it turned into commercially motivated permissiveness that is in fact contrary to the city's Calvinistic roots. Abroad, Amsterdam is first and foremost associated with liberal attitudes towards sex and drugs, and this has become its niche in the competitive world of tourism. (155-6)

Nijman argues that it is not so much tolerance but commercialism that is the enduring trait in the city. Despite the apparent mix between tourist attractions and ordinary life, most of the city center has turned into a kind of sex and drugs 'theme park' for mainly low-budget young tourists.

Nijman's rather grim characterization ultimately deplores the superficiality and vulgarization of urban identities. While it is certainly the case that Amsterdam has a persistent reputation as 'Europe's established good time city' (Holcomb 65), tourists do combine different acts of consumption in the city. Amsterdam's historic city center attracts tourists on the basis of architectural and cultural heritage as well as coffee shops and the Red Light District. Nonetheless, Nijman rightly observes patterns of inclusion and exclusion within the city center, described as mainly inhabited by ethnically Dutch and the upwardly mobile, and not welcoming to the elderly or families with young children (159). I will return to this point shortly.

The period since Nijman's observations has generated further expansion of city-branding with the launch of the 'I Amsterdam' slogan and campaign in 2004. What makes this successful concept so clever is that – unlike the famous 'I Love NY' logo declaring the tourist's fondness for the Big Apple – the visitor can inhabit the subject position of being a temporary Amsterdam dweller. The 'I' is also in keeping with the contemporary ideology of individualization, which takes the form of personalizing one's experience of Amsterdam. 'I Amsterdam' has expanded beyond its initial campaign with public posters and souvenirs, and includes hotel booking offices, sponsorship, and a web portal. It is also a place to visit, with a public statue of the logo situated prominently at the Museum Square. By visiting these enlarged letters, close to the main museum attractions, tourists can have the tactile experience of standing against or inside the enlarged letters. In this aesthetics of play, visitors can perform their presence in Amsterdam by means of photography, and perhaps be made to even feel at home. The English-language phrase of 'I Amsterdam' offers the image of a welcoming, inclusive, and international Amsterdam. Thus, it might be said that, even as tourism breaks down into niche markets, there is demand for a unified discourse, which appeals to the mainstream with the language of creativity and personalization.

Despite the feel-good ethos generated by 'I Amsterdam', with its appeal to the experience economy, the competition to attract both (upmarket) tourists and business investors in Amsterdam has led to development agendas that enforce new displacements and exclusions. Indeed, the launch of city-marketing campaigns often goes hand in hand with patterns of urban regeneration and property development. As Klunzman pointed out in 2004, 'each story of regeneration be-

8.1. The IAmsterdam sign at the Museumplein, in front of the Rijksmuseum in Amsterdam. (Photo: C. Birdsall)

gins with poetry and ends with real estate' (qtd. in Evans, 'Measure' 959). This is illustrated by the 'Top City' policy, which has the explicit aim to promote urban regeneration and property development, as part of a bid to ensure that Amsterdam remains competitive within the international economy. According to the policy, 'creativity is the motor behind the city's ability to attract continued investment and interest' (City of Amsterdam). Among the projects launched by the city government and its partners is the development of 'Art Factories' in former industrial and office spaces, with 'interim use' programs to generate cultural capital for subsequent property development. Indeed, one of the major consequences of Richard Florida's influential 'creative city' thesis – that defines ideal environments for creatives to set up businesses – is that it only validates certain types of creativity. As Alan Blum points out, Florida's normative vision posits creativity as a mainstream activity, which reduces its negative or oppositional character (80).

The developments in Amsterdam reflect the adoption of a neoliberal urban policy, where city governments get involved in real estate development and partnerships with private investors. High-profile examples include large-scale property and commercial developments on the northern IJ foreshores (IJ-oeveren), the South Axis district (Zuidas), and in the Western Garden Cities (Amsterdam West). In all three cases, the search for business investors and wealthier residents has led to the driving out of the less wealthy or educated, particularly from the inner suburbs (Oudenampsen). The urban theory collective BAVO has critiqued the way that Dutch urban policy is increasingly guided by soft techniques of power (222-4). In the past, gentrification often occurred in places where artists and bohemians lived, which was followed by increase in rent and housing prices, and the displacement of these and other lower income residents (Zukin *Loft*). In the current neoliberal situation, when neighborhoods are forcibly regenerated:

> Artists, designers or architects, often with urban art institutions acting as mediators or temp agencies, organize cool cultural projects that have to soften the blow on local community life and public space of the creative destruction. (BAVO 223)

The willing participation of artists and art institutions in such initiatives thus leads to a depoliticization of the urban process. In the case of Amsterdam's historic inner city, the cooperation of artists is nowhere more apparent than in the now-notorious Project 1012. In the bid to 'clean up' the Red Light District, the city government forced owners of prostitution windows to sell around 100 of the total 500 properties. In a commercial deal with property developers, the city government rezoned the buildings, with some windows allocated to interim use by artists and fashion designers, as Joyce Goggin discusses in her chapter in this book. While it was hoped that the district could be remolded with residential and lifestyle provisions, the council has since lost millions of euros and had to pay damages to several housing corporations (Middelburg).

Such gentrification and growth-driven projects do not only attempt to change the physical space of the city. They also suggest the generation of a particular image and imagination tied up with the city center (in terms of protected heritage), and a projection of the kinds of tourists and new residents the council are actively trying to attract. The attempts to clean up the inner city and attract upmarket tourists also reflect a distancing from the predominant reputation of Amsterdam in the global tourism circuit. Nonetheless, if one – like Nijman – mourns the loss of the 'authentic' Amsterdam to tourism, it might be tempting to forget that locals consume the city too, in everyday activities, media consumption, and through public and cultural events. This brings me to my second section about how locals try to create special and extraordinary 'underground' experiences with arts and culture in the inner city.

Enchantment and Consumption within the Night-time Cityscape

One of the significant ways that cities are sold and consumed – for tourists and locals alike – is through the organization of large events (Rennen). In Amsterdam, this may include Sail Amsterdam, the annual Gay Boat Parade, or the many cultural events and festivals in the city. An international concept that has gained popularity since its introduction in 2000 is the annual Museum Night (Museumnacht), where around forty museums stay open until late. This ticket-only event provides museums and art galleries the opportunity to dispense with its stuffy, high-culture reputation and to attract younger, predominantly local visitors, usually by featuring DJs and encouraging a party atmosphere.

Over time, Museum Night has expanded in its scope and ambition for facilitating experience and play in familiar and unusual environments. In 2010, eight thematic routes were established: Mokums Mayor, The Socialite, Art Smart, Nutty Professor, Urban Explorer, Soldier of Love, Globetrotter, and Playing Tourist. Most relevant for this discussion was the Playing Tourist route, which passed by the Anne Frank House and Rembrandt House to the Museum Square. Here, in the Stedelijk Museum, visitors were encouraged to rest and feel at home with slow food, minimalist music, and yoga workshops. The main attraction, near the 'I Amsterdam' statue, was a life-size version of Rembrandt's *Nightwatch*, constructed from sixty thousand lollypops. The creators, British street art duo The London Police, revealed in an interview that the American company Chupa Chups – which sponsors artists for free publicity – had provided materials, and there were company representatives on site to talk to journalists (Verkerk).

In sum, what these activities suggest is that visitors were invited to feel at home while moving through city spaces, as well as to try out alternative urban identities (the mayor, the scientist, the wealthy elite, the nomad, the tourist, and so on). The event was designed to create buzz in the city, with museums and galleries filling up with young people and 'nightlife', thereby creating a special – though partially branded – experience of the city at night as beautiful and enchanted.

Exit Through the Gift Shop also draws attention to this somewhat sentimental discourse about urban nightlife. During an early scene in the film, Thierry Guetta follows and films Parisian street artists at night-time. In this sequence, set to the synthesizer Muzak sounds of the French band Air, Guetta informs the viewer that this first encounter with the creative production of art in urban space was fascinating and enchanting. Discovering this authentic subculture – coded with grainy black and white, hand-held footage – is inferred as illicit and thrilling, not least since these vanguard artists are just a few steps ahead of the law. As we see the group zooming away from police on their scooters into the Paris night, a BBC-style voiceover emphasizes the underground status of street art movements.

Thierry, who is so enamored by the creation of street art at night-time, reminds us of a long-held trope in modernity about the almost mythical associations with the beauty of the night. The fascination can be linked to the creation of the 'nocturnal city' in the nineteenth century following the introduction of modern street lighting (Schlör). Yet the enchantment with light also marked the emergence of ambivalent associations with the night-time city. Historically, the night is a site of social conflict and moral panics about criminality and sexuality. The contemporary city after dark is still considered unsafe, as the time of day for theft, attacks, fights, and general illicit or drunken behavior. In particular, the justified concerns about safety for women at night in the city led to initiatives, such as 'Reclaim the Night', which sought recognition and solidarity through night-time protests. These trends suggest a background to the night in (late) modernity as a source of enchantment and wonder, but also as a source of conflict and oppositional stances.

In the case of contemporary Amsterdam, an interesting expression of these investments in the night can be delineated with the activities of the function of the *Nachtburgermeester* (or night-time mayor), as an unofficial representative for nightlife in the city. In Amsterdam, it is a two-year appointment and until recently, the position was shared by Josine Neyman and Kristel Mutsers, who together form the 'Club zonder Filter' event-management group. Upon their appointment, Neyman and Mutsers said that they would like to lobby the city council for longer opening hours and better zoning laws, suggesting that nightlife should be better promoted along with creating a 24-hour economy in the city (Böhm). Soon after, Neyman and Mutsers announced that they would like to start an Amsterdam edition of the all-night festival concept Nuit Blanche in Amsterdam to facilitate one night per year as a showcase for 'creative projects' that would usually be impossible due to inflexible city bureaucracy.

Nuit Blanche (or 'white night') is a dusk-until-dawn arts and culture festival which gained popularity as a result of the festival held in Paris, which has been organized by the local government since 2002 and rapidly increased to attracting around two million visitors each year to galleries, museums, and public spaces, primarily in the center of the city. This concept has since been picked up in other cities across Europe and North America. In a recent analysis, Graeme Evans has shown how, even though the local objectives sometimes differ in focus, the Nuit Blanche brand clearly sets out objectives in its European charter (Evans 'New Events'). Alongside key elements such as free entry and encouraging reflection about the urban night, the charter declares the importance of using places 'that are usually closed or abandoned, outlying areas, prestigious locations or places that form part of the city's cultural heritage, revisited in an unusual way by artists' (qtd. in Evans, 'Measure' 162). The Nuit Blanche concept appears to contribute to the tourist and night-time urban economy, if not the potential implication of creatives in fuelling the growth and development strategies discussed in the previous section.

In the case of Amsterdam, the Paris event also provided the initial inspiration for night-time mayors Neyman and Mutsers. The Nuit Blanche concept, as they said, 'seemed suited perfectly to what we wanted: a festival that could clear the way for establishing food and hospitality, innovative projects and creativity in Amsterdam' (qtd. in Böhm). The main difference was that the Paris event is considered 'highbrow', whereas the mayors claimed that their event would be less touristy, and thus more 'underground' (Boersma, 'Nachtfestival'). Yet there are similarities with Museumnacht in that it almost only attracts hip people in their twenties and thirties and encourages visitors to consume and experience wonder in the ordinary spaces of their city. The aesthetics of the underground are suggested by the 2009 festival logo, which presented the festival title in graffiti overlaid on the image of Centraal Station, and which was part of the 'Paint the City' interactive project with laser pointer and videomapping at night-time.

In 2010, the discourse shifted a little from their original aim to lobby the council, with the duo claiming that the event had something for everyone: 'from the Amsterdam socializers (*nachtvlinders*) to the council aldermen and municipal officers, tourists and real Jordaan types' (Nuit Blanche Amsterdam). This is quite suggestive of the ambivalence toward the council in public statements. Initially, Neyman and Mutsers complained that the city council had a misconceived notion of the night, and should adapt to their own rhetoric of discovery, inspiration, and play. Even though the organizers were so keen to emphasize the underground nature of their event, we can discern the way that those working in arts and culture also have their own stake in hyping and promoting the so-called 'creative city'. In keeping with the city council's 'I Amsterdam' campaign, Nuit Blanche sets itself apart from Amsterdam's usual tourist image: 'no red lights, coffee shops and that sort of thing' (Nuit Blanche Amsterdam).

Despite the repeated efforts of the night mayors to gain the support of the city government, the Nuit Blanche organization had to rely heavily on the council's institutional co-operation and sponsorship. The sponsor list shows that both the 2009 and 2010 events were sponsored by Amsterdam Topstad, 'I Amsterdam', the city and district councils, along with various alcohol and food sponsors, cultural institutions, and newspapers. While this reliance on prominent sponsors aligns the event with mainstream city-marketing, it also becomes apparent that 'Club zonder Filter' is partly a marketing agency. Elsewhere, Neyman and Mutsers describe themselves as cultural entrepreneurs and 'maverick marketers', who conduct marketing and branding to complement standard advertising campaigns. Their creative services – viral marketing, brand events, and lifestyle promotion – have been offered to large multinational clients like Nike, Diesel and Bacardi. Even though Amsterdam's Nuit Blanche event is comparatively small, it thus also alerts us to the strong presence of large brands and the international advertising industry in Amsterdam, which in turn has influenced the orientation of cultural entrepreneurship and creative networks since the 1990s (Röling).

The work of 'Club zonder Filter' may be better understood in line with the phenomenon of brand strategists, who adopt the subversive strategies of protest movements and recruit artists as a means of hacking into subcultures and trendsetting. As Friedrich von Borries and Matthias Böttger have argued, these strategists 'are important actors in today's city, although their intervention in the architecture and use of the urban space is an operation hidden from view' (138). Such a critique may suggest a leftist resignation to marketing and neoliberalization, yet these authors argue that there is potential in the call for urban justice within the current situation. In the examples discussed above, locals are heavily involved in the consumption of special sensory and aesthetic experiences in their own city – in this case the enchanted city at night. In what follows, I will suggest an aesthetics involving camouflage or partial visibility that does not necessarily have to lend itself to undercover branding or viral marketing.

Sonic Variations, Inaudible Interventions

Place-selling usually revolves around a city's sights, and thus *visual* distinctiveness, with tourist experiences of the city bound up with the visual gaze and related practices of photography (Urry, *Tourist Gaze*). Yet I would like to probe the visual logic of modern tourism, not least due to the historical relationship between (popular) music and place-selling. In the 1960s, as post-war tourism was established, the music recording industry began to release records with lounge or background music that would convey the feeling of faraway places, whether tropical islands, Alpine mountaintops, or European cities. To cite an example, the liner notes to the album *In Love in Paris* promoted the notion of imagined travel through sound: 'Montmartre, the Champs Élysées, The Seine – all speak of the romance of Paris. Here is a musical journey to Paris by night ... Renaud with the World of Strings is your passport to Paris' (qtd. in Connell and Gibson 198). This is suggestive of the role of music as a means for imagining other places and other lives, often in the form of fantasies of exotic locales. Simultaneous to the rise of music-based place-selling was the rise of portable recording and listening devices from the 1950s. Western consumers could listen to music while travelling in their cars, taking a mobile device along for a daytrip, or even using tape recorders to create 'sound souvenirs' of their holidays (Bijsterveld and Van Dijck).

Many tourist activities in the current global era involve kinesthetic movement and share parallels with other, contemporary forms of traveling or 'mobile culture'. In response, John Urry has partially revised his earlier thesis on the primarily *visual* nature of tourism experience (*Tourist Gaze* 146). It is not only visual landscapes that attract tourists, but also soundscapes (in music-motivated tourism), smellscapes (of natural environments), tastescapes (in the consumption of food), or even geographies of touch (in physical activities like rock climbing). Interest in the sensory dimensions to global travel has been echoed by *Holland Herald*, the KLM in-flight magazine, which in recent years has pursued special issue themes including light, fast, sweet, water, and natural. In 2010, it became clear with 'The Sound Issue' that sound and audio culture has gained broader currency within tourism marketing. The issue includes more established concepts of music pilgrimage, such as visiting Liverpool due to its 1960s pop music heritage. Indeed, for cities like Liverpool and Manchester, the promotion of urban regeneration with cultural tourism in the 1990s was primarily based on their respective reputations for rock and club music (Connell and Gibson 248).

In one of the most striking articles from 'The Sound Issue' – titled 'The Art of Noise' – a young urban subject is illustrated sitting with headphones, although supposedly also opening his ears to the pleasures of the immersive urban soundscape (McKenzie). In this image, we see an overlap between the mobile and privatized urban subject (symbolized by iPod listening) and practices of tourist consumption (as also involving sensory experience). In the article, KLM passengers on their way to Amsterdam are encouraged to download soundwalks, in order to 'open your ears to every sound in your immediate environment' (27). Soundwalks are presented here as quite neutral, with (musical) sound posited as aesthetic and pleasurable, even therapeutic. Its stress on sound art and festivals bypasses the ways that music – and sound more broadly – are frequently used in the urban everyday to condition consumer and work spaces (such as Muzak) or are integrated into surveillance and control tactics (Kassabian). In the present day, sonic modes of urban control can take the form of PA systems (with two-way communication) or loudspeakers (playing classical music) to ward away unwanted groups, and sonic weapons like sound bombs and LRAD (long range acoustic devices).

The *Holland Herald* article implies that the city should not only be consumed

8.2. 'The Sound Issue' in *Holland Herald* (December 2009), the in-flight magazine for Dutch airline KLM, which was produced by Ink Global

8.3. Main article illustration for Simone McKenzie, 'The Art of Noise' in *Holland Herald* (December 2009).

through postcards or photography, but also through (mediated) listening experience. Indeed, listening and sound technologies are already integrated into existing tourist activities in Amsterdam, such as boat tours (with prerecorded multi-lingual commentary), bus tours (with microphone PA systems), guided bike or segway tours (with spoken commentary), and groups on foot (with wireless headsets receiving microphone commentary). In some of these instances, visitors can still hear the other sounds of the city around them, in others the urban soundscape is masked or sealed off.

Interestingly, this idea of subjects experiencing the city in their own audio bubble has been reworked as a commercial concept within tourism. Audio tours or audio guides – usually in a linear narrative form – have long been fixtures of museums. However, the consumption of Amsterdam has been upgraded with more personalized versions of the city tour. Among the handful of companies offering tours, all appeal to consumers on the basis of not being herded around in a group or standing out in the crowd:

> With audio city tours you can have an affordable private tour guide. Stroll through the city without looking like a tourist. At your own pace you will experience the unique mix of local history, trivia, gastronomy, architecture, night life, cuisine, culture and much more that we have selected for you. You should be in control, know the hotspots and why not blend in like a local. Our audio tour with a twist is a new fun way to experience a city. (Audio City Tours Productions)

In the case of Amsterdam, alongside affordability, comfort, and acquiring knowledge, it is suggested that the narrator – comedian Ryan Gowland – will make the experience of discovering Amsterdam light-hearted and accessible. The narrator's text, however, illustrates how a studio-recorded audiotour can deny the soundscape of the city for the listener. When he introduces the Muntplein tower – noting that its bell melody has been the same since 1669 – no source or background sounds are heard. 'If you want to order this ringtone, just let us know', Gowland quips. This statement, although intended as a joke, draws attention to a cynical treatment of Amsterdam's urban soundscape, which remains muted for the duration of the audiotour.

Against the commercial development of individual audio tours in the city, I would like to reflect on several artistic projects that offer small interventions in generating user agency with mobile listening activity in and around central Amsterdam. A sound-based work in Amsterdam which we might turn to as a way to break with the linear presentation and restricted movement through the city is Edwin van der Heide's 2004 project 'Radioscape' at De Balie cultural center in Amsterdam. Much of Van der Heide's work is concerned with sound, space, and questions of (listener) interactivity. For this project, situated in the busy Leidseplein tourist area, radio transmitters were distributed on buildings around the main square (an area of around one square kilometer). Each of these transmitters emitted a part of the main 'composition' to a range of 50 to 200 meters. Participants used headphones and tracking devices for picking up the frequencies from the transmitters, which they themselves modulated. Due to this modulation and movement between transmitters, no one listened to the same thing or moved around the area in the same way:

> By navigating the city, the audience generates their own sonic order, combinations and timing of the composition. By interacting with the environment, the visitors become 'inhabitants' of the organized transmitted signals. The visitors reorganize the area and assign new meanings to places. (Van der Heide 16)

In other words, each exploration of these multiple sound fields was unique, with varied sound quality according to exact positioning, weather conditions, and forms of interference. The soundscape – extended across around twelve blocks – could be traversed in any number of ways, and its musical composition did not include verbal commentary or instructions.

Van der Heide's 'Radioscape' project had some limitations, and participants were sealed off from other city sounds around them due to their headphones. Yet, this exploration escapes the visual logic of city-branding, and allows for both locals and visitors to mix and manipulate signals, and make their own choices about how to move around this mainly tourist and leisure district. The sounds of the work cannot be replicated or sold in CD format, and were generated in a site-specific environment, but do not lend themselves to place-selling or hype.

In a recent sound art project, 'Zuidas Symphony' (2009) created by Justin Bennett, a more explicit response is made to the current state of urban policy and cultural politics in Amsterdam. Bennett's soundwalk in and around the Zuidas (or South Axis) development forms part of the project 'Soundtrackcity' (Huijsman and Zentschnig), which commissioned eight soundwalks by local and foreign artists, each investigating a different area of the city. The one-hour soundwalk begins at the World Trade Center (Zuidplein) and proceeds through a residential area to the Beatrixpark, before returning through the underground tunnel to the Zuidas site.

From the outset, Bennett asks what exactly the sound of the Zuidas is, and whether sound can aid in the task of creating public space. For this task, he interrogates the rhetoric around this elite business district, and its explicit strategies to use art and culture in urban planning: 'The buildings are the hardware, the culture is the software' (Bennett). Initiatives include Virtual Museum Zuidas (where Bennett himself was an artist in residence) and Contemporary Art Screens Zuidas. At the heart of the Zuidas, the use of composers names (the Vivaldi complex, the Ravel area, Stravinsky house, and streets named after George Gershwin and Gustav Mahler) make reference to 'power and tradition, modernity or a new verve. These associations with culture give credibility to the project development' (Bennett). Bennett observes that other plans for cultural infrastructure at the site have been thwarted: plans for a large commercial theater ended in a fraud investigation, and proposals to relocate the Rietveld Academy and a design museum were also resisted.

The piece shows a similarity to soundwalks by artists like Janet Cardiff, who tries to open up a gap between what is seen and heard. The piece begins with a

8.4. The Soundtrackcity project, a collection of eight soundwalks in Amsterdam.

woman's voice, which sounds like it is echoing through a PA system. She reads out terms from promotional material distributed by Project Bureau Zuidas, which try to promote the development as an international place for working and living:

> Popular, inspiring, accessible, changing, competitive, sporty, leisurely, energetic, residential, commercial, cosmopolitan, sustainable, ambitious, solid, modern, spacious, cultural, multilingual, educational, developing, profitable, aspirational, innovative, interesting, exceptional, safe, green, beautiful, inspiring, central. (in Bennett)

Rather than evaluate this marketing discourse, Bennett provides a collage of vox pop clips from locals and internationals, who – in their own words – describe it as a virtual environment, a business district that is convenient but too somber and orderly, devoid of normal life, nature, and social interaction. Bennett proposes to investigate whether there are signs of public space and room to play. In the spirit of Constant and the Situationists (discussed in Andrew Hussey's chapter in this book), the listener is encouraged to go on a *derive* – to wander and listen to the history and sounds of the South.

In one of the first stops, Pi de Bruijn, one of the leading architects involved in the Zuidas project, is quoted: 'The central premise of urbanity is that there is something for everyone, and that everyone is welcome' (in Bennett). This statement prompts Bennett to leave the Zuidas area, and look for surrounding sites of urbanity and urban creativity, including Berlage and socialist-inspired buildings, and a former cloister complex, which was later squatted by musicians and artists, used by art students, non-profit organizations, and an organic restaurant. The soundwalk proceeds into the Beatrixpark, designed in 1938 and described as 'a different planet' to the Zuidplein. Public parks, as Bennett points out, have their own sounds (wind, streams, birdsong), and absorb and filter the sounds of the city, and allow for rest, play, and private conversation. Bennett's commentary gives space for contemplation, and the following sequence – the sounds of dance music and chatter from the beach café Strandzuid – continue for several minutes without commentary.

As the listener returns in the direction of the Zuidas, Bennett notes the contrast from the peaceful park to the sounds of the freeway, trains, and metros. As part of the 'Composer Project', these transport routes will be rerouted underground, thus creating large expanses for above-ground property development. Bennett investigates one of the main justifications for this government-funded infrastructure development: reducing noise for residents. The soundscape will not improve, he argues, since other noises will be unmasked, such as airplanes and air conditioning systems.

Venturing into the Zuidas, Bennett investigates the uses and denials of public space, noting, for instance, a staircase leading to a rooftop garden that was closed for safety reasons. He suggests that the ambitions of architects to create public space and interaction at the Zuidas or any large project are often thwarted by their collaboration with 'people who want to earn a lot of money and do not have patience for consultations, environmental reports, and community participation' (Bennett). The listener is encouraged to look into some of the buildings, and observe contrasts between the visual order of people working and exercising, and the prevalent noise of air-conditioning units. The sound of capital, it is suggested, is perhaps inaudible, but we are encouraged to imagine the white collar crimes of real estate fraud and controversial investments into armed conflict and weapon production by the ABN AMRO and ING banks.

The constructed and constricted nature of Zuidas seems to call for a renewed plea for public space as a site of collective participation, where all forms of public events can take place. The listener is instructed to sit on one of the outdoor chairs, close their eyes, and take part in an experiment. Bennett introduces the sounds of skateboarders, followed by passersby, and a busker setting up a sound system. We hear musicians tune their instruments and more people stop by and crowd in, while a group of old ladies protests against bankers, with banners that say 'Where is my pension?' Art students and their teachers call to rescue the Rietveld from relocation, the friends of the Beatrixpark protest to save the VU Hortus garden. A school recorder ensemble joins in, and a group of anarchical young people bring a banner 'Be creative, squat the Zuidas now!'

Bennett's 'Zuidas Symphony' provokes the listener to imagine sounds and rhythms of a broad spectrum of locals, as they call for their right to their city (and for corporate responsibility), and take over the semi-private space of the Zuidas. The piece concludes with Bennett himself taking to the public microphone, noting that all resemblances with reality are coincidental, and reads out a

8.5. Justin Bennett's "Zuidas Symphony" (2009), a soundwalk created in and around the Zuidplein or South Axis development. (Photo: Soundtrackcity)

list of sponsors. This ironic statement – not unlike a public service announcement – reminds the listener of the limits to Bennett's own intervention and the funding of his residency by Zuidas itself. Bennett's foregrounding of the 'creative city' policies of project developers is thus also self-critical, and he reminds his listeners of their own participation: 'And us? We are also complicit. I create a soundwalk, you are listening to it. With each step, we also contribute to the credibility of the project developers. I talk the talk. You walk the walk' (Bennett). Sound is used here to create a parallel space *within* Zuidas for critical reflection, and the piece seeks to re-politicize the urban process in Amsterdam. It neither invites the disinterested stare of the everyday iPod users (who try to take distance from their surroundings), nor the audio tour listener (who expects humorous anecdotes and sightseeing itineraries). In this sense, it differs strongly from, for instance, a Red Light District audio tour, which may in fact defuse urban politics and social justice, both by facilitating the tourist gaze and perhaps affirming the city council's desire to clear the way for safer spaces of leisure and consumption.

Both Van der Heide and Bennett's projects go against the grain of commercial appeals to sensory experience. If not the *underground*, then both at least engage with the theme of (in)audibility, and offer small interventions in generating mobile and critical listening activity in prominent sites within central Amsterdam. Bennett's piece invites reflection on what one hears, sees, and reads in and about the Zuidas, and the power structures underpinning such large-scale urban development. In unearthing the silences and silencing of this project, Bennett reminds us that sound and music are not only aesthetically appealing, but highly bound up in patterns of power and ideology. The intervention of the soundwalk, reaching out to one urban subject at a time, is modest, but marks a clear departure from the efforts of cultural entrepreneurs to invest wonder and enchantment in the branded city, as outlined earlier in this essay. In an era of Art Factories and Creative Cities, Bennett encourages skepticism toward the simulated activism and lifestyle propaganda generated by projects like Zuidas. Though whether all this falls on deaf ears is another thing. As of recently, all those coming to the Zuidas are encouraged on the area's official website to come and listen to Bennett's soundwalk.

9. Red Lights and Legitimate Trade: Paying for Sex in the Branded City

Joyce Goggin

Introduction

As the articles in this volume all in some way argue, the 'underground' is an ambiguous concept. On the surface, the word itself has a number of meanings and can refer to location, as in 'the Paris metro' or catacombs; to sketchy and sometimes illegal practices, such as drug dealing and prostitution; or to the avant-garde, as in 'The Velvet Underground'. And the 'underground' can move in and out of its marginalized position over time and under various conditions. For example, as an expression of the avant-garde, the underground can cross over into the mainstream, and underground activities like prostitution and drug use can be tolerated to a greater or lesser extent depending on the historical juncture in which they occur, or the location in which they operate. So given that the many meanings of 'underground' are not entirely stable or straightforward, the term is an uneasy fit with anything it may be used to describe, such as Amsterdam's Red Light District, which is the subject of this essay.

To further muddy the waters, Amsterdam's centuries-old Red Light District is, in many respects, as complex and convoluted as the winding canals and narrow streets in which it is located. For example, the history of the Dutch tolerance for both prostitution and the district itself is as varied as the notion of what, exactly, was or is being tolerated. In this case, moreover, tolerance also involves the question of exactly how far underground red-light practices are driven. For example, centuries ago tolerance meant turning a blind eye to prostitution if it was conducted in a designated area, although this *laissez-faire* attitude could quickly veer off into sporadic round-ups whenever prostitutes became the subject of civic debate. And although in the seventeenth century 'prostitution was widespread in Dutch society in contrast to other European counties [it was] characterized by a relative absence of soliciting in streets and a tendency to disguise brothels as something else' (Israel 682). In other words, as long as it was kept more or less underground and within the parameters of a district that contained brothels to conceal the business within, this specialized neighborhood was permitted to operate at the very heart of Amsterdam's busy port, and service the bourgeois population as well as seafaring traffic.

In the Netherlands, prostitution went from being tolerated to being legalized in 2000, which moved the Red Light District forcefully out of the underground, although a tantalizing racy aura continues to surround it. A sort of special reverence for prostitution is present in contemporary Dutch culture and this is reflected in various popular media, including, somewhat surprisingly, the University of Amsterdam student weekly magazine. In November of 2010, *Folia* featured an article entitled 'Je moet wel van seks houden als je een baantje in de prostituie wilt' ('You Have to Like Sex If You Want a Job in Prostitution'), about two female students who were financing their university studies by working as call-girls. The article's byline laments that one cannot put a job in prostitution on one's CV, while the author wonders if this might not be the ideal student job ('*ideale studentenbaan*').

One of the issues lurking behind the gritty image that accompanied this feature article has to do with the notion of 'authenticity'. Both visitors to Amsterdam and residents of the city relate the Red Light District, and its 'cool' aura of 'underground' panache, to a time before the advent of political correctness and Starbucks, as a kind of last frontier that resists Disneyfication, homogenization, and standardization. This nostalgic view of authenticity informs much of popular musing on the topic, as one 2008 blog entry entitled 'Amsterdam – So Colorful' attests. The author urges the reader to 'get over and enjoy the brothels in the Red Light District of Amsterdam while you can' since 'new laws are changing the area, in response to an increase in crime and trafficking from Eastern European pimps who are getting out of hand', and concludes by lamenting the authenticity of the 'good ol' days'.

9.1. 'You have to like sex if you want a job in prostitution', cover of *Folia*, a weekly news magazine for students and staff members of the University of Amsterdam. 19 November, 2010. (Photo: Pascal Tieman)

The 'good ol' days' that the author of this blog invokes are part of a temporal duality or disjunction, often associated with the 'authentic' experience that (former) underground urban areas may stimulate. As Sharon Zukin has observed in *Naked City*, on the streets of such areas one can feel the presence of another kind of time:

> The Greeks called it *kairos*; a sense of the past that intrudes into and challenges the present ... The streets and buildings ... are reminders of an alternative time that [provides] 'a sense of authentic origin and justification for present hopes' ... Such neighbourhoods supply the visitor with a sense of 'a history of artistic energy and resisting authority'. (101)

Importantly, however, the aura of resistance and bohemian hipness that hangs around Amsterdam's Red Light District is also tempered with the more banal consideration of commerce and the kind of monetary transaction that drives prostitution. As Jean-François Lyotard once explained, the economy of prostitution is based on the transformation of 'the client's *jouissance* into money, which converts 'the surplus of pulsional energy scattered in society, and dangerous to it ... into money, and then into commodities ... bringing about the return of these "lost" expenditures into the circuit of social exchanges' (157). Far from the romance of underground culture, which is often synonymous with the notion of anti-commercialism, the Red Light District is then a center for financialized sexual transaction. Add to this Amsterdam's privileged relationship with commerce since the seventeenth century as a center for banking and trade, and the Red Light District takes on a much more 'business-as-usual' air. Seen in this light, the toleration of prostitution has more to do with its potential as an economic driver than any special relationship to authenticity or the underground.

Ironically, the secularized commercial climate that made Amsterdam famous for its red lights may well be the one force that, after these many centuries, spells its demise. In an effort to clean the area up and diversify its offering by adding more mainstream attractions for the contemporary tourist, the city bought up about one-third of its red-lit windows and began a process of conversion in 2007. The desired effect of this strategy is best demonstrated by an entry entitled 'Amsterdam: Sex, Drugs and Civilized Living' in *Time Out: The World's Greatest Cities*. This entry on Amsterdam begins with prostitution and commerce, explaining that visitors will 'find themselves endlessly looping back – just like randy sailors did in the seventeenth century when the city was the richest port in the world – to Amsterdam's near geographic center, the Red Light District' (24). The *Time Out* guide then apologetically notes that 'it is true that Amsterdam still has a certain reputation' and quickly moves on to advertising the city's clean-up and gentrification campaign:

> The recent 'I Amsterdam' city-branding campaign has done much to distract the global imagination away from the sex and drugs and towards the 'creative capital', once home to Rembrandt, now abuzz with designers and advertising companies. Meanwhile, the city is gentrifying quickly as the authorities are

committed to making what is already the safest Red Light District into an area more conducive to wine bars and sushi joints. (24)

This plan to open the district for other forms of city experience and entertainment is perfectly in keeping with trends that scholars working in urban studies have noted. As Zukin explains, the 'gritty' vibe that the Red Light District communicates can be used to create a 'desirable synergy between underground cultures and the creative energy they bring to both cultural consumption and city growth' (*Naked City* 53). As part of this effort to make the 'area more conducive to wine bars and sushi joints', and to enhance the city's creativity profile, the 'Red A.I.R.' (Artists in Residence) program was launched, through which artists were allotted space in the brothels that the city had purchased. The idea was to short-circuit squatters who might have occupied the buildings if left empty until the properties could be redeveloped for high-end housing and boutique retail space. Using the buildings as temporary ateliers and gallery spaces was thought to have the added benefit of boosting Amsterdam's image as a 'creative capital' known for its heritage brand that spans the centuries from Rembrandt to Van Gogh.

In what follows, I will unpack various aspects of the ongoing developments which I have just briefly enumerated. All of these developments are in some way involved in the gentrification of Amsterdam's Red Light District, and throughout my analysis I will be particularly mindful of the historical developments in both commerce and culture that led the city to adopt its current branding strategy. Part of this analysis will also involve a discussion of those elements of Amsterdam's cultural heritage that intersect with the city's most notorious 'underground' neighborhood and its shifting reputation.

It is important to note, however, that writing about the Red Light District in the limited space of one chapter necessarily means selecting certain topics above others, such as the straight history of prostitution as opposed to the current problem of slave trade in sex workers, or other kinds of prostitution on offer in the district. And while a detailed financial geography of the area would also be useful, this chapter will provide a discussion of city-branding that has to forego the obvious benefits that such a study would entail. Therefore, my argument in the following sections will focus largely on straight prostitution in the Red Light District as it has been cast in cultural production, and particularly in painting, beginning with the seventeenth century. My aim is to discuss the contradictory aims of the Red A.I.R. project and the perception that creativity is the answer to the bristling bouquet of issues plaguing the district.

Historical Notes: Painting and Prostitution

In analyzing Amsterdam's Red Light District and the services it provides, one might be tempted to begin with the contestable psychoanalytical notion that (sexual) desire is predicated on lack, or the craving for some impossible object of fulfillment. Prostitution effectively inverts this axiom by making the seemingly unobtainable readily available for a price, so that transactions between johns and hookers render the impossible object of desire fully attainable, thereby temporarily satisfying drives and impulses with straightforward lust fulfillment. As one blogger explained in a post from 2010 titled 'Dating Amsterdam Prostitutes', he 'really enjoys the no-strings-attached screw … the fast-forward-to-the-juicy-bits [of the] semi-anonymous … fuck, [and] the freedom from social and emotional monitoring that comes along with purchased whoopee.' As he goes on to explain, it 'is a different and pleasant feeling that is also beautiful and nice now and again', yet he feels oddly compelled to refer euphemistically to purchasing sex as 'dating an Amsterdam prostitute who feels well-paid'.

Amsterdam has long been known as a center where sex with strangers is on offer for a price. According to Reuters Online, 'prostitutes have plied their wares in the narrow alleys of the old center of Amsterdam for centuries ... [where] they used to attract sailors and merchants in the city's heyday as the heart of a global trading empire' (Thomasson). For hundreds of years, seamen arriving in Amsterdam stopped first in the port to make a sexual transaction before penetrating into various arteries of the city where more legitimate trade and commerce would be conducted. This tradition of exchange is so deeply embedded in the culture that the expression '*ouwehoeren*', or 'old whoring', is still commonly used in Dutch to refer to idle verbal intercourse.

The brothel and the procuress were also frequent subjects of seventeenth-century Dutch genre paintings that featured the popular music houses, or 'musicos' ('*speelhuizen*') where men could gamble, drink, dance, and enjoy the company of available young women. Located primarily in Amsterdam and Rotterdam, these settings for merry companies 'were schools of vice, just as home was the great school of virtue' (Schama 467). It was here that one found a world of drunkenness, immoderation, and carnality that 'inverted humanism's domestic norms [of] cleanliness, honesty, comfort, sobriety and moderation' (Schama 467).

These upside-down seventeenth-century microcosms boasted a workforce of girls, many of whom had traveled to Amsterdam to ply their trade as seamstresses, knitters, or lace makers only to become part of a rowdy anti-family, conducting business in a reversed version of domesticity. Ironically, or perhaps appropriately, these young women who had started out as migrant textile workers were subject to incarceration in the Spinhuis, where they were put to work spinning or knitting as punishment for prostitution. While these unfortunate women were incarcerated in the Spinhuis, upstanding citizens could pay money to stand and peer in at them, just as they had captured titillating glimpses of them working as prostitutes in houses of pleasure or in genre paintings.

When Mandeville visited Amsterdam early in the eighteenth century, he concluded that brothels were tolerated in certain zones so that 'honest housewives might go unmolested by what would otherwise be the uncontrollable licentiousness of the maritime population' (qtd. in Schama 467). The government, he wrote, is 'always endeavouring, though unable, to suppress what it actually tolerates'(467), whereby the upstanding and the derelict maintained a kind of mutually beneficial interdependence. According to Simon Schama, this was typical of Dutch seventeenth-century 'moral pluralism', whereby virtue and vice are permitted to coexist for the 'sake of effective social management', resulting in a 'prophylactic

9.2. Jan Steen, *In Luxury, Look Out* (ca. 1663).
(Courtesy of Kunsthistorisches Museum,Vienna)

approach to civic morality' (468). Hence it was the very presence of a segregated, corrupted, inverted world order – or underground – that made it possible to maintain the ostensible virtue, cleanliness, and thrift of the rest of society.

Until very recently, these two realms continued to co-exist in Amsterdam in remarkably unchanged intimacy, which is why, according to art historian Svetlana Alpers, Amsterdam bordellos have been constructed 'on the model of the domestic house' (64). In 1987 Schama wrote of the coziness of red-light establishments in Amsterdam, and their gaudy version of '*gezelligheid*' (coziness) that amounts to a 'travest[y] of the Dutch bourgeois household or the bric-a-brac bibelot shop, full of knickknackery, lace curtains, ... and potted plants' (467). Similarly, in his 1984 novel *Small World*, David Lodge remarked that two things prevented the Amsterdam traffic in prostitutes from being merely sordid:

> The first was that the interiors of the houses were spotlessly clean, and furnished in a cosy petit-bourgeois style, with upholstered chairs, embroidered antimacassars, potted plants, and immaculate linen turned down on the bed that could usually be glimpsed at the rear. The second thing was that ... the women were ... in many cases ... passing their time in the homely occupation of knitting. (201)

According to Lodge, one was still able in 1984 to glimpse a prospective scene of lust through the petit-bourgeois interiors of the Red Light District, just as one suddenly spots the copulating dogs in Van Mieris's otherwise tame and tidy brothel scene of 1658.

9.3. Frans van Mieris de Oude, *Bordeelscène* (1658). (Courtesy of Mauritshuis Museum)

For some time then, historians and art historians, including Svetlana Alpers, have concurred that Amsterdam has tolerated vice and a booming underground at its very hearth and heart as a means of preserving 'good women's virtue' and civic hygiene (Schama 467-8). It was also here in the seventeenth century that the economic necessity of maintaining a thriving port, open to unseemliness as well as to wealth, and the moral imperative of nurturing a decent, hardworking citizenry, became the subject of copious genre paintings (such as Van Mieris's pictured here above) that circulated in a booming free art market. As recorded in the travelogues of those who visited Amsterdam in the seventeenth and eighteenth centuries, homes of the wealthy and the lower classes alike were festooned with affordable paintings, as were taverns, brothels, butchers, bakers, and even stables. 'Such is the generall Notion, enclination and delight that these Countrie Natives have to Painting', wrote one traveler of the Dutch in 1640, that pictures seemed to cover every available surface in private homes and public places (qtd. in Fuchs 42). Therefore, given the imperative, or privilege, of producing saleable art for the market, artists who no longer relied solely on wealthy patrons produced genre paintings intended to intrigue and titillate the virtuous while providing a point of identification for purveyors of vice, as both were now potential buyers.

Re-Writing Heritage, Re-Branding the City

Some claim that Amsterdam has been famous for prostitution for 800 years, and indeed the city's red-light districts have been prophylactically located in the same areas at least since the fifteenth century. The geographic stability of the red-light districts – and particularly of the world-famous Wallen – coupled with the deep cultural embeddedness of prostitution to which I have been referring, make it a powerful urban signifier and a huge tourist draw. Yet while prostitution has organically become an essential part of the city's identity, Amsterdam is currently engaged in a campaign to re-brand itself as part of a new kind of 'global trading empire', under the English-language slogan 'I Amsterdam'. While this slogan seems to imply that everyone belongs in Amsterdam – that I, too, am Amsterdam – the city's branding makeover campaign involves re-purposing all of the red-light districts, and thereby necessitating the partial exclusion of one particular class of the city's citizens, namely the prostitutes themselves.

Since 2007 the city has been concertedly acquiring and reselling buildings in the district to commercial developers, and has launched a program to replace a number of the windows where prostitutes were formerly on display with chic apartments, upmarket shops, galleries, and high-quality hotels and restaurants, along with outlets for young fashion designers. Although the extent of the gentrification and its impact has, as yet, been neither fully assessed nor achieved, Charles Geerts, who sold 18 of his properties in 2007, claimed that there were 250 windows in the city and that the sale of his 18 buildings meant the loss of 51 windows, or 20% of the Red Light District's venues. Former mayor Job Cohen announced plans to halve the number of brothels, and estimated that the 51 windows the city had taken over amounted to one-third of the total.

But there have been obvious and predictable objections to this grand-scale gentrification. For example, Mariska Majoor, a former prostitute who now runs an information center in the Red Light District, asks 'where the women should go' and fears that hundreds of women would be put out of work or forced 'underground' were the district disintegrated and replaced with standard tourist fare ('Window Brothels'). Metje Blaak, who runs a support group for prostitutes, has stated that without the exposure and ostensible protection afforded by the windows, prostitutes 'may end up in a back room somewhere where we can't reach them' ('Window Brothels'). Blaak sees the clean-up as 'a big mistake' since, without the windows which have now taken on a sort of reverse panopticular function, no one could 'keep tabs on the women by looking at the windows to see if they are there' ('Window Brothels').

The other, perhaps more obvious, objection to the complete dissolution of the Red Light District, is that Amsterdam relies heavily on tourism and this sector accounts for about 70 million euros a year. So the question that arises is this: what is a city to do, faced with increasingly unfavorable attitudes toward human trafficking and forced to compete with other cities that have joined the second wave of experience economics? How does a city appeal to consumers in a race to offer high-class, emotional experiences while competing with the kind of aggressive urban branding going on in other cities and tourist destinations?

What Amsterdam, like many other cultural capitals, has to offer is, according to Zukin in *Naked City*, 'an authentic *experience* of local character [which] becomes a local *brand*' (121). In this case, however, a major part of that local character is an 800-year-old reputation for a particular brand of 'sleaze', which does not appeal to family tourism and high-end visitors, nor does it sit comfortably with a number of feminist and political concerns. As just noted, the strategy thus far has been one of half measures involving moving other kinds of businesses into the Red Light District, and advising visitors to 'take a walk there nowadays, and you can admire Dutch couture next door to the well-known girls of pleasure' (HTNK). But while the hope is that the Red Light District will become an international hotspot for design tourists, when asked about this development, Majoor replied that 'the story about the fashion industry coming to the Red Light District is laughable. This is definitely not going to turn into some wonderful Walt Disney story' (qtd. in 'Amsterdam to Clean Up').

I would hasten to raise another objection, however, that has nothing to do with commercialization, Disneyfication, or authenticity, and everything to do with the basic dynamics of attracting and assisting tourism. As it is well known, travellers and indeed customers of all kinds use their 'cognitive maps' – and their expectations – to guide them from one axis or hub of interest (i.e., a red-light district) to the next. Once internalized, these points or markers help visitors to navigate any city with the confidence of a 'sleep-walker feeling safe and at home' (Mikunda 18). This is why axes, hubs, mnemonic points, and districts have become part of every 'experience world' and most cities in the branding race map space to assist visitors as they navigate.

Interestingly enough, this is what Amsterdam's city gentrification project has avoided doing with the Red Light District by adding clothing designers and other kinds of venues to the mix. Hence, while the 'randy sailors' to which the *World's Greatest Cities* referred above now find it difficult to find the Red Light District, other tourists not interested in the sex trade are often surprised to turn a corner and find themselves confronted suddenly with a woman in a g-string in a red-lit window. In other words, this move to mix offerings would appear to go against the grain of standard city-branding techniques designed to guide visitors comfortably from one experience location to the next.

Artists, Pimps, and Whores

In one online article that discussed what to do with the Red Light District, bizarrely entitled 'How to Turn Prostitutes into Artists', the author asks, 'if your city is overrun with prostitutes, what do you do?'. The answer, it goes on to explain, is simple: 'just replace them with artists.' In the RED A.I.R. project, the government has joined forces with private enterprises to install artists temporarily in bordello spaces, and to replace prostitutes in windows with artists and the products of their creativity. The goal is to turn the Red Light District into an artistic area like SoHo, the East Village, or Chelsea. Yet in the face of all the new space that gentrification has created, artist Niels Vis lamented, 'It feels a bit like

9.4. Designer dress shop next to a brothel in Amsterdam's Red Light District. (Photo: Tess Jungblut)

we pushed the prostitutes out. Only one prostitute window is left on the Korsjespoortsteeg' (qtd. in 'Amsterdam Brothels'). Similarly, Laurence Aëgerter, who was involved with RED A.I.R. and was originally assigned Korsjespoortsteeg 23, chose not to use the space as a studio, but rather as a place to question her role as an artist in the city's political plans for the gentrification of Amsterdam. In other words, this attempt to repurpose the district seems to have resulted in anger, frustration, and discontent on the part of artists and sex workers alike.

Yet in spite of all the somewhat predictable objections, the notion of throwing artists and prostitutes together is based on a tacit yet popular tradition that links the two, at least since artists began explicitly painting prostitutes in the seventeenth century. This carries through to the nineteenth century and the romantic concept of the starving artist sharing urban space with prostitutes and bohemians, hence Toulouse-Lautrec's supposedly authentic renderings of prostitutes, and the use made of prostitutes as models by academic painters such as Gérôme and Manet. Yet I would like to suggest that there is a deeper, subtler similarity or association to be made between these two professions, which emerges when erotics and aesthetics are commercialized in Western culture.

Between 1946 and 1949, Georges Bataille wrote *La part maudite*, in which he elaborated on Marcel Mauss's *Essai sur le don* (Essay on the Gift) of 1922. In particular Bataille was interested in 'potlatch', a premodern form of economic exchange that Mauss had heard existed among people like the Haida natives of British Columbia, involving a meeting of tribes in which one tribe gives enormous gifts to the other without any clear reciprocal arrangement. Although goods certainly do circulate and come back, Mauss contrasted this form of economic exchange with modern forms that have now replaced it in so-called developed nations where utility and accumulation are the backbone of economy. For Bataille, although potlatch economics have been supplanted by notions of utility in modern societies, he argues that instances of potlatch break through economic regulation in the form of seemingly non-utilitarian expenditure such as fireworks which cost a great deal of money but produce nothing but sensual enjoyment; unsanctioned, non-procreative sexuality; and aesthetic production that has no aim other than to be visually pleasing. This might help to explain why we tend to think, deep down, that recreational sexuality and artistic production should be 'free' of the workaday world and that artists should live hand-to-mouth on grants, producing 'priceless' works of art. This is why, when erotics and aesthetics start to look like business, as in the sex trade or the art market, we tend to invent figures that make it all seem okay, like the whore with the heart of gold who would really give it away if she only could, or the starving artist who dies penniless in the name of Beauty.

Andy Warhol is one famous artist who challenged this notion, claiming that he wanted to be 'an Art Businessman or a Business Artist', and that his fantasy was to one day overhear someone saying 'There goes the richest person in the world', as he walked by. He also claimed that he would not be happy until all museums had become department stores, and his own career began with commercial window dressing in New York in the late 1950s. In a similar vein, Claes Oldenburg periodically presented exhibitions titled *The Store* at his storefront studio on New York's Lower East Side, for which he would fill the space with manufactured objects he bought and coated sloppily with commercial enamel paint.

But the relationship between art and the department store got underway long before Warhol, with the opening of Le Bon Marché in Paris in 1852, designed by L.C. Boileu and Gustav Eiffel, which featured impressive architecture embellished with priceless masterpieces. Five years later, Macy's opened in the United States with elaborate displays of commodities, fashions, and fine art, and in 1913 the Gimbel brothers took to displaying Cézannes, Picassos, Braques, Constables, Reynolds, Turners and even the occasional Titian in their stores alongside goods and in their impressive window displays. The path of influence between the department store window and the modern gallery became blatantly reciprocal in 1914 when the Metropolitan Museum of Art hired Richard Bach to develop commercial products, and again in 1927 when the Met co-sponsored an exhibition at Macy's devoted to modern art and sales (Taylor, 33-34). More recently Thomas Hoving, a former director of the Met, hired Gene Moore, whose Tiffany's window displays had made him famous, thereby inverting Warhol's notion of turning the store window into a museum by turning the museum into a store window.

Moreover the practice of window shopping is modern, commercial, and aesthetic at the same time and is entirely predicated on the invention of plate glass late in the eighteenth century. While urban centers had been bristling with commercial markers and signage since the middle ages, the display window made the sumptuous arrangement of goods and art objects possible, coalescing in the erotic desire for consumption, hence the French expression '*lèche-vitrine*' for window shopping, meaning literally to 'lick the store window'. In red-light districts, the powerful display afforded by the technology that produced plate glass moves the window shopper's desire along the libidinal scale from consumption to consummation. And by placing artists' work in red-lit windows, the developers who choose to do so, whether consciously or not, are effectively reiterating the tradition of merging libidinal and aesthetic economies, while reinforcing the developments I have been outlining here.

Plate glass also had a serious impact on the urban experience of the stroller or, in Walter Benjamin's terms, the thoroughly modern figure of the *flâneur*. For Benjamin the modern urban experience entailed being subjected to a constant barrage of images, announcements, and advertisements, and this ultimately led to a new kind of consciousness and aesthetic vision. According to Anne Friedberg, the shop window is quite literally a show window, so that 'from the middle of the nineteenth century, ... the shop window succeeded the mirror as a site of identity construction, and then – gradually – the shop window was displaced and incorporated by the cinema screen' (66). In other words, the shop window becomes our experience of the aesthetic, and as city-branders know, the trick is to keep pedestrians moving from one highly emotional and enhanced point of purchase to the next, by means of landmarks, concept lines, axes, hubs, mnemonic points, and areas such as the Red Light District. All of this is calculated to provide tourists with a compelling, emotional experience as well as one that is thoroughly commercialized. In short, the casual stroll has now become part of what economists refer to as the 'financialization of everyday life', whereby every aspect of our lives has been colonized by pricing, commodification, instruments of credit, insurance, and points of sale (Martin).

In this regard, it is interesting to contemplate the notion of a red-light chain that would form part of the new Amsterdam brand, with standardized prices for various services, so that the pre-modern, romanticized practice of haggling, which bloggers claim is still a part of paying for sex, would be entirely eliminated. Recall the blogger with whom I began, who insisted on referring to paid sexual transactions as 'dating', thereby returning this intimacy to the order of the gift exchange, at least in his imagination. Indeed, we have a knee-jerk reaction to the notion that every nook and cranny of our existence is susceptible to being standardized and financialized, just as we are loath to face the commerciality of art. In a similar vein, Pierre van Rossum, one of the clean-up campaign's project managers, described a butcher who ran a few brothel rooms on the side. 'He was selling cold meat and warm flesh at the same time', van Rossum explains, invoking once again the hominess of the seventeenth-century brothel which co-existed with and supplied the 'decent' household, thereby acting as a bastion of domesticity ('Window Brothels').

And finally, consider Love Club Thai 21, whose owner invited a journalist inside, saying 'come see, we are a normal business', before giving the reporter a tour of his small office, fitted with a computer, a washing machine, and a row of drying towels – hardly the romantic image of an old-timey bordello. Similarly unromantic was the club owner's insistence that Love Club Thai 21 'ha[s] a license' and 'pay[s] taxes' (qtd. in Thomasson). As the city mayor insists that he does not want 'to get rid of prostitution entirely, since it is part of the area's history and a major tourist draw for the city' (qtd. in Thomasson), the status of the Red Light District, how it is marketed and its uneasy fit with the 'I Amsterdam' brand is likely to become increasingly complex.

Conclusion

Since I began research on the Red Light District, there have been countless developments associated with the city's ongoing efforts to gentrify this dynamic historic neighborhood. For example, I participated in an 'Inspiring Cities' workshop organized in 2010 by an international network for cities and culture whose goal was 'searching for the soul of the city', by which, in this case, they meant the Red Light District. Also in 2010 the Amsterdam Historical Museum, under the curatorship of Annemarie de Wildt, hosted an exhibit entitled 'The Hoerengracht'. This enormous installation, created by American artists Ted and Nancy Kienholz between 1983 and 1988, measured over 13 by 4 meters, and provided viewers with a 'walk-through reinterpretation of a section of Amsterdam's Red Light District' ('The Hoerengracht'). For Kienholz, the narrative he thought he was creating with the piece 'was supposed to make the viewer feel uncomfortable' as he or she views 'society's rejects' depicted in an 'awkward and challenging' way (qtd. in 'The Hoerengracht'). Previously, this 'world-famous' installation was on display in the National Gallery in London, where it also drew viewers in, 'to peer into the windows and doorways in order to discover the secrets concealed within' this 'superb example of assemblage art' and 'monument to the Wallen of the 1980s' ('The Hoerengracht').

Whether the installation, safely on view as a simulacrum of one of Amsterdam's neighborhoods in the city's own historical museum, manages an effective critique or celebration of the Red Light District is open to question. Yet however one wants to read this piece, it remains as strange and complex as the district itself. At the same time the piece also seems to herald at least one possible future fate of the Red Light District, namely that it becomes sanitized, historicized, and placed on view as a monument to a part of the city's past that, after 800 years, is ceding to urban and economic pressures to be offered as a safe tourist destination, part of the new Amsterdam brand of experience, and a reminder of its own underground past.

10. Visibly Underground: When Clandestine Workers Take the Law into Their Own Hands

Anna-Louise Milne

The underground I am interested in is not a space sought out or cultivated in opposition to the law. Rather it is a situation of clandestinity either generated *by* or in some sense *despite* the law. Yet this does not mean to say that this underground is devoid of any political charge. On the contrary – although it is frequently the case that this zone of *non-droit* is framed as a *human* disaster, rather than as an issue of both political and ontological consequence. The humanitarian frame for much discussion of illegal migration around the world reflects the fact that it is but very rarely opposition to the law in the so-called 'host' country that constitutes the primary impetus for this 'underground movement'. Yet the challenge brought to the law by the ever more numerous candidates for illegal migration becomes political and, as such, is apt to generate forms of mobilization and association that weave into other, perhaps more self-consciously constituted networks of political resistance. In other words, existing without papers in '*le pays des papiers*', as young Algerian *harragas*, or clandestine immigrants, like to call France, is rarely intended as a political act, though the idea that this act might always be an act of desperation needs to be questioned too. But it becomes a political issue, not merely in the sense that politicians are summed to answer the specific forms that this plight takes exactly, but more exactly an occasion to think politics again (Brun, 'Les sans-papiers' 104).

In this respect, I want to argue that attending to what is present in the lack – in the lack of papers or the lack of so-called 'useful' qualifications and skills – is both to acknowledge the limitations of the political system, or the law, and to participate in the appeal or, more intransigently, in the demand that inhabits that lack. So the lack is also a plus: something like the sort of 'supplement' or 'movement' that Rancière identifies as '*le politique*', in opposition to '*la politique*' of the institutionalized management of population flows. Instead of denouncing the aberrant evolution of the law, which has reduced some people previously living legally in France to illegality, or criticizing the increasingly stringent formulation of the law, or the unbending application of the law, as the majority of pressure and support groups tend to do, Rancière's thinking involves a more disarming reconceptualization of the life of the '*cité*'. It disarms the impetus and organizing principles of a certain form of socially-motivated action, which may critique specific aspects of state 'reason', but does not ultimately question the reason of the state and the supposed 'self-evidence' of an expression such as Michel Rocard's oft-quoted public appeal to 'common sense': '*La France ne peut pas accueillir toute la misère du monde*' ('France cannot accommodate all the misery of the world').

More fundamentally, Rancière is particularly significant here because he also loosens the connection between two conceptions of the avant-garde that tend to remain locked together, and by extension reshapes the frame of underground contestatory activity. These two conceptions are, on the one hand, a notion of the avant-garde as forerunner that embodies the intelligence of the moment and the possibility of determining the future forms of history, and, on the other, the notion of the avant-garde, or non-conformism, as engaging in finding new forms of life, in modifying what Rancière would term the '*domaine du sensible*'. In distinguishing these two conceptions of the avant-garde, and rejecting the teleological structure of the former, Rancière's work participates in, and constitutes one of the most important articulations of, a vibrant scene that wants to think otherwise than within the frame of a Hegelian dialectic.

In this chapter, I want to shuttle between that level of abstraction and some very local instances of work that have been produced in Paris in relation to the nebula of protest and resistance clustering around the *sans-papier* movement. This shuttling is not a bid to situate something specific about the *sans-papier* situation in Paris within a broad intellectual or socio-political context, if that process is understood as a measuring of the particular against some greater level of generality. Rather, it is a heuristic device to locate what we might term 'Paris' in terms of practices that have no particular location and that can in that sense be described as transnational. Illegal migration is a global phenomenon, and though it is important to distinguish between different legal regimes operating in different national spaces and the different cultural affects that freight specific journeys, the actual movement of migrants suggests the very relative significance of these distinctions when set against frontiers such as those that keep apart Europe and North Africa, or the United States and Mexico, or those with papers and those without within '*le pays des papiers*'.

Academic discourse in the humanities is also largely a transnational phenomenon, of which this book is a good instantiation. At both these levels, it is not immediately obvious why it might be worth making a distinction between Paris and Amsterdam in today's global economy. But this book is also a good instantiation of the fact that this distinction is everywhere apparent to us, and that historical and/or socio-political terms and considerations are not sufficient to think it. So it is to that end that I need the shuttling between what we might term theory and socio-demographic reality. Because the specifics lie not in a particular social reality, or in a particular and new – or vanguard – mode of thinking, but in how thinking and living rub off on one another, and the sort of culture that accrues around that rub.

So this chapter is part of a larger endeavor to think the specificities of a city, not so much despite the global processes that traverse it but rather in light of these processes. And its claim is that there is a specific texture and energy to the question of 'papers' in France, which needs more of an explanation than can be derived from focusing on the details of the law of that nation, and in turn offers more of an *occasion* for thinking.

I propose to substantiate these claims by staying quite close to two different ways in which actual moments of struggle by and with clandestine workers have been accompanied by efforts to enable this necessarily short-lived pressure on the law to be translated into different forms of visibility. The first endeavor grew out of the longish occupation of the Bourse du Travail building in the 4th arrondissement of Paris, a large block of offices in a Haussmannian building, which belongs to the Confédération Générale du Travail (CGT), and which was occupied by the Collectif des Sans-Papiers from May 2008 to July 2009 following the announcement that a certain number of regularizations would take place and the CGT positioned itself to ensure that its members without papers would be top of the list.

This choice of location is significant, over and above the not negligible factor that the building offered un-used space in a central location with electricity and plumbing. The CGT has long been a key locus of oppositional energy in France and is still closely associated with extreme-left organizations such as the Nouveau Parti Anti-Capitaliste as well as the Parti Communiste Français. But its record on supporting the *sans-papiers* is much less positive: its position had tended to echo the view that illegal immigrants are a threat to the job prospects of French citizens, thus aligning itself with the position of 'common sense' that requires a regretfully stringent application of quotas and a necessary removal of elements that slip through anyway.

The decision to occupy the Bourse du Travail put the government, under President Sarkozy, and the CGT on the same side of the fence. Moreover, the occupation was significant because, like other large-scale occupations, it flaunted the illegality of its participants, drawing attention to people who were not necessarily known to the *préfecture* and who thereby increased their chances of deportation. But unlike the much-mediatized occupation of the Saint-Bernard church in 1996, which ended with violent clashes and numerous arrests and deportations, here the Collectif did not have the theoretical protection of the Church and the CGT ended up doing the work of the police by strong-arming the *sans-papiers* out. The latter took refuge in another strategic location in the 18th arrondissement, in the empty premises of the French Social Security administration, the CPAM, where they founded the Ministry for the Regularization of All the Sans-Papiers. Once again the movement ran the risk of visibility, with a *permanence* set up on the street and large banners hung from the building. The men lived on the ground floor so as to establish continuity with the street, and separate quarters were established for the women and children on the second floor.

In this instance, the overt but passive contestation of the law collapsed in the face of the law's intransigence: despite the official circulars that define due processes for the regularization of applicants on the basis of particular forms of evidence, all regularizations in Paris had ceased. The law had responded to exception with exception; physical inertia met with bureaucratic inertia; the bid to 'void' the law and 'ape' government 'ministry' by making the intrinsically selective process of 'regularization' universal and applicable to 'all' met with the self-silencing of the law as its implementation slowed to a complete halt. And in order to secure the proper functioning of the law, the movement left the premises, despite suggestions of dissension. The situation, at the end of 2010, was effective dispersal, with sporadic demonstrations that received little media attention, such as the occupation of the Cité de l'Immigration museum, which went virtually unremarked in the press despite the fact it forced one of the largest new cultural centers in Paris to close its doors for a significant period of time.

This 'vacillation' of the law is worth considering more closely. One of the reasons why the properly political dimension of the *sans-papiers* situation is often ignored stems from the fact that the actors involved tend to get cast as individuals seeking individual solutions that will enable them to disappear fully into the anonymous mass of legitimate citizens. What sort of political force can a heterogeneous group of people all bound on proving at all cost their capacity for integration possibly constitute? By definition their plight commits them to a form of consensus, and social and political militants active in this and related areas such as housing and access to education often express the difficulty of consolidating any action with such a fluctuating population whose relation to the struggle is conditioned by their success in making the law work to their own end, particularly in the face of evidence that, for the state too, the law is a flexible tool and not an autonomous structure (Brun 'Sans-Papiers aux guichets'; Fassin 78-9). Being a *sans papier* is after all hopefully a mere phase in the life of an individual; it is not a matter of conviction.

In the course of a fascinating study that charts the experiences of a diverse group of Algerian men, primarily all living illegally in France, although some were raised in that country, Marie-Thérèse Têtu-Delage describes the frustrations of 'French' militants: '[the young migrants] don't tend to accept the way French organize their associations [*la vie associative*]... meanwhile the "French" will express surprise at the way the *sans-papiers* behave among themselves, the very fragile nature of the bonds they form, their mutual mistrust and tendency to put one another down' (164, author's translation). Lurking within this sort of frustration is often a sense of the unreliability of the *sans-papier* – here today demanding assistance, gone tomorrow, late for appointments, willing to take clandestine work even though it may mean jeopardizing the dossier that has painstakingly been put together by a local support group. The characterization of the unstable, self-interested, potentially unscrupulous character runs deep, generating the characterization of the *sans-papier* militant as a chameleon, as Ababacar Diop was described by *Le Monde* after he led the very noisy occupation of the Saint-Bernard church (see Fassin 83).

The pressure that this potentially unapologetic manipulation of the law places on 'our' consensual conception of the democratic process is perhaps expressed most clearly in the way young Algerians tend to translate the Arabic word *harragas*: in French they call themselves '*grilleurs*': '*on grille les trains*', '*on grille les contrôles*', '*on grille son nom.*' But it is precisely within what can too easily be reduced to a form of delinquency that the affirmation of self-determination needs to be heard, and not where it is more comfortably muted in the evocations of hapless victims of a new world order. That these '*grilleurs*' are victims of shrinking economic, social, and political possibilities is not in question; but they are not only victims. The choice of illegal immigration is experienced as an act of self-definition, which is also an act of shared significance: an adventure that resonates strongly for those still 'back home' who write the names of the *harragas* on the walls of the *medina*, thereby generating the sort of mythology that Arjun Appadurai has analyzed as productive of localities, or lived worlds constituted by relatively stable associations, and often opposed to the forms of belonging offered by the nation-state.

In the past twenty years or so, and more intensely since the post-2001 restrictions on global mobility for certain social categories, the self-perception of the migrant has shifted significantly and in ways that are articulated through a comparison with the previous generation seeking opportunities for work. This distinction operates at the level of self-designation as part of some larger group, as one particularly rich declaration by one of the young *harragas* interviewed by Têtu-Delage reveals:

> Immigrants, the ones with papers, call us *blédards* [from '*le bléd*' or hometown/village in Algeria] or *clandos* [from 'clandestine']. They were the first generation. We've since learnt about the law, about applying for asylum. We know how to go round things, how to go in the opposite way from the others, how to open up paths. For example, head over to Hamburg with a fake passport, apply for asylum in Germany because you're entitled to housing benefit. In Germany there are no squats full of Arabs, only the homeless live in squats. Then you head up to Holland, then into Denmark. If you're worried about getting back into France, no worries, there is always Greece, or Spain, or Portugal. There's always some way through. (qtd. in Têtu-Delage 21, author's translation)

Where the generation of their fathers and uncles is perceived as caught in a structure of exploitation, with the only redress possible being recognition of their 'place' within that structure – whether in the form of army pensions, residency permits, papers for dependents etc. – what this comment articulates is a strikingly fluid sense of some sort of shared underground agency, an agency that subverts the structure, that uses the law, that is smarter than the law, with the key value being at all times the capacity to move and to outwit. In its expression of its unfreedom, it also declares another future which is not only that of 'regularization'.

The same young man will also express feelings of extreme dejection in the course of Têtu-Delage's deep ethnographic study, and the account of his activities leaves us in no doubt as to the difficulty of his choice. But the irrepressibility of his declaration, with its claim to inventiveness and creativity, is inseparable from the knowledge of what objectifies him or what 'holds' him in a marginal and acutely vulnerable category, that of the putative asylum seeker. Where the state can only perceive a form of disturbance, and humanitarian groups deplore the actions of criminal networks exploiting the desperation of individuals, we need to contend with the idea that persistent efforts to outwit the law, and the connections that happen in and through this effort, also open up a sense of possibility around frontiers. This is not, however, to lapse into some sort of post-structuralist celebration of nomadism or transnationality. It would be naïve to suggest that the actual frontiers of economic and political division are any the less imposing as a result of what is also perhaps nothing more than the bravura of a young *apache*. But the expression of that defiance and what is involved in hearing it as an expression of possibility generates some sort of friction, or rub, somewhere between the smooth functioning of the law and the fantasy of unhindered circulation on the part of the illegal migrant who knows the secret passages in fortress Europe.

This brings me back to Paris as a site, then, of encounters where the forms of expression have a particular tone, such as '*griller*' with its evocation of a lawlessness that has strong roots in a *poète damné* tradition and the listening in turn also draws on a specific range of resources. And more precisely it brings me back to the first of the projects I want to mobilize here: the project that grew into its title 'Vas-y montre ta carte' ('Go On, Show Your Papers') initiated and developed by Fabien Breuvart throughout the occupation of the Bourse du Travail. This project papered the walls around the main Place de la République with cheaply printed A4 pictures of two people, one usually of African origin and the other of more varied social and physical profile. Together the two people held up an identity card, which on close inspection – though the photo did not always make this inspection possible – turned out to be the ID card of one of the people pictured.

As portraits, Fabien Breuvart's photos were fascinating for the sort of '*brouillage*' or disruption that they provoked, in a mild, almost surreptitious way. The idea of surreptitiousness is important to me here to catch something of this project's mode of visibility and readability. In contrast as much with the widely mediatized and aestheticizing images of migrants produced, for example, by the Paris-based Brazilian photographer Salgado, as with the criticism famously leveled at them by Susan Sontag in her work on regarding the pain of others, these photos have none of the reifying, brooding intensity that tends to transform misery into a form of spectacle, but nor do they offer a means of reconstructing what Sontag felt was abstracted out of Salgado's stills, that is the 'concreteness' of politics and history. They are not interested in the specific trajectory of the migrant photographed, nor in his or her name. They are interested in what perhaps remains a fleeting moment of interaction that occurs by means of an interpellation that constitutes both of the objects of the lens through the summation to show papers.

Indeed, the informal 'tu' of the address, '*Vas-y montre ta carte*', shifts across the divide of menacing challenge and civic invitation, generating a subversion of the powerful fiction that papers underwrite identity. Of course, papers do in very real senses underwrite all sorts of possibilities, but what the light gesture of suspending the ID card between two distinct hands and two distinct bodies suggests is the disjunction between this 'fiction' and the bodies it tries to order and control. It also flickers with possibilities of stories between people, especially when the photos are viewed in series and the bodies seem variously together, or together variously, either constrained, or almost affectionate, laughing, portentous. A certain sort of community is figured in this togetherness, and Fabien Breuvart explained to me how people came often from quite a distance specifically to the Bourse du Travail to participate in the project, responding to a need to inscribe themselves in this story. He also related how quickly and easily people handed over their ID cards, and one of the things that is suggestive about these photos when viewed serially is the range of ways of holding the card and who holds it most forthrightly.

More important perhaps than these variations within the act of loosening the monadic structure of ID-based social organization is the formal quality of this project that becomes more apparent if we contrast it, say, with the relatively common practice of '*parrainage*' or 'sponsoring', whereby a fully-paid-up member of civic society assists a migrant or asylum seeker with his or her process of integration, initiating him or her into the ways and means of the 'host' country. In those contexts what is lent in terms of knowledge and even in terms of goods and clothes gives a very thick sense to the 'identity' of the community gradually created, even though the sharing may involve a degree of reciprocity. In Fabien Breuvart's photos, however, what is shared, even though very provisionally, is precisely what cannot be shared, and the 'flat' collectivity of two hands on one card intervenes between the embodied differences of destiny, or of place in the structures of civil society.

It is the doubling that is interesting, behind the card that declares singularity. It creates the sense of the pressure of bodies rubbing shoulders while also collapsing any impression that the photo offers up the full presence of a unified subject, as portraits in the traditional sense are often perceived to do. Instead, the presence we gauge here occurs across a distance, that of the ID card, generating the implication that we are all held together, though apart, by the structure of papers, those with as much as those without, and by extension this gesture implicates us, as we look, casually caught by the interpellation from the wall: 'Go on, show your papers'.

Let me shuttle back now to the level of abstraction, because what perhaps needs underscoring here is that these photos, which squarely frame the impoverished victims of global capitalism and put them on view for police and spectators, seem nonetheless to sidestep the accusation addressed in all number of forms to the image as a mere simulacrum that we unwittingly take for presence. In his introduction to Anabell Guerrero's *Aux frontières*, a collection of photos taken in the Sangatte migrant camp near Calais, John Berger stages this dilemma: how do you catch a living shadow on camera while also avoiding the cat-and-mouse strategy of revelation and censure, shared by the national media and the state police? Between aesthetics and information, or between disembodied forms, circulating without weight in 'our' world, and sociological facts, what we need is a production of knowledge that prompts us to show our cards, provoked in our own unfreedom to think carefully about the postures we might adopt when holding them out. Defiance, apology, anxiety: perhaps we are not fully sure of being '*en règle*' ('in order') ourselves.

What I want to emphasize here is a mode of apprehension of the production of identity that happens as much within the body as it does in some sort of reflective process: it is no more freely imagined than it is fully ascribed. Rather, the fiction of the disinterestedness of the law is crossed by feelings of discomfort or discrepancy – 'not me, you don't mean me' – in its reception. Our own implication in this interpellation is also an experience of our resistance to it, which tends to take the form of a flood of emotions, subsequently relived as stories told of intransigent police officers, influential friends, things that go really wrong, stories bound together with shame, or defiance, or laughed off loudly. It is rare that one's tussles with the identity police do not involve the experience of exception, where our place within the law is overwritten by other realities, where we *take exception* to the form which the experience is assuming.

Fabien Breuvart expressed a version of this when describing the impetus for his project, which he claimed would not have happened if it had not been '*dans ma rue*' ('in my street'). The archetypal structure of belonging within the culture of Paris – '*mon quartier*', '*ma rue*' – is right in the foreground here, particularly as voiced by a local shopkeeper such as Breuvart, who is a *quartier* photographer first and foremost, making most of his income from ID pictures and family prints. It resounds with two distinct sounds: a sense of outrage – how can people be reduced to living in these conditions on *my* street – but also a recognition of responsibility. In his terms, it was not possible to remain unmoved by this event. The emergency was as much his emergency as that of the *sans-papiers* themselves, and as we talked on in the local market café, where he often meets one of the main leaders of the Bourse du Travail occupation who has cleaned the aisles of the market for over 15 years, his account of what was caught up in this imperative bled out into other sources of grievance, both local and more existential.

This notion of 'taking exception' – and by extension, the feeling of entitlement in taking the law into one's own hands – echoes through the other project I want to discuss here: the film work made by Sylvain George, a relatively young French film-maker whose focus on the trajectories of illegal immigrants has recently caught significant attention at a number of festivals. In one of George's early short pieces, entitled *No Border* (2005-2008) and built around images of the liminal presence of migrants in Paris, Benjamin's famous 8th 'Thesis on Philosophy' occupies the screen:

> The tradition of the oppressed teaches us that the 'state of emergency' in which we live is not the exception but the rule. We must attain to a conception of history that is in keeping with this insight. Then we shall clearly realize that it is our task to bring about a real state of emergency, and this will improve our position in the struggle against Fascism. (257)

The standard English translation of this passage opts for the notion of a 'stage of emergency', but in many ways the concept of a 'state of exception' is perhaps closer to the political tradition within which Benjamin was writing. Giorgio Agamben has offered the fullest engagement with Benjamin's thesis on the state of exception in his sequel to *Homo Sacer*. There he rejects the idea that the state of exception occurs outside the frame of law as a moment of disruption that subsequently founds a regime, as in a revolutionary upheaval that then legitimizes the constituent assembly. Instead he elaborates a reading of exceptionality which claims, echoing Benjamin, that we live in a permanent state of exception, understood, not as untrammelled force, but rather as a structure or tension that holds together in one body – the state – the two forces of life and the law. The first, also analyzed as *autoritas*, operates with impunity, the second, *potentas*, maintains and enforces the law. While these two forces have been conceptually distinct in earlier regimes, the modern state has entered a permanent state of exception by welding them together. In other words, what characterizes the modern state is its now generalized tendency to act outside the law while continuing to sustain the fiction of the law's sovereignty.

The significance of Agamben's analysis lies in the way it opens up another mode of exceptionality that must be understood as operating on and with the law, rather than erasing the law. Instead of conceptualizing resistance to a government-driven state of exception as requiring force to meet force, thereby generating some sort of dialectical resolution, Agamben advances the idea of a 'deposing' of the law. Not its suppression, but its transformation through acts of study or play. He is interested in actions that seek only to manifest themselves and, in so doing, to reveal the disjunction between law and life, not so as to reveal a priority of one over the other, but as a 'possibility of reaching a new condition' (Agamben 88).

Thus, Agamben posits a form of 'pure violence' whereby action does not bind and neither commands nor prohibits, but rather loosens the law from its role as juridical structure in a way that finds a particular resonance with the loosening of ownership of one's 'ID' in the photos produced by Breuvart. This pure 'play' reveals the non-necessity of the law, or its lack of purchase without *autoritas* to ensure its application. In its combination of defiance and flippancy it mirrors the overt flaunting of the law by state power, which also risks exposing the limits of the law. In other words the notion of exceptionality as demonstrated by the state is faced with another mode of exceptionality, which I will proceed to explore further by means of Sylvain George's film-work, speaking to the latter's own mobilization of Benjamin in the opening shots of his film, but also shuttling back *away* from this level of abstraction, and indeed Agamben's strenuous efforts to dislodge from any particular institutional frame the forces that compose civil society, by turning our attention to the close grain of George's attempts to figure the pressure of exceptionality. Or, to put it another way: to the forms George produces to enable the underground to be seen.

What is perhaps most striking about George's films is the way they move fluidly between highly formalizing, almost writerly, strategies and oblique snatches of documentation of brutal reality, surveying the sorts of makeshift encampments in disused lots in the city, particularly behind the Gare de l'Est, or dwelling on bodies cursorily washing in the cold at a water tap in the street. The camera lingers on the rubbish, the rags, the cardboard, the plastic bags, all signs of transience and the dematerialization of social life. But these signs are not merely empty, as if emblematic of the commodification of labor. They are in some instances quite literally occupied, but the motion of his films is still not exactly about making 'concrete' the processes of capital or the bodies on the streets. What is more important is the ebb and flow of presence through the films, or the way 'empty' forms gain weight, then retreat again into mere shadows, like the lights on the water between France and England, or the plastic bags full of all one owns, then abandoned in order to make a dash. There is a long tradition in France of fascination with the way the city harbors its capacity to shock, a tradition that could bear lots of names, but perhaps most resonantly that of Baudelaire, for whom the city, its 'old stones', and its obscure and abandoned '*déchets*' offered supremely the occasion to '*penser à des choses qui ne sont pas de la terre*' ('think of things that are not of this earth') (42). Baudelaire, and particularly Baudelaire read with Benjamin in mind, is one of the principle resources with which George appears to apply himself to listening and seeing in Paris. But this does not mean to suggest that his work is about exegesis, any more than it is about representing with sociological accuracy the patterns and processes of migrancy. Rather it is about a construction of the self or a construction of a certain knowing, in which a literary culture – perhaps a specifically Parisian *lexus* – is what both enables and is transformed by the effort to see an 'underground' reality.

Like Breuvart, this process is affirmed as fundamentally political precisely in the fact that it operates outside the frame of 'traditional' or institutionalized politics, or in that it operates as some sort of exception to the categories that regiment social life. Breuvart emphasized an experience of '*cassure*' ('breakage'), something irredeemably lost. George in turn resists any designation as militant, if that means an association with a recognizable and stable political formation. The limited nature of the fluctuating, liminal '*collectif*' of the *sans-papiers*, generated in the face of specific emergencies and intended to play a role in situations of crisis – such as deportation – that do not have a vocation to endure, is in this respect a significant element in understanding both these endeavors. The pressure they bring to bear on the ordered control of bodies in space is intermittent, a seizure or shock that disrupts the habitual flow of information and processes. But this interruptive flare of emergency is not fully blinding, and this might be another way of saying that it is not primarily aesthetic or poetic: it has shape, it reveals a process, it articulates sounds that fill space. In George's film, it has what I want to call a particularly Parisian urban tone, that of the lightening gaze of the *passante* (passerby), or that of the pestilent crowd's heaving body. These are the forms that re-emerge through the flare, while also being what ignites that flare.

'N'entre pas sans violence dans la nuit' – 'Show Your Cards'

This chapter has strayed far from the 'traditional' notion of the underground, and I want to conclude by bringing it back within that frame via discussion of another of George's films, *N'entre pas sans violence dans la nuit* (2005-2008), which participates in the events that ensued when an identity check in the Château d'Eau area of Paris prompted a small riot. The film opens with the arrival of the police, but contrary to the energy and momentum we might expect with this sort of emergency, the law hovers and floats across the screen as an abstract form before emerging into its incontrovertible force. The street hurls around us, and yet the whole scene is suspended, '*crispé*', as people camp their indignation in its imminent overflow into uncoordinated action, as if its time had suddenly got thicker. George's *montage* wrong foots the sense of unfolding, and in that suspension it generates an openness, a possibility. And if violence, or resistance, is what we are invited to effect, it is a very specific mode of violence. Not a directed, purposeful attack on an identifiable target, but a bristling of the self, as if sprouting nervy antennae.

The film is squarely *in* Paris here; it ends its long sequences of defiant but uncoordinated action with a hand slapping a sticker announcing revolution on one of the iconic art-nouveau metro entrances as the body disappears below ground. But it does nothing to imply that this riot will be anything other than an 'incident', ignored by most, but nonetheless of the greatest urgency: a *visible*, direction-less suspension of the law. In Paris, any attempt to re-locate this 'moment' or 'space' clearly on a map is problematic. Instead of a consolidated city, mapped, mined, or mirrored by its underground, we will have found ourselves shuttling between different frequencies, observing something like the crackle between them, and it is only in so doing, I would like to suggest, that we can know something today of what constitutes clandestine Paris.

11. Archaeology of the Parisian Underground

Stephen W. Sawyer

> *... Parisien de base ... je tiens dans la main ce qui me tient a distance; je domine du regard ce qui me domine du regard.*
> (Latour and Hermant)

> *L'histoire des hommes se reflète dans l'histoire des cloaques.*
> (Hugo 1283)

Introduction: Digging in the Underground

In his book *Laboratory Life*, Bruno Latour asks how it is possible to build a 'bridge' between the sciences and social experience. He then writes:

> The word 'bridge' is not quite right ... the social world cannot exist on one side and the scientific world on the other because the scientific realm is merely the end result of many other operations that are in the social realm. (13)

When applied to our contemporary urban experience in general and the *underground* in particular, Latour's claim suggests that a certain self-consciousness may be necessary to apprehend key aspects of contemporary urban life – we must, at some level, think about ourselves thinking about the underground.

If we accept that the underground necessarily appears on the margins, covered over in some way, that it thrives when it is hiding from our analytical gaze, then I would like to suggest that the underground is a particularly useful analytical field for investigating the self-reflexivity suggested above. The tension inherent in the underground between presence and absence, overflow of expression and the void of a certain kind of *mass* presence, means that the underground must at some level remain outside of our grasp if it is to remain *underground*. These specific characteristics of the underground suggest that locating and analyzing it (or investigating and mapping the discourses on and around it) may provide a particularly strong insight into both the promise and limits of our contemporary understanding of cities.

Indeed, when we are called to think about the underground as an urban scene, we are confronted not with the question of bringing yet another urban object or experience under our scientific gaze. Rather, we are confronted with investigating how our understanding of the urban experience is constructed as well as the very limits of our knowing something about the city itself. Moreover, the ever-elusive nature of the underground further suggests the importance of recognizing those limits in order to say something meaningful about the experience of the contemporary city.

From a social scientific perspective, the key question for the underground then becomes: in what ways is investigating the underground also a means of asking how we construct the inside and the outside of cities as analytical objects, what they do and how we know this? In what follows, I would like to suggest that where we construct epistemological fault lines around, within, and outside cities, including what we can and cannot know, is essential to understanding how we plan and how we conceive them. This chapter then seeks to place the limits of any social scientific apprehension of the underground at its center, uncovering it through two discourses that have attempted to focus on the underground as a field that can tell us something about the city – specifically in Victor Hugo's discussion of the souterrain in his 1862 novel *Les Misérables* and a 2010 guidebook entitled *Paris Underground*. I then take lessons from these two investigations into the underground to make maps of the contemporary underground in Paris. These maps do not so much locate the underground. Rather, they are designed to show the intersection of a spatial representation of 'Paris' and discourses that are formulated about and within the underground. They open up how discourses on the city might be grasped from an urban sociological view that takes seriously its own epistemological limits as the foundation for knowing something about cities.

From *Souterrain* to Underground: A Brief Archaeology

I open then with a brief (extremely partial) archaeology of the Paris underground by juxtaposing two moments in its history, the *monde souterrain* of Hugo and the post-Fordist contemporary consumer experience of the underground in a 6-euro *Paris Underground* guidebook. By proposing an archaeology of these two moments, I am suggesting that the underground is less an analytical object that can be apprehended and should be studied as such, than a site where meaning about the city is made and unmade; knowledge of the underground is constructed as much by what we claim to be able to know about it and we argue it can tell us as what may or may not be contained within it. In this sense, as Foucault suggested of any archaeology in *The Archaeology of Knowledge*, 'its unity is variable and relative. As one questions that unity, it loses its self-evidence; it indicates itself, constructs itself, only on the basis of a complex field of discourse' (23). Sounding out two moments in the construction of the discourse of the underground can then open up the possibility of establishing a field within which the underground experience gains its meaning. This in turn should render the underground and its relationship to a larger container called 'the city' less apparent and therefore more useful as we start digging, mapping, and elaborating what the underground can tell us about the city.

Hugo's *souterrain* is defined less by the fact that it is hidden, than through the specificity of what it can tell us about the city and how it tells us these things. It is the space within which the city reveals itself, in a peculiar, but potent way. The underground appears in this mid-nineteenth-century metropolis of over 1 million inhabitants, whose surface was undergoing the great emblematic reconstruction of the nineteenth century, as a place where what is knowable about the city is reversed.

In *The Hunchback of Notre Dame*, Hugo famously described the city of Paris of the July Monarchy from the towers of Notre Dame as a checkerboard displayed out before him:

> I do not despair that Paris, seen from a balloon, should one day present that richness of line, that opulence of detail, that diversity of aspect, that hint of the grandiose in the simple and unexpected in the beautiful, which characterizes a checkerboard. (qtd. in Clark 32)

Hugo's irony in 1831 offered one of the essential images for the strangle-hold of rationality on a city caught up in the powerful winds of modernity. However, this sarcastic image from above of rationality, beauty, opulence, and linearity found its counterpart in the Paris souterrain. In his chapter on the *souterrain* in *Les Misérables*, he once again stood above Paris, gazing down, imagining the city: 'One can imagine lifting the cover off of Paris ... and below would appear something like branches grafted onto the two sides of the river' (1283, author's translation). Branches stretching out from the river, he suggested, fed and were fed by the underground world creating a sinuous set of passages. The fundamental opposition between Hugo's two visions as he soared above the city, between the checkerboard and the sinuous branches, the rational and the organic, already suggested the difference between the two worlds and what they might indicate about the city.

And yet, Hugo quickly corrects himself, 'This figure is only half-right', he writes. Searching for a more appropriate metaphor to describe the souterrain, he adds 'the right angle which is common in this type of underground construction is very rare in the world of vegetation' (1285, author's translation). Hugo's quick reappraisal merits investigation as does the image he offers in its place. Indeed, unsatisfied with his organic metaphor, he offers a new image from above:

> One would have a more accurate idea of this strange geometric plan by imagining a bizarre alphabet from the orient, laid out flat on a background of shadows, scrambled into a mess. Its deformed letters would be welded to each other in a random way, sometimes by their angles and sometimes by their extremities. (1285, author's translation)

At first glance, then, Hugo's second view of the underground from above is no less promising. It offers, perhaps, a more accurate image, but this accuracy only serves to render it completely unintelligible, transforming the city into an illegible letter of some oriental alphabet. Hugo, romantic author and urban observer *par excellence*, in the deepest orientalist vein, has aestheticized the underground into a written language that becomes entirely incomprehensible when it is encountered from above.

However, Hugo does propose that the underground can be comprehended. It only appears illegible, a letter from an unknown oriental alphabet, precisely because of the point of view from which it is apprehended: the abstract view from above. Its illegibility then is the product of the position *from which it is observed*, not the underground itself. The fact that the underground cannot be apprehended from above, in some abstract position, therefore, does not imply that it is entirely incapable of offering meaning – quite the reverse. It is the view from above that *under*-mines (in the sense of being incapable of completely mining the wealth below it) the urban observer's experience.

To this extent, Hugo's thinking aligns with Latour and Hermant's assertion about understanding the city in *Paris: ville invisible*:

> No bird's eye view may grasp, in one simple shot, the multiplicity of sites ... there are no panopticons any more than there are panoramas; there are only richly colored dioramas, with multiple branches, whose different lines cross each other. Under the sidewalks, in the tunnels of the metro, attached to the vaults of the sewers. (author's translation)

Any attempt to grasp the unity of the underground from above or as a whole, reveals the weakness of the gaze itself instead of revealing some logic hidden in the object under study. The underground when grasped from above obscures and inspires, but it does not speak. (Discovering an oriental alphabet, the underground is an extension of the 'Alph', that underground source, 'meandering' and 'mazy' below Coleridge's 'Xanadu' which inspired so many romantics. But Hugo is going one step further; he is looking for more than inspiration.)

It is for this reason that Hugo suggests that to understand the underground 'the social observer must enter into these shadows. They are part of his laboratory' (1287, author's translation). What is his method in exploring this underground world? 'Philosophy is the microscope of thought. Everything seeks to step outside of it, but nothing can escape it' (1287, author's translation). The narrow focus of the sewers becomes the microscope, the tubular view on a specific object that has tried to resist decay, but has inevitably ended below ground. One can only apprehend the underground by entering into it, never by standing above it. As a result, when seen from the underground, the city must be apprehended from the bottom up, or rather as a form of deduction and not a pure totalizing observation. The underground provides meaning because it carries a trace, a remainder of what sits above from which the rest can be reconstructed.

Hugo's purposeful gaze into the underground, then, uncovers a relationship and an impossibility: a relationship between what is seen and unseen in the city. One can see the city above ground, as a whole, from the towers of Notre Dame and understand the rationalist push that was rebuilding it. Similarly, from those towers one can also see the *souterrain*. However, one cannot make sense of both at the same time or according to the same method. The gaze from above allows one to make sense of the pressures toward rationalization that would guide Haussmann's reconstruction, but from this perspective, the underground is illegible, a mere inspiration. The underground is just as essential for grasping the city as an object of investigation, but it requires the specific experience of the underground itself. As if the urban were constructed out of two parts, the seen and the unseen, the above and the below, the fragment and the whole, '*la pourpre et le haillon*', on (or by) its underside, or what is underneath – and each requires its own method.

A Guide through the Paris Underground

It is with no small measure of irony (a feature that is often essential to underground scenes) that one puts down Hugo to purchase (for 6 euros) the guidebook *Paris Underground*, edited in 2010. The juxtaposition of the Paris underground and the Paris souterrain suggests the distance traveled from 1861 to the 2010 guide subtitled: 'Art, fashion, music, militancy: all the addresses you need to go out, read, and clothe yourself like nobody else' (author's translation). The underground in this guidebook is a series of images and experiences, set up, one next to the other. What is the connection? The guidebook here becomes access, revealing not only the secrets of the underground, but its location and its contours. Under this light, the city appears an archipelago. As opposed to some other aspect of urban culture that one could know through a cold, rational analysis – here we circulate, jumping from one scene to the next.

As weak evidence that we are in the same discursive field as that of Hugo, note that at the beginning of our young century, the Paris souterrain is still a part of Paris underground. Open to page 80 in the guidebook: 'The Catacombs: More underground than this and you're dead! Don't even try to write a guide on the underground world without discussing the underground [*souterrain*]' (author's translation). The repetition of the term 'underground' in the English translation reveals that the underground has been doubled in our contemporary city. Where we once had unity, we now have multiplicity – the object has shifted, or one could say has been fractured and classified. The *souterrain* becomes the underground when it is divided, hierarchized into those aspects that are truly *underground* and those that are just under the ground:

> Obviously, we are not referring to the official catacombs. Those under Denfert Rochereau, which you can even visit as a family. No, to feel the frightful experience of the unknown and discover a truly strange world, you must head into the 'off' galleries of Paris. (Besse 80, author's translation)

The discursive field of the underground is now larger than it was in the context of Hugo: it contains what is below, but simply being below is insufficient to make it 'underground'. There is a process of hierarchizing and prioritizing what is *underground* within what is literally under the ground.

And yet, this new vision of the underground concurs with Hugo in that the hierarchy structuring the new underground can only be apprehended through experience. This is precisely the aim of the guidebook. It is a book about access, opening what is hidden or closed, prioritizing, listing, classifying, creating knowledge by establishing a path, moving through the city, through and to the *underground*. It is a question of access through knowledge-experience. In this sense, the drive to read and write such a book is no doubt one of the best examples of the democratization of knowing or gaining access to what is theoretically inaccessible and resistant to abstract comprehension.

In this attempt to gain access, the underground appears to be at once vertical and horizontal: the vertical axis is structured by levels of knowledge and thus levels of access. According to the book's epigraph: 'To be underground is to know how to take a step to the side' (Besse, author's translation). The expression merits reflection: to be underground means to know something. The underground does not produce per se in this work; it is a question of knowing or of being 'in the know'. The more you are 'in the know' the more you have access to the secret world of the underground. The horizontal axis stems from movement across the city offered by the underground experience, 'to the side' to gain access to this vertical world of knowledge. In the case of the (6-euro) guide, each of these entries is an experience that stands alone and can be consumed in any order, but always from the side. They are fundamentally incommensurable in that they are particular experiences, happenings that share nothing more than an oblique approach as one spreads across the city in search of underground experiences.

Let me signal then two strange features of this movement through the underground. First, it would seem to be endless. It is unclear whether this guide to the underground stops on page 103 because that is the end of the *underground* road, or because the editor decided that the Parigramme guides would only be around 100 pages in length. No doubt the latter, but what is striking is that the necessary incompleteness does not necessarily take away from the credibility of the information contained on the underground. It is as if its partiality and the editorial limits suggest that the underground continues beyond what Besse has been able to present in his small guide.

Second, the legitimacy of the guide is troubled much more by its physical presence, by the very fact that it exists, than by what it does not contain. The underground would seem to have a very short half-life. It appears ephemeral, resistant to the durability of institutions, and any urban dweller would seem to be dubious of a guide that guarantees it can deliver the marginal experience of the underground to a mass audience:

> All of our efforts to give you the best possible information will not prevent the Earth from turning and certain addresses from changing between the moment we publish this book and the moment you have it between your two hands. (Besse, front matter, author's translation)

In this sense, the materiality of the work would seem to be in competition with the very thing it is leading us toward. Indeed, the underground has a particular relationship to any materialization, like architecture. Take, for example, the factory Pali-Kao in the 20th arrondissement, self-declared center of the underground culture in the early 1980s. An abandoned factory in a neighborhood waiting to be redeveloped, the greatest testament to its being *underground* being the fact that it has since been destroyed and is now a school – a place to learn or perhaps to know through.

No doubt, a lack of ethereality, too much knowledge, or too many people knowing about any specific underground site undermines the site's credibility as an underground space – as if durability and common knowledge about a given underground space generate a void where there was an experience. Knowledge makes the space accessible, and yet its very nature makes this knowledge at some level useless: what is the value of knowing something about something that everyone knows something about and that will soon disappear? Thus, the underground is hidden away and knowledge of the underground means access to it, but it cannot be cumulative. Rather it is archaeological in the deepest sense of the term. So the urban analyst is left with the fact that the underground's inaccessibility, or marginality, that is a certain hiddenness, is a condition of our knowing something about it. But this raises a more fundamental question: how does one grasp the urban experience when essential portions of it are always and already hiding? Is it possible to grasp the entirety from the fragment? Is it possible to move through, constructing knowledge of the city through experiences that will someday not be worth knowing without posing the unity of this underground or its verity? In short, is it possible to map the underground from above?

Mapping the Underground

Mapping the Paris underground forces us to stand alongside Hugo, taking a step back and upward and to the side, in an attempt to 'see' the underground world that Besse has offered us in his guide. From this perspective, we can observe the sites he has listed, much like Hugo observing the *souterrain* from above. A quick aggregation of all the underground sites listed in Besse's guidebook in each arrondissement generates the map in Figure 11.1.[1]

This map attempts to provide insight into where Besse's underground is located. But, much like Hugo's recognition of the limits of his first simile of the *souterrain* as a set of branches, this vision of the Paris underground would also seem to have too many right angles, to be too distant, too abstract to capture the underground as a contemporary phenomenon – imaging the Paris metropolitan region as something that could be a continent, filled with tall rectangular columns. Thus, when gazing upon the underground from this epistemological position, our perspective is totalizing: it does in a fundamental sense capture all of the underground sites, but much like Hugo's critique of so many right angles, the rectangular forms, the crude aggregation, the 'sterile piles' (recalling Louis Sullivan on skyscraper architecture) would all seem to make it incomprehensible. We might even go so far as to re-quote Hugo's assessment of his own first attempt to apprehend the underground from above: 'the right angle which is common in this type of underground construction is very rare in the world of vegetation' (1285, author's translation).

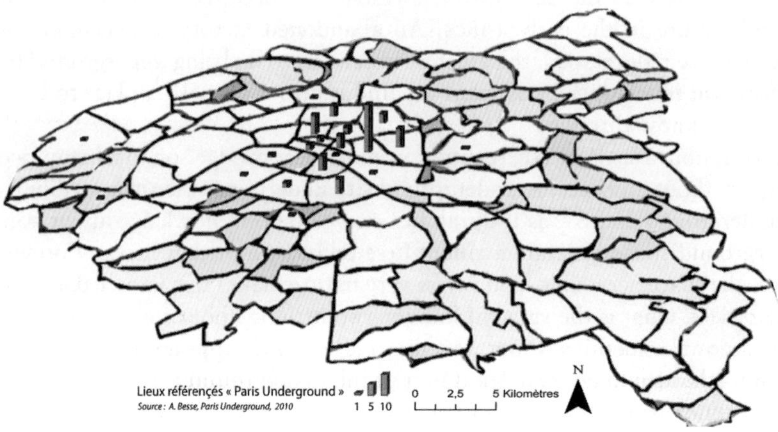

11.1. Map of all the 'underground' sites as listed in Antoine Besse's guidebook *Paris Underground* per district.

Again, like Hugo, we search then for a second representation. And this time, we enter. Instead of looking at the underground from above, we attempt a map that 'steps aside' by attempting to map the experience, or at least the type of experience that is communicated by Besse. From this perspective, the stacks of amenities shift from sterile piles into a *scene*. Grasping the underground as a scene means abandoning the mere aggregation of sites and attempting to understand what these sites convey; the experience they generate; the feelings they evoke. It is precisely in this way that Besse wants to guide us, describing and therefore capturing what is specifically underground about a given site. Besse systematically observes but also constructs his sites as underground. He describes the locations in his underground as 'out there' ('*hors norme*') 'bizarre' ('*bizarre*'), 'crazy'('*déjantés*'), 'different' ('*différents*'), 'where passion replaces the bottom line' ('*où la passion remplace la rentabilité*'), 'esoteric' ('*ésotériques*'), 'little known' ('*confidentiels*'), and 'improbable' ('*improbables*'). Building on these discursive assessments by Besse, it is possible to make an entirely different type of map.

These other maps attempt to locate the discourses used to define a specific site or amenity as 'underground'. That is, we attempt to map not just a list of amenities, as we did in the previous map, but the experience conveyed by a specific amenity: is it 'different', 'out there', or somehow *transgressive*? Is it a space that is 'crazy', 'bizarre', or defies *traditional* codes? Is it a place where passion replaces *utility*? To make maps of this sort, we took over 100 different types of amenities in the Grand Paris, including everything from *bar/tabacs* and *boulangeries* to sex shops and tattoo parlors. We then coded them according to fifteen dimensions divided into three broad categories derived from classical sociology: legitimacy (tradition, utilitarianism, self-expression, egalitarianism, charisma), authenticity (exhibitionism, transgression, glamour, formality, neighborliness), theatricality (locality, ethnicity, corporate, state, rationality). We ask ourselves if a given type of amenity is more or less traditional, giving it a positive numerical score if it is and a negative numerical score if it is not.[2] Doing this for every type of amenity, we generate maps of what we are calling *traditional* Paris, *transgressive* Paris, *utilitarian* Paris. Using the discourses proposed by Besse, we then mix these various dimensions: superimposing a map of transgressive Paris onto a map that highlights the areas that are less utilitarian and traditional, for example. Mixing these dimensions generates the map of underground Paris in Figure 11.2. If we assume that the underground cannot be seen as such – that it is, as Besse and Hugo would seem to suggest, something that we must enter to understand – then perhaps this map is more useful. Our mapping, here, is not necessarily a step toward an abstract position from above. It is rather an attempt to map the actual locations that could be considered part of the underground.

The underground in both of the texts discussed above is both a place and a mechanism for revealing something about the city itself. Mapping the discourses on the underground therefore means mapping the places through which these discourses may or may not be materialized. The aim then of mapping the underground as a scene is not to stand on the towers of Notre Dame and look down, adding the various amenities that are underground or not, but rather to grasp the underground as simultaneously a series of specific experiences and a specific perspective on the city. To see the city from the underground is to see it in a spe-

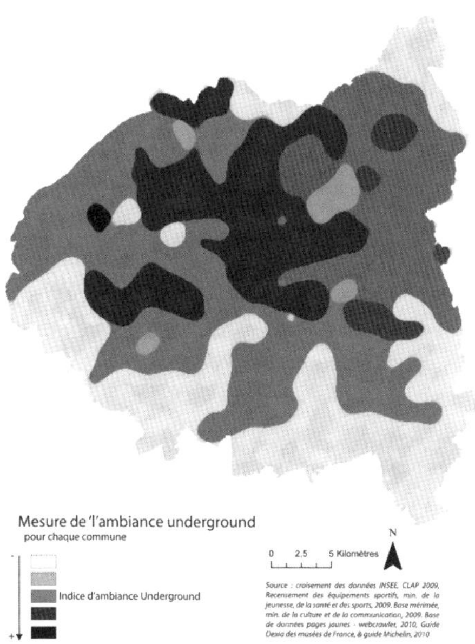

11.2. Map of ambiances ascribed to different places in Paris, according to Antoine Besse's guidebook *Paris Underground*.

cific way. It means looking for what cannot be seen, formulating what cannot be formulated outside of a specific experience. The city becomes a series of hidden spaces that must be discovered or perhaps un-covered. The city is no longer a given, which presents itself before you, but is rather something that will necessarily produce the elusive, the hidden that must be known. In this sense, the above map does not so much map where the underground is, because it is always and already hidden, but rather presents the spaces that may be declared underground or hidden from view.

It is in this sense that grasping the underground is also an attempt to say something more global about the contemporary urban experience and how we may know something about that experience. To quote Bruno Latour again:

> The totality does not present itself as a fixed framework, like a context that is always and already present, but is obtained through a work of totalization, which is itself localized and must be pursued again and again. Paris is neither big nor small. The sites without dimension find themselves provisionally given dimension through the movement of rules, comparisons, classifiers, explorers. (*Paris*, author's translation)

In our work, then, we are both literally and figuratively giving dimension to the Paris underground. It is precisely in the process of striving for totalization, in the attempts to map the places and the discourses that are generated about them, that the underground acquires form and scale.

By way of conclusion, I would like to make reference to a cartoon: in the image, a man described as paranoid is standing in front of a street map. He reads out loud, 'You are here' and then thinks to himself: 'How did they know that!' These maps should, perhaps, provoke the opposite reaction. The two discourses we explored in our brief and necessarily partial archaeology established that the underground could not be seen from above. The attempt to grasp the underground, the attempt to show where the underground 'is', then, should only comfort the most paranoid undergrounder.

So what *can* such a map tell us? Perhaps it can tell us as much about how we may know our city as it does about the objects and experiences of the city itself. Such a map reveals its own limits in its attempt to totalize the urban experience. These maps are not showing us the way or locating the underground specifically. Rather, they are designed to locate an intersection of a discourse on the city and the sites around which those discourses may be produced. It is in this sense that they are totalizing. They find their *raison d'être* in their materialization of an intersection between two worlds that construct the urban experience. Our social scientific gaze, then, does not grasp an urban experience, but it does open up its discourses for analysis. Those discourses do not, cannot, tell us 'where' we are any more than a stack of books on the underground at 6 euros each in your local bookstore can bring to light a cultural phenomenon that is as central to our contemporary urban experience as it is ungraspable. Mapping the underground scene is precisely an attempt to totalize the urban experience, out of the particular discourses that are produced around it. In the terms of Jean Baudrillard, who

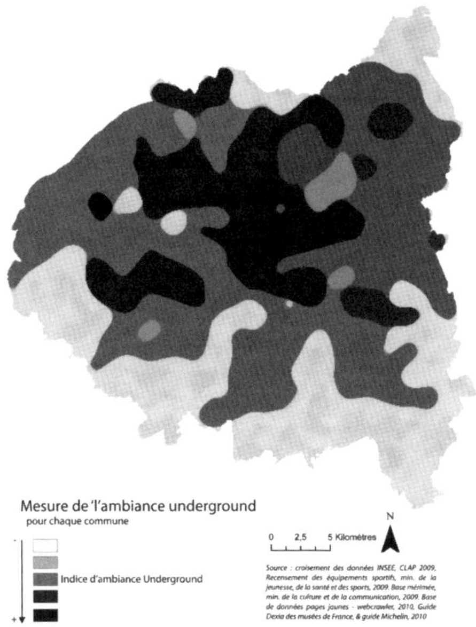

'One would have a more accurate image of this strange geometric plan by imagining a bizarre alphabet from the orient laid out flat on a background of shadows, scrambled into a mess. Its deformed letters would be welded to each other in a random way, sometimes by their angles and sometimes by their extremities' (Hugo 1285, translation: S.W. Sawyer). (Map produced by Mathias Rouet)

11.3. Map of ambiances set alongside Hugo quotation.

famously announced that the map now precedes the territory, we are mapping the maps that precede the territory.

This brings us back to our point of departure and one final image. Figure 11.3 once again shows the map of Besse's discourse on the city, only now set alongside the key quotation from Hugo. Perhaps unsurprisingly, Hugo's reading is more useful than ever. When his description of the underground is brought side by side with our map of the underground scene, it too appears to be a character from an 'oriental alphabet'. What we have mapped, then, or tried to map, is precisely an approach to the underground, an attempt to grasp it with the scientific means available to us. Considering however that the underground has been constructed as an object that is forever-unknown, such a map does as much to reveal the limits and conditions of our production of knowledge about the city as it does the actual underground itself.

Notes

1 The maps reproduced in this chapter were produced by Mathias Rouet in the context of a two-year research project funded by the city of Paris and directed by Stephen Sawyer. For more information on how the maps were produced and for a complete 'scenes' analysis of metropolitan Paris, see Sawyer.

2 This method was developed by Daniel Silver. To code, we ask a series of questions of each amenity. On the theory of scenes see, Silver, Clark, and Navarro Yañez.

Bibliography

30 jaar Metro: Verleden, toekomst. Een tentoonstelling over de ontwikkeling van Amsterdam als Metrostad. Amsterdam: Gemeente Amsterdam, 2007.

Agamben, Giorgio. *State of Exception.* Trans. Kevin Attell. Chicago: University of Chicago Press, 2005.

Alpers, Svetlana. 'Picturing Dutch Culture'. *Looking at Seventeenth-Century Dutch Art: Realism Reconsidered.* Ed. Wayne Franits. Cambridge: Cambridge University Press, 1997. 57-68.

Althusser. Louis. 'Ideology and Ideological State Apparatuses'. *Lenin and Philosophy and Other Essays.* Trans. Ben Brewster. New York: Monthly Review Press, 1971.

Amin, Ash, ed. *Post-Fordism: A Reader.* Oxford: Blackwell, 1994.

'Amsterdam Brothels Become Art Studios in Clean Up'. 1 May 2009. *nrc.nl.* 28 June 2011.

'Amsterdam – So Colorful'. 24 Feb. 2008. *f21village.blogspot.com.* 28 June 2011.

'Amsterdam to Clean Up Red Light District'. 11 Feb. 2009. *cbsnews.com.* 28 June 2011.

Appadurai, Arjun. 'Patriotism and Its Futures'. *Modernity at Large: Cultural Dimensions of Globalization.* 1996. Minneapolis: University of Minnesota Press, 2003. 158-178.

Asso, Raymond. 'Zazou Menace'. *La Globe*, 18 December 1942.

Audio City Tours Productions. *audiocitytours.com.* 23 June 2010.

Augé, Marc. *Non-places: Introduction to an Anthropology of Supermodernity.* Trans. John Howe. London: Verso, 1995.

Bakker, Henk. 'De Amsterdamse metro en de moraal voor de planologie'. *Rooilijn: Mededelingen van het Planologisch en Demografisch Instituut* (1996): 121-6.

Baudelaire, Charles. 'Sculpture'. *Salon de 1859: Lettres à M. le Directeur de 'La Revue Française'.* Collections Litteratura.com.

BAVO. 'Democracy and the Neoliberal City: The Dutch Case'. *Urban Politics Now: Re-Imagining Democracy in the Neoliberal City.* Ed. BAVO. Rotterdam: NAi Publishers, 2007. 212-33.

—, ed. *Urban Politics Now: Re-Imagining Democracy in the Neoliberal City.* Rotterdam: NAi Publishers, 2007.

Benjamin, Walter. 'Theses on the Philosophy of History' (1949). Rpt. in *Illuminations.* Trans. Harry Zohn. New York: Schocken, 1969. 253-65.

—. *The Origin of the German Tragic Drama.*1928. Trans. George Steiner. London: Verso, 1990.

Bennett, Justin. 'Zuidas Symphony'. *Soundtrackcity: 8 Geluidswandelingen in Amsterdam*. Ed. Michiel Huijsman and Renate Zentschnig. Zwolle: d'jonge Hond, 2009. CD/DVD.

Benstock, Shari. *Women of the Left Bank*. Austin: University of Texas Press, 1986.

Berrebi, Sophie. 'Paris Circus New York Junk: Jean Dubuffet and Claes Oldenburg 1959-1962'. *Art History* 29.1 (2006): 79-107.

Besse, Antoine. *Paris Underground: Art, mode, musique, militantisme: Toutes les adresses pour ne plus sortir, lire, s'habiller ni penser comme tout le monde*. Paris: Parigramme, 2010.

Bijsterveld, Karin, and José van Dijck, eds. *Sound Souvenirs: Audio Technologies, Memory and Cultural Practices*. Amsterdam: Amsterdam University Press, 2009.

Bizot, Jean-François, ed. *Underground: L'Histoire*. Paris: Denoel, 2001.

Blatt, Noelle. 'Rupture et deplacement dans l'oeuvre de William Burroughs'. *Revue française d'études américaines* 1 (1976): 12-21.

Blum, Alan. 'The Imagination of Self-Satisfaction: Reflections on the Platitude of the "Creative City"'. *Circulation and the City: Essays on Urban Culture*. Ed. Alexandra Boutros and Will Straw. Montreal and Kingston: McGill-Queen's University Press, 2010. 64-95.

Boersma, Maaike. 'Nachtfestival "met kunst enzo", gratis'. 18 June 2010. *depers.nl*. 22 June 2011.

Boersma, Pieter. *Onverklaarbaar bewoonde woning: Afbraak, verzet en nieuwbouw in Amsterdam – van Nieuwmarkt tot Bijlmer*. Amsterdam: De Verbeelding, 2010.

Böhm, Frank. 'Interview: Nachtburgemeesters Amsterdam'. 23 Dec. 2009. *partyscene.nl*. 22 June 2011.

Borries, Friedrich von, and Matthias Böttger. 'False Freedom: The Construction of Space in Late Capitalism'. *Urban Politics Now: Re-Imagining Democracy in the Neoliberal City*. Ed. BAVO. Rotterdam: NAi Publishers, 2007. 128-40.

Bosma, Jitske, Pieter Boersma, and Tineke Nijenhuis. *De beste aktiegroep ter wereld ... 40 dorpsverhalen uit de Nieuwmarkt*. Amsterdam: Wijkcentrum d'Oude Stadt, 1984.

Boyarin, Daniel, and Jonathan Boyarin. 'Diaspora: Generational Ground of Jewish Identity'. *Critical Inquiry* 14.2 (1993): 693-725.

Boyarin, Jonathan. *Storm from Paradise: The Politics of Jewish Memory*. Minneapolis: University of Minnesota Press, 1992.

Breebaart, Matthijs. 'De Noord-Zuidlijn als kind van zijn tijd'. *Rooilijn: Mededelingen van het Planologisch en Demografisch Instituut* (1996): 230-4.

Broyard, Anatole. 'A Portrait of the Hipster'. *Beat Down to Your Soul: What Was the Beat Generation?* Ed. Ann Charters. London: Penguin, 2001. 43-9.

Bruckner, Pascal. *Fourier*. Paris: Seuil, 1975.

Brun, François. 'Sans-papiers aux guichets: échec au droit ?' *A la lumière des sans-papiers*. Ed. Antoine Pickels. Brussels: Complexe, 2002. 71-88.

—. 'Les sans-papiers: simple affaire d'humanité ou (aussi) question politique ?' *Migrations Société* 18.104 (2006): 103-20.

'Burroughs' Statements at the 1962 International Writers Conference'. *realitystudio.org*. 2 June 2011.
Burroughs, William S. *Cities of the Red Night*. New York: Holt, Rinehart and Winston, 1981.
—. *Naked Lunch: The Restored Text*. Ed. James Grauerholz and Barry Miles. New York: Grove, 2001.
Burroughs, William S., and Brion Gysin. *The Third Mind*. New York: Viking, 1978.
Buruma, Ian. *Murder in Amsterdam: The Death of Theo van Gogh and the Limits of Tolerance*. London: Atlantic, 2007.
Calis, Piet. *Venus in minirok: Seks in de literatuur na 1945*. Amsterdam: Meulenhoff, 2010.
Cardinal, Roger. *Outsider Art*. London: Studio Vista, 1972.
Castells, Manuel. *The Rise of the Network Society*. Oxford: Blackwell, 1996.
Caulfield, Philip. 'Gay Protesters in Spain Greet Pope Benedict with Massive "Kiss-in" to Signal Defiance to Church Laws'. 7 Nov. 2010. *articles.nydailynews.com*. 2 July 2011.
Chevalier, Louis. *L'Assassinat de Paris*. Paris: Calman-Lévy, 1977.
Chtcheglov, Ivan. 'Formulaire pour un urbanisme nouveau'. *Internationale Situationniste* 1 June 1958.
City of Amsterdam. 'Ambition'. *www.topstad.amsterdam.nl*. 22 June 2011.
Clark, Timothy J. *The Painting of Modern Life: Paris in the Art of Manet and His Followers*. Princeton: Princeton University Press, 1986.
Clifford, James. 'Travelling Cultures'. *Cultural Studies*. Ed. Larry Grossberg, Paula Treichler, and Cary Nelson. London: Routledge, 1992. 96-116.
Coll, Steve. 'Leaks'. *The New Yorker*. 8 Nov. 2010. 27-8.
Connell, John, and Chris Gibson. *Sound Tracks: Popular Music, Identity and Place*. London and New York: Routledge, 2003.
Constant. *Pour une architecture de situation*. Amsterdam, 1953.
—. Interview with Andrew Hussey. 6 April 2001. Unpublished.
—. Interview with Benjamin Buchloh. 'A Conversation with Constant'. *The Activist Drawing: Retracing Situationist Architectures: From Constant's New Babylon to Beyond*. Ed. Catherine de Zegher and Mark Wigley. MIT Press, 2001. 23-30.
—. Interview by Linda Boersma and Sue Smit, *Bomb* 91 (2005).
Corso, Gregory. 'Bomb'. *Happy Birthday to Death*. New York: New Directions, 1960.
Davis, Mike. *City of Quartz: Excavating the Future in Los Angeles*. London and New York: Vintage, 1992.
Damisch, Hubert. *Fenêtre jaune cadmium ou les dessous de la peinture*. Paris: Seuil, 1984.
—. 'Entrée en matière'. *Jean Dubuffet*. Saint-Paul: Fondation Maeght, 1985.
'Dating Amsterdam Prostitutes'. 17 March 2007. *amsterdam-red-light-district.info*. 28 June 2010.
Debord, Guy. 'Rapport sur la construction des situations et sur les conditions de l'organisation et de l'action de la tendance situationniste internationale'. Pre-

paratory text for the Cosio d'Arroscia conference, July 1957. Rpt. in *Documents rélatifs à la fondation de l'internationale situationniste: 1948-1957*. Ed. Gérard Bérreby. Paris: Editions Allia, 1985.
—. *Panégyrique*. 1989.
—. *Society of the Spectacle*. Trans. Donald Nicholson-Smith. New York: Zone, 1995.
—. *La Poésie au service de la révolution*, Paris, 2002.
—. *Correspondance: Vol. 'O', septembre 1951-juillet 1957: Complèté des 'letteres retrouvées' et de l'index général des noms cités*. Paris: Arthème Fayard, 2010.
—. *Correspondance: Vol. 1, juin 1957-août 1960*. Paris: Arthème Fayard, 2010.
Debord, Guy and Constant. 'The Amsterdam Declaration'. *Internationale Situationniste* 2 Dec. 1958.
De Groot, Gerard. *The Sixties Unplugged: A Kaleidoscopic History of a Disorderly Decade*. London: Pan, 2009.
Deleuze, Gilles, and Félix Guattari. *Anti-Oedipus: Capitalism and Schizophrenia*. Trans. Robert Hurley, Mark Seem, and Helen R. Lane. Minneapolis: University of Minnesota Press, 1983.
—. *A Thousand Plateaus: Capitalism and Schizophrenia*. Trans. Brian Massumi. Minneapolis: University of Minnesota Press, 1987.
Develing, Enno. *De maagden*. Brussel and Den Haag: Manteau, 1968.
Doane, Mary Ann. *The Emergence of Cinematic Time: Modernity, Contingency, the Archive*. Cambridge, MA and London: Harvard University Press, 2002.
Dubuffet, Jean. *Prospectus aux amateurs de tout genre*. Paris: Gallimard, 1946.
—. 'Avant-projet d'une conférence populaire sur la peinture' (1945). Rpt. in Jean Dubuffet. *Prospectus et tous écrits suivants*. Vol. 1. Paris: Gallimard, 1967. 31-53.
—. 'L'Art Brut préféré aux arts culturels' (1949). Rpt. in Jean Dubuffet. *Prospectus et tous écrits suivants*. Vol. 1. Paris: Gallimard, 1967. 198-202.
—. 'Plus modeste' (1945). Rpt. in Jean Dubuffet. *Prospectus et tous écrits suivants*. Vol. 1. Paris: Gallimard, 1967. 89-93.
—. *Correspondence Dubuffet-Paulhan: 1944-1968*. Paris: Gallimard, 2004.
Dumontier, Pascal. *Les Situationnistes et Mai 68*. Paris: Ivrea, 1994.
Duivenvoorden, Eric. *Magiër van een nieuwe tijd: Het leven van Robert Jasper Grootveld*. Amsterdam: Arbeiderspers, 2009.
Duyves, Mattias. Message to Allen Hibbard. 4 Dec. 2010. E-mail.
Epstein, Gerald A. *Financialization and the World Economy*. Northampton: Edward Elgar, 2005.
Evans, Graeme. 'Measure for Measure: Evaluating the Evidence of Culture's Contribution to Regeneration'. *Urban Studies* 42.5/6 (2005): 959-83.
—. 'New Events in Historic Venues: A Case of London'. *Rivista di Scienze del Turismo* 2 (2010): 149-66.
Fabre, Michel. *La rive noire: De Harlem à la Seine*. Paris: Lieu commun, 1985.
—. *From Harlem to Paris: Black American Writers in France, 1984-1980*. Urbana-Champaign: University of Illinois Press, 1993.
Fainstein, Susan S., and Dennis R. Judd. 'Global Forces, Local Strategies, and

Urban Tourism'. *The Tourist City*. Ed. Susan S. Fainstein and Dennis R. Judd. New Haven and London: Yale University Press, 1999. 1-17.
Fassin, Didier. '"Clandestins" ou "exclus"? Quand les mots font les politiques.' *Politix* 9.34 (1996). 77-86.
Featherstone, Mike. 'City Cultures and Post-Modern Lifestyles'. *Post-Fordism: A Reader*. Ed. Ash Amin. Oxford: Blackwell, 1994.
Fekkes, Jan. *De God van je tante ofwel het Ezel-proces van Gerard Kornelis van het Reve*. Amsterdam: Arbeiderspers, 1968.
Ferdinandusse, Rinus, Jan Blokker and Dimitri Frenkel Frank. *Zo is het toevallig ook nog eens een keer*. Amsterdam: Van Ditmar, 1966.
Florida, Richard. *The Rise of the Creative Class: And How It's Transforming Work, Leisure, Community and Everyday Life*. New York: Routledge, 2002.
—. *Cities and the Creative Class*. New York: Routledge, 2005.
Ford, Simon. *The Situationist International: A User's Guide*. London: Black Dog, 2005.
Foucault. Michel. *Discipline and Punish*. Trans. Alan Sheridan. New York: Random House, 1975.
—. *Histoire de la Sexualité: La volonté de savoir*. Vol 1. Paris: Gallimard, 1976.
—. *Power/Knowledge*. Ed. and Trans. Colin Gordon. New York: Random House, 1980.
—. *The Archaeology of Knowledge*. Trans. Alan Mark Sheridan-Smith. New York: Pantheon, 1982.
Frank, Thomas. *The Conquest of Cool: Business Culture, Counterculture, and the Rise of Hip Consumerism*. Chicago: University of Chicago Press, 1997.
Franke, Simon, and Evert Verhagen, eds. *Creativity and the City: How the Creative Economy is Changing the City*. Rotterdam: NAi Publishers, 2005.
Friedberg, Anne. *Window Shopping: Cinema and the Postmodern*. Berkeley: University of California Press, 1994.
Fuchs, R. H. *Dutch Painting*. London: Thames and Hudson Ltd., 1978.
Ginsberg, Allen. *Kaddish and Other Poems, 1958-1960*. San Francisco: City Lights, 1961.
Goodman, Steve. 'Audio Virology: On the Sonic Mnemonics of Preemptive Power'. *Sonic Mediations: Body, Sound, Technology*. Ed. Carolyn Birdsall and Anthony Enns. Newcastle: Cambridge Scholars Press, 2008. 27-42.
Goudsblom, Johan. *De nieuwe volwassenen*. Amsterdam: Querido-Salamander, 1959.
Green, Jonathon. *All Dressed Up: The Sixties and the Counter-Culture*. London: Jonathan Cape, 1998.
Greif, Mark, et. al. *What Was the Hipster? A Sociological Investigation*. Brooklyn, NY: n+1, 2001.
Grunberg, Serge. *A la recherché d'un corps*. Paris: Éditions du Seuil, 1979.
Hamon, Hervé and Patrick Rotman. *Génération, Tome 1: Les années de rêve*. Paris: Gallimard, 1997
Harris, Oliver, and Ian MacFadyen, eds. *Naked Lunch@50: Anniversary Essays*. Carbondale: Southern Illinois University Press, 2009.
Harvey, David. 'From Managerialism to Entrepreneurialism: The Transforma-

tion in Urban Governance in Late Capitalism'. *Geografiska Annaler* 71.1 (1989): 3-17.

Hegel, Georg Wilhelm Friedrich. *The Phenomenology of Spirit*. Trans. A. V. Miller. Oxford: Clarendon Press, 1977.

Hekma, Gert. 'Kermis in Amsterdam of de cultuur van de seksuele revolutie'. *Het verlies van de onschuld: Seksualiteit in Nederland*. Ed. Gert Hekma, Bram van Stolk, Bart van Heerikhuizen, and Bernard Kruithof. Groningen: Wolters-Noordhoff, 1990. 103-20.

—. *De roze rand van donker Amsterdam: De opkomst van een homoseksuele kroegcultuur 1930-1970*. Amsterdam: Van Gennep, 1992.

—. 'The Drive for Sexual Equality'. *Sexualities* 11.1 (2008): 51-5.

Hekma, Gert, Bram van Stolk, Bart van Heerikhuizen, and Bernard Kruithof, eds. *Het verlies van de onschuld: Seksualiteit in Nederland*. Groningen: Wolters Noordhoff, 1990.

Hibbard, Allen, ed. *Conversations with William S. Burroughs*. Jackson: University Press of Mississippi, 1999.

Hoeben, Frans, dir. *Schroeiplekken: Geen buizen maar huizen*. TV documentary, RVU 1997.

Holcomb, Briavel. 'Marketing Cities for Tourism'. *The Tourist City*. Ed. Susan S. Fainstein and Dennis R. Judd. New Haven and London: Yale University Press, 1999. 54-70.

Houtum, Henk van, and Bas Spierings. 'Barcode Humans: On The Fabrication of Consumers in the Super-Market Society'. *Urban Politics Now: Re-Imagining Democracy in the Neoliberal City*. Ed. BAVO. Rotterdam: NAi Publishers, 2007. 182-96.

'How to Turn Prostitutes into Artists'. *www.causecast.org/news_items/7368-how-to-turn-prostitutes-into-artists*. 24 August 2011.

HTNK, 'Red Light Fashion Amsterdam'. *http://www.htnk.nl/?p=36*. 24 August 2011.

Hugo, Victor. *Les Misérables*. Paris: Gallimard, 1951.

Huijsman, Michiel, and Renate Zentschnig, eds. *Soundtrackcity: 8 Geluidswandelingen in Amsterdam*. Zwolle: D'jonge Hond, 2009. CD/DVD.

Huizinga, Johan. *Homo Ludens: A Study of the Play-Element in Culture*. Boston: Beacon Press, 1955.

Hussey, Andrew. 'Abolish Everything!', *London Review of Books*, 2 September 1999. 34-43.

—. *The Game of War: The Life and Death of Guy Debord*. London: Cape, 2001.

—. '"Paris Is about the Last Place ...": William Burroughs In and Out of Paris and Tangier, 1958-60'. *Naked Lunch@50: Anniversary Essays*. Ed. Oliver Harris and Ian MacFadyen. Carbondale: Southern Illinois University Press, 2009. 73-83.

Israel, Jonathan I. *The Dutch Republic: Its Rise, Greatness, and Fall, 1477-1806*. Oxford: Oxford University Press, 1995.

Jean Paulhan à travers ses peintres. Paris: Éditions des Musées Nationaux, 1974.

Jameson, Fredric. *Valences of the Dialectic*. London: Verso, 2009.

—. *The Hegel Variations: On the Phenomenology of Spirit*. London: Verso, 2010.

Johnson, Bruce, and Martin Cloonan. *Dark Side of the Tune: Popular Music and Violence*. Aldershot and Burlington, VT: Ashgate, 2008.
Jolles, Allard, ed. *Stadsplan Amsterdam: Toekomstvisies op de ruimtelijke ontwikkeling van de stad, 1928-2003*. Rotterdam: NAi; Amsterdam: Gemeente Amsterdam, 2003.
Kassabian, Anahid. 'Would You Like Some World Music with Your Latte? Starbucks, Putomayo, and Distributed Tourism'. *Twentieth-Century Music* 1.2 (2004): 209-23.
Kaufmann, Vincent. *Guy Debord: La Révolution au service de la poésie*. Paris: Fayard, 2001.
Kempton, Richard. *Provo: Amsterdam's Anarchist Revolt*. New York: Autonomedia, 2007.
Ketting, Evert. *Van misdrijf tot hulpverlening. Een analyse van de maatschappelijke betekenis van abortus provocatus in Nederland*. Alphen aan de Rijn: Samson, 1978.
Klein, Naomi. *No Logo: No Space, No Choice, No Jobs – Taking Aim at the Brand Bullies*. London: Flamingo, 2000.
Kloosterman, Robert. 'The Creative Hype'. *Creativity and the City: How the Creative Economy Is Changing the City*. Ed. Simon Franke and Evert Verhagen. Rotterdam: NAi Publishers, 2005. 56-65.
Kooy, G.A., et al., eds. *Sex in Nederland: Het meest recente onderzoek naar houding en gedrag van de Nederlandse bevolking*. Utrecht and Antwerp: Spectrum, 1983.
Latour, Bruno, and Emilie Hermant. *Paris: Ville invisible*. http://www.brunolatour.fr/virtual/index.html. 5. Dec. 2011.
Latour, Bruno, and Steve Woolgar. *Laboratory Life: The Construction of Scientific Facts*. Princeton: Princeton University Press, 1979.
Le Dernier Metro. Dir. François Truffaut. United Artists Classics,1980. Film.
Lefebvre, Henri. *Le droit à la ville*. Paris: Anthropos, 1968.
—. *La vie quotidienne dans le monde modern*. Paris: Gallimard, 1968.
Lodge, David. *Small World: An Academic Romance*. London: Penguin, 1984.
Lyotard, Jean-François. *Libidinal Economy*. Trans. Iain Hamilton Grant. Bloomington: Indiana University Press, 1993.
Maas, Nop. *Gerard Reve: Kroniek van een schuldig leven* Vol. 1. Amsterdam: Van Oorschot, 2010.
Mailer, Norman. *The White Negro*: *Superficial Reflections on the Hipster.* New York: City Lights Books, 1957.
Mak, Geert. *Een kleine geschiedenis van Amsterdam*. Amsterdam: Atlas, 1995.
—. *Amsterdam: A Brief Life of the City*. Trans. Philippe Blom. London: The Harvill Press, 2001.
Mamadouh, Virginie. *De stad in eigen hand. Provo's, kabouters en krakers als stedelijke sociale beweging*. Amsterdam: SUA, 1992.
Marcus, Griel. *Lipstick Traces*, London: Secker and Warburg, 1999.
Marelli, Gianfranco. *L'Amère victoire du situationnisme: Pour Une Histoire Critique de L'Internationale Situationniste 1957-1971*: Arles: Sulliver.
Marshall, Peter. *Demanding the Impossible*. London: Harper-Collins, 1992.

Martin, Bernice M. *A Sociology of Contemporary Cultural Change*. Oxford: Blackwell, 1985.
Martin, Randy. *Financialization of Daily Life*. Philadelphia: Temple University Press, 2002.
Massey, Doreen. *World City*. Cambridge: Polity Press, 2007.
McCann, Eugene and Kevin Ward, eds. *Mobile Urbanism: Cities and Policymaking in the Global Age*. Minneapolis: University of Minnesota Press, 2011.
McDonough, Tom. *Guy Debord and the Situationist International: Texts and Documents*. Cambridge, MA: MIT Press, 2002.
—. 'Metastructure: Experimental Utopia and Traumatic Memory in Constant's New Babylon', *Grey Room* 33 (2008): 84-95.
McKenzie, Simone. 'The Art of Noise'. *Holland Herald* [Sound Issue]. Dec. 2010. 27-9.
Meiners, J.L.J. 'De Amsterdamse metro gaat rijden na een bewogen geschiedenis vooraf'. *Ons Amsterdam* 29 (1977): 198-206.
Metropijn. Kritisch onderzoek naar de geplande Noord-Zuid-metro van Amsterdam. Amsterdam: Wijkcentrum d'Oude Stadt, 1995.
Middelburg, Bart. 'Hoerenpanden Megastrop: Gemeente Verliest Tientallen Miljoen op Aangekochte Bordelen'. *Het Parool*. 12 Nov. 2010. 1.
Mikriammos, Philippe. *William S. Burroughs*. Paris: Seghers, 1975.
Mikunda, Christian. *Brand Lands, Hot Spots and Cool Spaces: Welcome to the Third Place and the Total Marketing Experience*. London: Kogan Page, 2004.
Miles, Barry. *The Beat Hotel: Ginsberg, Burroughs, and Corso in Paris, 1958-1963*. New York: Grove, 2000.
Milne, Anna Louise. *The Extreme In-Between: Jean Paulhan's Place in the Twentieth Century*. Oxford: Legenda. 2006.
Morgan, Ted. *Literary Outlaw: The Life and Times of William S. Burroughs*. New York: Henry Holt and Co., 1988.
Murphy, Timothy S. 'Exposing the Reality Film: William S. Burroughs Among the Situationists'. *Retaking the Universe: William S. Burroughs in the Age of Globalization*. Ed. Davis Schneiderman and Philip Walsh. London: Pluto, 2004. 29-57.
Nabrink, Gé. *Seksuele hervorming in Nederland*. Nijmegen: SUN, 1978.
Naeyé, Jan. *De sterke arm. Tekstboek behorende bij een video onderzoek naar de rol van de Amsterdamse politie en justitie in het Nieuwmarktkonflikt over de periode 1973-1987*. Amsterdam: VU Boekhandel, 1979.
Nancy, Jean Luc. 'Paysage avec dépaysement'. *Au fond des images*. Paris: Galilé, 2003. 100-18.
Nardi, Sarah. 'Slow Money'. *Adbusters*, n.p. n.d.
Nijman, Jan. 'Cultural Globalization and the Identity of Place: The Reconstruction of Amsterdam'. *Ecumene* 6.2 (1999): 146-64.
Noordhoff, J.D., et al., eds. *Sex in Nederland*. Utrecht and Antwerp: Spectrum 1969.
Nuit Blanche Amsterdam. *nuitblancheamsterdam.nl*. 22 June 2011.
Oosterhuis, Harry. *Homoseksualiteit in katholiek Nederland*. Amsterdam: SUA, 1992.

Osborne, Peter. *The Politics of Time: Modernity and Avant-Garde*. London: Verso, 1996.
Oudenampsen, Merijn. 'Amsterdam™, the City as a Business'. *Urban Politics Now: Re-Imagining Democracy in the Neoliberal City*. Ed. BAVO. Rotterdam: NAi Publishers, 2007. 110-27.
Pas, Niek. *Imaazje! De verbeelding van Provo (1965-1967)*. Amsterdam: Wereldbibliotheek, 2003.
Paulhan, Jean. *Guide d'un petit voyage en Suisse*. Paris: Gallimard, 1947.
Peck, Jamie. 'Recreative City: Amsterdam, Vehicular Ideas and the Adaptive Spaces of Creativity Policy'. *International Journal of Urban and Regional Research* 36.3 (2012): 462-85.
Pike, David. *Subterranean Cities: The World beneath Paris and London, 1800-1945*. Ithaca: Cornell University Press, 2005.
Pinder, David. *Visions of the City: Utopianism, Power and Politics in Twentieth-Century Urbanism*. Edinburgh: Edinburgh University Press, 2005.
Prinzhorn, Hans. *Artistry of the Mentally Ill: A Contribution to the Psychology and Psychopathology of Configuration*. Trans. Eric von Brockdorff. Vienna and New York: Springer-Verlag, 1995.
Qu'ils reposent en révolte (figures de guerres). Dir. Sylvain George. Noir Production. 2010. Film.
Rambonnet, Danielle de Loches. *De Nieuwmarktbuurt: Veranderingen van een Amsterdamse stadsbuurt*. Amsterdam: Bureau Monumentenzorg en Uitgeverij Architectura & Natura, 1995.
Rancière, Jacques. 'Le corps du philosophe: les films philosophiques des Rossellini'. *Les écarts du cinéma*. Paris: La Fabrique éditions, 2011. 92-108.
Rapport van de Enquêtecommissie Noord/Zuidlijn. Den Haag: Sdu, 2010; Amsterdam: Gemeente Amsterdam, 2009.
'Reality Studio: A William S. Burroughs Community'. *realitystudio.org*. 7 May 2011.
Recourt, Annemiek. 'Je moet wel van seks houden als je een baantje in de prostitutie wilt'. *Folia*, 19 Nov. 2010: 18-19.
Rennen, Ward. *CityEvents: Place Selling in a Media Age*. Amsterdam: Amsterdam University Press, 2007.
Rheingold, Howard. *Smart Mobs: The Next Social Revolution*. New York: Basic Books, 2002.
Röling, Hugo. 'Samen of alleen. Initiatief en overgave in "Wij willen weten" (1938-1985)'. *Het verlies van de onschuld: Seksualiteit in Nederland*. Ed. Gert Hekma, Bram van Stolk, Bart van Heerikhuizen, and Bernard Kruithof. Groningen: Wolters-Noordhoff, 1990. 85-102.
Röling, Robert. W. 'Amsterdam Advertising: The Rise and Growth of an International Advertising Industry'. Diss. University of Amsterdam, 2011.
Rumney, Ralph and Alan Woods. *The Map Is Not the Territory*. Manchester: Manchester University Press, 2001.
Sadler, Simon. *The Situationist City*. Cambridge, MA, and London: MIT Press, 1998.
Said, Edward. *Out of Place: A Memoir*. New York: Knopf, 1999.

Saldanha, Arun. 'Music Tourism and Factions of Bodies in Goa'. *Tourist Studies* 2.1 (2002): 43-62.
Sandbrook, Dominic. *White Heat: A History of Britain in the Swinging Sixties.* London: Abacus, 2007.
Savage, Jon. *England's Dreaming*. London: Faber, 2005.
Sawyer, Stephen W., ed. *Une cartographie culturelle de Paris: Les ambiances du Paris-Métropole.* Report submitted to City of Paris, 2011.
Schama, Simon. *The Embarrassment of Riches: An Interpretation of Dutch Culture in the Golden Age.* London: Fontana Press, 1987.
Schlör, Joachim. *Nights in the Big City: Paris, Berlin, London, 1840-1930.* London: Reaktion, 1998.
Seem, Mark. 'Introduction'. *Anti-Oedipus: Capitalism and Schizophrenia.* Trans. Robert Hurley, Mark Seem, and Helen R. Lane. Minneapolis: University of Minnesota Press, 1983. xv-xxiv.
SI. 'The Adventure (1960)'. *Situationist International Anthology.* Ed. and trans. Ken Knabb. Berkeley: Bureau of Public Secrets, 2006. 79-81.
—. 'The Bad Days Will End (1962)'. *Situationist International Anthology.* Ed. and trans. Ken Knabb. Berkeley: Bureau of Public Secrets, 2006. 107-13.
Silver, Daniel, Terry N. Clark, and Clemente Jesus Navarro Yañez. 'Scenes: Social Context in an Age of Contingency'. *Social Forces* 88 (2010): 2293-324.
Simmel, Georg. 'The Metropolis and Mental Life'. *Simmel on Culture.* Ed. David Frisby and Mike Featherstone. London: Sage, 1998.
SmartMobs. 'About the Book'. *smartmobs.com.* 9 May 2011.
Soja, Edward. *Thirdspace: Journeys to Los Angeles and Other Real and Imagined Places.* Cambridge, MA: Blackwell, 1996.
Somer, Kees. *The Functional City: The CIAM and Cornelis van Eesteren, 1928-1960.* Trans. Peter Mason. Rotterdam: NAi, 2007.
Sontag, Susan. *On Photography.* New York: Farrar, Straus & Giroux, 1977.
Steenbeek, Kristien. *Kunst in het metrostation Nieuwmarkt*, BA thesis in Art History, University of Amsterdam, 1982.
Tacussel, Patrick. *L'Imaginaire radical.* Dijon: Presses du Réel, 2007.
Taylor, Mark C. *Confidence Games: Money and Markets in a World Without Redemption.* Chicago: University of Chicago Press, 2004.
Terhorst, Pieter, and Jacques van de Ven. 'The Economic Restructuring of the Historic City Center'. *Amsterdam Human Capital.* Ed. Sako Musterd and Willem Salet. Amsterdam: Amsterdam University Press, 2003. 85-101.
Têtu-Delage, Marie-Thérèse. *Clandestins au pays des papiers: Expériences et parcours de sans-papiers algériens.* Paris: La Découverte, 2009.
'The Hoerengracht'. *hoerengracht.amsterdammuseum.nl.* 29 June 2011.
Tielman, Rob. *Homoseksualiteit in Nederland. Studie van een emancipatiebeweging.* Meppel: Boom, 1982.
Time Out: The World's Greatest Cities. London: HSBC, 2009.
Thomasson, Emma. 'Amsterdam to Clean Up "Red Light" District'. 17 Dec. 2007 *reuters.com.* 28 June 2011.
Twaalfhoven, Anita, ed. *Festivals.* Special issue of *Boekman: Tijdschrift voor Kunst, Cultuur en Beleid* 83 (2010).

Urry, John. *The Tourist Gaze: Leisure and Travel in Contemporary Societies.* London: Sage, 1990.
—. 'Sensing the City'. *The Tourist City.* Ed. Susan S. Fainstein and Dennis R. Judd. New Haven and London: Yale University Press, 1999. 71-86.
—. *The Tourist Gaze.* 2nd ed. London: Sage, 2002.
Van Blokland, Simon, ed. *Nieuwmarkt in beeld: 1900-2000.* Amsterdam: Stadsuitgeverij, 2003.
Van der Heide, Ervin. Portfolio. 2009. *www.evdh.net.* 28 June 2011.
Van der Klein, Marian, and Saskia Wieringa, eds. *Alles kon anders. Protestrepertoires in Nederland, 1965-2005.* Amsterdam: Aksant, 2006.
Van Duijn, Roel. *Provo: De geschiedenis van de provotarische beweging 1965-1967.* Amsterdam: Meulenhoff, 1985.
—. *Netherlands: The Second Liberation.* Amsterdam, 1998.
Van metro tot beeldbuis, Werkgroep Kunstzaken Metro Amsterdam. Amsterdam: Stadsdrukkerij, 1983.
Van Waveren, Guus, dir. *Groeten uit de Nieuwmarkt.* TV documentary, NOS, 1980.
Van Weerlee, Duco. *Wat de provo's willen.* Amsterdam: Bezige Bij, 1966.
Verhagen, Hans. *De gekke wereld van … Hoepla: Opkomst en ondergang van een televisieprogramma.* Amsterdam: Bezige Bij, 1968.
Verkerk, Connie. 'Kunst is Vaak Veel te Serieus'. *Het Parool.* 8 November 2010. 13.
Verstraete, Ginette. *Tracking Europe: Mobility, Diaspora and the Politics of Location.* Durham, NC: Duke University Press, 2010.
Viénet, René. *Enragés and Situationists in the Occupations Movement, France, May '68.* New York and London: Autonomedia and Rebel Press, 1992.
Vivant, Elsa. 'How Underground Culture Is Changing Paris'. *Urban Research & Practice* 2.1 (2009): 36-52.
—. 'The (re)Making of Paris as a Bohemian Place?' *Progress in Planning* 74.3 (2010): 107-52.
Vuijsje, Marja. *Joke Smit. Biografie van een feministe.* Amsterdam: Amstel Uitgevers, 2008.
Ward, Stephen W. *Selling Places: The Marketing and Promotion of Towns and Cities, 1850-2000.* New York: Routledge, 1998.
Wark, Mackenzie. *The Beach beneath the Street: The Everyday Life and Glorious Times of the Situationist International*, London: Verso, 2011.
Westermann, Mariët. *A Worldly Art: The Dutch Republic, 1585-1718.* New York: Harry N. Abrams, Inc. 1996.
Wigley, Mark. *Constant's New Babylon: The Hyper-Architecture of Desire.* Rotterdam: 010 Publishers, 1998.
Williams, Rosalind. *Notes on the Underground: An Essay on Technology, Society, and the Imagination.* Cambridge, MA: MIT Press, 1990.
'Window Brothels Replaced by Redlight Fashion'. *http://amsterdam-red-light-district.info/news/45-window-brothels-replaced-by-redlight-fashion.html.* 24 August 2011.
Wood, Robert. 'Gerard Reve'. *glbtq.com.* 7 May 2011.

Zeldenrust-Noordanus, Mary. *Slotrede*. N.p., 1967.
Zukin, Sharon. *Loft Living: Culture and Capital in Urban Change*. New Brunswick, NJ: Rutgers University Press, 1989.
—. *The Culture of Cities*. Cambridge: Blackwell, 1995.
—. 'Urban Lifestyles: Diversity and Standardization in Spaces of Consumption'. *Urban Studies* 35.5/6 (1998): 825-39.
—. *Naked City: The Death and Life of Authentic Urban Places*. Oxford: Oxford University Press, 2010.

Illustrations

Contributors

Sophie Berrebi is Assistant Professor in the history and theory of photography at the University of Amsterdam, where she teaches contemporary art and cultural analysis. She is also a curator and an art critic. Her written work has appeared in publications such as *Frieze*, *Afterall*, and *Metropolis M*. She is completing a book on the role of visual documents in contemporary art entitled *The Document Reversed: Photography as Theoretical Object*, and a study about Jean Dubuffet's complex relationship with modernism, entitled *Modernism Undone: The Work of Jean Dubuffet*, for which she received a postdoctoral grant from the Getty Foundation.

Carolyn Birdsall is Assistant Professor of Media Studies at the University of Amsterdam. Her research interests are in the fields of media and cultural history, with a particular focus on radio, film, and television sound, documentary, and urban studies. Her recent publications include *Nazi Soundscapes* (2012) and the edited collections *Inside Knowledge* (2009) and *Sonic Mediations* (2008).

Sudeep Dasgupta is Associate Professor of Media Studies at the University of Amsterdam. He works in the fields of critical theory and visual culture, aesthetics and politics, postcolonial and queer theory, philosophy and media. His book publications include *Constellations of the Transnational: Modernity, Culture, Critique* (2007) and *What's Queer about Europe?* (forthcoming).

Joyce Goggin is Associate Professor of Literature at the University of Amsterdam where she also teaches film and new media. She is also a contributing emeritus member of Amsterdam University College where she served as Head of Studies for the Humanities from 2008 to 2010. Her research focuses on literature, film, painting, and new media, which she approaches from an economic perspective, and she has published articles on gambling, addiction, and finance in various cultural media. Her other interests include comic books and graphic novels and she recently co-edited a collection of essays entitled *The Rise and Reason of Comics and Graphic Literature: Critical Essays on the Form* (2010).

Gert Hekma is Assistant Professor of sexuality and gender studies at the Department of Sociology and Anthropology at the University of Amsterdam. His specialization is the history of homo/sexuality and he now works on the sexual revolution. Among his (co-edited) books are *The Pursuit of Sodomy* (1989), *Gay Men and the Sexual History of the Political Left* (1995), *Sexual Cultures in Europe* (1999), *Homoseksualiteit in Nederland van 1730 tot de moderne tijd* (2004), *ABC van de perversies* (2009), and *A Cultural History of Sexuality in the Modern Age* (2011).

Allen Hibbard is Professor of English and Director of the Middle East Center at Middle Tennessee State University. He has written two books on Paul Bowles (*Paul Bowles: A Study of the Short Fiction* [1993], and *Paul Bowles, Magic & Morocco* [2004]), edited *Conversations with William S. Burroughs* (2000), and published a collection of his own stories in Arabic (1994). His research and teaching interests include modernism, postmodernism, literary theory, the novel, translation, transnational movement, and globalization, with a focus on interactions between the United States and the Arab world.

Andrew Hussey OBE is Professor and Dean of the University of London Institute in Paris. He is the author of two books about Georges Bataille: *The Beast at Heaven's Gate: Georges Bataille and the Art of Transgression* (2006) and *The Inner Scar: The Mysticism of Georges Bataille* (2000). His acclaimed biography of Guy Debord, *The Game of War*, was published in 2001, and named as an International Book of the Year by the Times Literary Supplement. *Paris: The Secret History* (2006) was shortlisted for the Prix Grandgousier (France) in 2008. He is currently writing a book entitled *The French Intifada: The Long War Between France and Its Arabs*.

Christoph Lindner is Professor of Media Studies and Director of the Amsterdam School for Cultural Analysis at the University of Amsterdam, where he writes about cities, globalization, and visual culture. He is also a Research Affiliate at the University of London Institute in Paris and founding Director of the Netherlands Institute for Cultural Analysis. His publications include *Fictions of Commodity Culture* (2003) as well as the edited volumes *Globalization, Violence, and the Visual Culture of Cities* (2010), *Revisioning 007* (2009), and *Urban Space and Cityscapes* (2006).

Anna-Louise Milne is Director of Postgraduate Studies in the Department of French and Comparative Studies at the University of London Institute in Paris. Notable publications are two books on Jean Paulhan (*The Extreme In-Between* [2006] and *La Correspondance Paulhan-Belaval* [2005]), a collection *May 68: Rethinking France's Last Revolution* (2011), and a contribution to the centenary of *La Nouvelle Revue Française* in the form of a special issue of the *Romanic Review* (99.1-2 [2008]). Her current research spins out of the center/periphery dynamic explored in construction of the literary field, to consider its modalities in twentieth-century visions of and for the city of Paris.

David Pinder is Reader in Geography at Queen Mary, University of London. He is the author of *Visions of the City: Utopianism, Power, and Politics in Twentieth-Century Urbanism* (2005), and editor of *Cultural Geography in Practice* (2003). He is also reviews editor for the journal *Cultural Geographies*.

Stephen W. Sawyer is Associate professor at The American University of Paris, Chair of the History Department, founder of the Urban Studies program, and co-director of a Mellon-funded program in Global Cities with the New School for Social Research. In 2009, he was awarded a two-year grant by the city of Paris to map cultural scenes in metropolitan Paris. His translation of previously unpublished lectures by Michel Foucault for University of Chicago Press is to appear in 2013.

Ginette Verstraete is Professor of Comparative Arts and Media and Head of the Division of Arts and Culture at the VU University Amsterdam. She has written on cultural studies, media and globalization, intermediality, and mobility. Among her recent publications are 'Media Globalization and Post-Socialist Identities' (special issue of *European Journal of Cultural Studies* 12.2 [2009]), *Tracking Europe: Mobility, Diaspora, and the Politics of Location* (2010), and 'Intermedialities: Theory, History, Practice' in *Acta Universitatis Sapientiae: Film and Media Studies* 2 (2010).

Index